DOE-HDBK-1013/1-92
JUNE 1992

DOE FUNDAMENTALS HANDBOOK

INSTRUMENTATION AND CONTROL

Volume 1 of 2

AF799877

UNITED STATES OF AMERICA · DEPARTMENT OF ENERGY ·

U.S. Department of Energy **FSC-6910**

Washington, D.C. 20585

This document has been reproduced directly from the best available copy.

Available to DOE and DOE contractors from the Office of Scientific and Technical Information. P. O. Box 62, Oak Ridge, TN 37831; (615) 576-8401.

Available to the public from the National Technical Information Service, U.S. Department of Commerce, 5285 Port Royal Rd., Springfield, VA 22161.

Order No. DE92019792

ABSTRACT

The *Instrumentation and Control Fundamentals Handbook* was developed to assist nuclear facility operating contractors provide operators, maintenance personnel, and the technical staff with the necessary fundamentals training to ensure a basic understanding of instrumentation and control systems. The handbook includes information on temperature, pressure, flow, and level detection systems; position indication systems; process control systems; and radiation detection principles. This information will provide personnel with an understanding of the basic operation of various types of DOE nuclear facility instrumentation and control systems.

Key Words: Training Material, Temperature Detection, Pressure Detection, Level Detection, Flow Detection, Position Indication, Radiation Detection, Process Control

FOREWORD

The *Department of Energy (DOE) Fundamentals Handbooks* consist of ten academic subjects, which include Mathematics; Classical Physics; Thermodynamics, Heat Transfer, and Fluid Flow; Instrumentation and Control; Electrical Science; Material Science; Mechanical Science; Chemistry; Engineering Symbology, Prints, and Drawings; and Nuclear Physics and Reactor Theory. The handbooks are provided as an aid to DOE nuclear facility contractors.

These handbooks were first published as Reactor Operator Fundamentals Manuals in 1985 for use by DOE Category A reactors. The subject areas, subject matter content, and level of detail of the Reactor Operator Fundamentals Manuals was determined from several sources. DOE Category A reactor training managers determined which materials should be included, and served as a primary reference in the initial development phase. Training guidelines from the commercial nuclear power industry, results of job and task analyses, and independent input from contractors and operations-oriented personnel were all considered and included to some degree in developing the text material and learning objectives.

The *DOE Fundamentals Handbooks* represent the needs of various DOE nuclear facilities' fundamentals training requirements. To increase their applicability to nonreactor nuclear facilities, the Reactor Operator Fundamentals Manual learning objectives were distributed to the Nuclear Facility Training Coordination Program Steering Committee for review and comment. To update their reactor-specific content, DOE Category A reactor training managers also reviewed and commented on the content. On the basis of feedback from these sources, information that applied to two or more DOE nuclear facilities was considered generic and was included. The final draft of each of these handbooks was then reviewed by these two groups. This approach has resulted in revised modular handbooks that contain sufficient detail such that each facility may adjust the content to fit their specific needs.

Each handbook contains an abstract, a foreword, an overview, learning objectives, and text material, and is divided into modules so that content and order may be modified by individual DOE contractors to suit their specific training needs. Each subject area is supported by a separate examination bank with an answer key.

The *DOE Fundamentals Handbooks* have been prepared for the Assistant Secretary for Nuclear Energy, Office of Nuclear Safety Policy and Standards, by the DOE Training Coordination Program. This program is managed by EG&G Idaho, Inc.

OVERVIEW

The *Department of Energy Fundamentals Handbook* entitled *Instrumentation and Control* was prepared as an information resource for personnel who are responsible for the operation of the Department's nuclear facilities. A basic understanding of instrumentation and control is necessary for DOE nuclear facility operators, maintenance personnel, and the technical staff to safely operate and maintain the facility and facility support systems. The information in the handbook is presented to provide a foundation for applying engineering concepts to the job. This knowledge will help personnel more fully understand the impact that their actions may have on the safe and reliable operation of facility components and systems.

The *Instrumentation and Control* handbook consists of seven modules that are contained in two volumes. The following is a brief description of the information presented in each module of the handbook.

Volume 1 of 2

Module 1 - Temperature Detectors

This module describes the construction, operation, and failure modes for various types of temperature detectors and indication circuits.

Module 2 - Pressure Detectors

This module describes the construction, operation, and failure modes for various types of pressure detectors and indication circuits.

Module 3 - Level Detectors

This module describes the construction, operation, and failure modes for various types of level detectors and indication circuits.

Module 4 - Flow Detectors

This module describes the construction, operation, and failure modes for various types of flow detectors and indication circuits.

Module 5 - Position Indicators

This module describes the construction, operation, and failure modes for various types of position indicators and control circuits.

Volume 2 of 2

Module 6 - Radiation Detectors

This module describes the principles of radiation detection, detector operation, circuit operation, and specific radiation detector applications.

Module 7 - Principles of Control Systems

This module describes the principles of operation for control systems used in evaluating and regulating changing conditions in a process.

The information contained in this handbook is by no means all encompassing. An attempt to present the entire subject of instrumentation and control would be impractical. However, the *Instrumentation and Control* handbook does present enough information to provide the reader with a fundamental knowledge level sufficient to understand the advanced theoretical concepts presented in other subject areas, and to better understand basic system and equipment operations.

Department of Energy
Fundamentals Handbook

INSTRUMENTATION AND CONTROL
Module 1
Temperature Detectors

www.KnowledgePublications.com

TABLE OF CONTENTS

LIST OF FIGURES ii

LIST OF TABLES iii

REFERENCES iv

OBJECTIVES v

RESISTANCE TEMPERATURE DETECTORS (RTDs) 1

Temperature 1
RTD Construction 2
Summary 4

THERMOCOUPLES 5

Thermocouple Construction 5
Thermocouple Operation 6
Summary 7

FUNCTIONAL USES OF TEMPERATURE DETECTORS 8

Functions of Temperature Detectors 8
Detector Problems 8
Environmental Concerns 9
Summary 9

TEMPERATURE DETECTION CIRCUITRY 10

Bridge Circuit Construction 10
Bridge Circuit Operation 12
Temperature Detection Circuit 14
Temperature Compensation 15
Summary 16

LIST OF FIGURES

Figure 1 Electrical Resistance-Temperature Curves 2

Figure 2 Internal Construction of a Typical RTD 3

Figure 3 RTD Protective Well and Terminal Head 4

Figure 4 Thermocouple Material Characteristics When Used with Platinum 5

Figure 5 Internal Construction of a Typical Thermocouple 6

Figure 6 Simple Thermocouple Circuit 6

Figure 7 Temperature-vs-Voltage Reference Table 7

Figure 8 Bridge Circuit 11

Figure 9 Unbalanced Bridge Circuit 12

Figure 10 Balanced Bridge Circuit 13

Figure 11 Block Diagram of a Typical Temperature Detection Circuit 14

Figure 12 Resistance Thermometer Circuit with Precision Resistor in Place of Resistance Bulb 15

LIST OF TABLES

NONE

REFERENCES

- Kirk, Franklin W. and Rimboi, Nicholas R., Instrumentation, Third Edition, American Technical Publishers, ISBN 0-8269-3422-6.

- Academic Program for Nuclear Power Plant Personnel, Volume IV, General Physics Corporation, Library of Congress Card #A 397747, April 1982.

- Fozard, B., Instrumentation and Control of Nuclear Reactors, ILIFFE Books Ltd., London.

- Wightman, E.J., Instrumentation in Process Control, CRC Press, Cleveland, Ohio.

- Rhodes, T.J. and Carroll, G.C., Industrial Instruments for Measurement and Control, Second Edition, McGraw-Hill Book Company.

- Process Measurement Fundamentals, Volume I, General Physics Corporation, ISBN 0-87683-001-7, 1981.

TERMINAL OBJECTIVE

1.0 Given a temperature instrument, **RELATE** the associated fundamental principles, including possible failure modes, to that instrument.

ENABLING OBJECTIVES

1.1 **DESCRIBE** the construction of a basic RTD including:
  a. Major component arrangement
  b. Materials used

1.2 **EXPLAIN** how RTD resistance varies for the following:
  a. An increase in temperature
  b. A decrease in temperature

1.3 **EXPLAIN** how an RTD provides an output representative of the measured temperature.

1.4 **DESCRIBE** the basic construction of a thermocouple including:
  a. Major component arrangement
  b. Materials used

1.5 **EXPLAIN** how a thermocouple provides an output representative of the measured temperature.

1.6 **STATE** the three basic functions of temperature detectors.

1.7 **DESCRIBE** the two alternate methods of determining temperature when the normal temperature sensing devices are inoperable.

1.8 **STATE** the two environmental concerns which can affect the accuracy and reliability of temperature detection instrumentation.

1.9 Given a simplified schematic diagram of a basic bridge circuit, **STATE** the purpose of the following components:
  a. R_1 and R_2
  b. R_x
  c. Adjustable resistor
  d. Sensitive ammeter

ENABLING OBJECTIVES (Cont.)

1.10 **DESCRIBE** the bridge circuit conditions that create a balanced bridge.

1.11 Given a block diagram of a basic temperature instrument detection and control system, **STATE** the purpose of the following blocks:
- a. RTD
- b. Bridge circuit
- c. DC-AC converter
- d. Amplifier
- e. Balancing motor/mechanical linkage

1.12 **DESCRIBE** the temperature instrument indication(s) for the following circuit faults:
- a. Short circuit
- b. Open circuit

1.13 **EXPLAIN** the three methods of bridge circuit compensation for changes in ambient temperature.

RESISTANCE TEMPERATURE DETECTORS (RTDs)

The resistance of certain metals will change as temperature changes. This characteristic is the basis for the operation of an RTD.

EO 1.1 DESCRIBE the construction of a basic RTD including:
a. Major component arrangement
b. Materials used

EO 1.2 EXPLAIN how RTD resistance varies for the following:
a. An increase in temperature
b. A decrease in temperature

EO 1.3 EXPLAIN how an RTD provides an output representative of the measured temperature.

Temperature

The hotness or coldness of a piece of plastic, wood, metal, or other material depends upon the molecular activity of the material. Kinetic energy is a measure of the activity of the atoms which make up the molecules of any material. Therefore, temperature is a measure of the kinetic energy of the material in question.

Whether you want to know the temperature of the surrounding air, the water cooling a car's engine, or the components of a nuclear facility, you must have some means to measure the kinetic energy of the material. Most temperature measuring devices use the energy of the material or system they are monitoring to raise (or lower) the kinetic energy of the device. A normal household thermometer is one example. The mercury, or other liquid, in the bulb of the thermometer expands as its kinetic energy is raised. By observing how far the liquid rises in the tube, you can tell the temperature of the measured object.

Because temperature is one of the most important parameters of a material, many instruments have been developed to measure it. One type of detector used is the resistance temperature detector (RTD). The RTD is used at many DOE nuclear facilities to measure temperatures of the process or materials being monitored.

RTD Construction

The RTD incorporates pure metals or certain alloys that increase in resistance as temperature increases and, conversely, decrease in resistance as temperature decreases. RTDs act somewhat like an electrical transducer, converting changes in temperature to voltage signals by the measurement of resistance. The metals that are best suited for use as RTD sensors are pure, of uniform quality, stable within a given range of temperature, and able to give reproducible resistance-temperature readings. Only a few metals have the properties necessary for use in RTD elements.

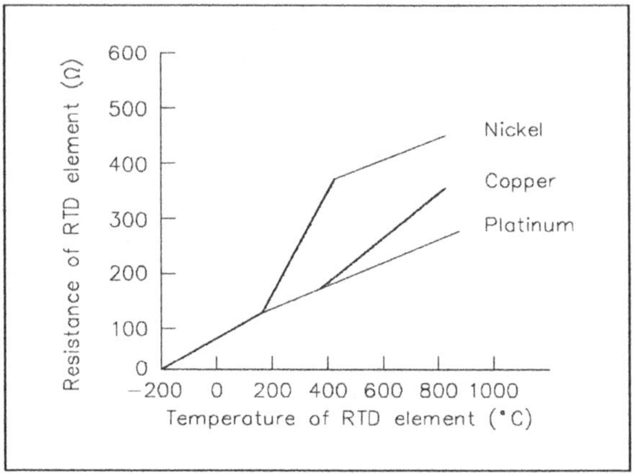

Figure 1 Electrical Resistance-Temperature Curves

RTD elements are normally constructed of platinum, copper, or nickel. These metals are best suited for RTD applications because of their linear resistance-temperature characteristics (as shown in Figure 1), their high coefficient of resistance, and their ability to withstand repeated temperature cycles.

The coefficient of resistance is the change in resistance per degree change in temperature, usually expressed as a percentage per degree of temperature. The material used must be capable of being drawn into fine wire so that the element can be easily constructed.

RTD elements are usually long, spring-like wires surrounded by an insulator and enclosed in a sheath of metal. Figure 2 shows the internal construction of an RTD.

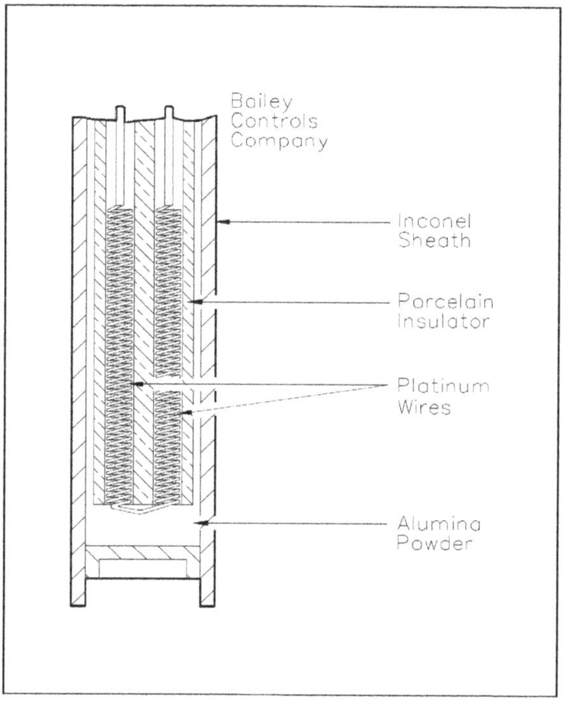

Figure 2 Internal Construction of a Typical RTD

This particular design has a platinum element that is surrounded by a porcelain insulator. The insulator prevents a short circuit between the wire and the metal sheath.

Inconel, a nickel-iron-chromium alloy, is normally used in manufacturing the RTD sheath because of its inherent corrosion resistance. When placed in a liquid or gas medium, the Inconel sheath quickly reaches the temperature of the medium. The change in temperature will cause the platinum wire to heat or cool, resulting in a proportional change in resistance.

This change in resistance is then measured by a precision resistance measuring device that is calibrated to give the proper temperature reading. This device is normally a bridge circuit, which will be covered in detail later in this text.

Figure 3 shows an RTD protective well and terminal head. The well protects the RTD from damage by the gas or liquid being measured. Protecting wells are normally made of stainless steel, carbon steel, Inconel, or cast iron, and they are used for temperatures up to 1100°C.

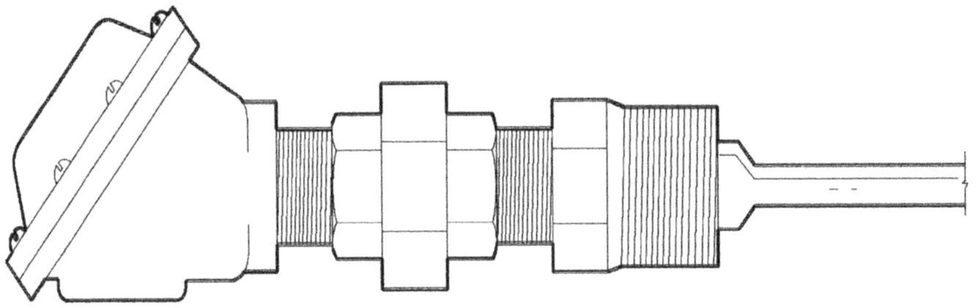

Figure 3 RTD Protective Well and Terminal Head

Summary

Resistance temperature detectors (RTDs) are summarized below.

RTD Summary

- The resistance of an RTD varies directly with temperature:
  - As temperature increases, resistance increases.
  - As temperature decreases, resistance decreases.
- RTDs are constructed using a fine, pure, metallic, spring-like wire surrounded by an insulator and enclosed in a metal sheath.
- A change in temperature will cause an RTD to heat or cool, producing a proportional change in resistance. The change in resistance is measured by a precision device that is calibrated to give the proper temperature reading.

THERMOCOUPLES

The thermocouple is a device that converts thermal energy into electrical energy.

EO 1.4 **DESCRIBE the basic construction of a thermocouple including:**
- **a. Major component arrangement**
- **b. Materials used**

EO 1.5 **EXPLAIN how a thermocouple provides an output representative of the measured temperature.**

Thermocouple Construction

A thermocouple is constructed of two dissimilar metal wires joined at one end. When one end of each wire is connected to a measuring instrument, the thermocouple becomes a sensitive and highly accurate measuring device. Thermocouples may be constructed of several different combinations of materials. The performance of a thermocouple material is generally determined by using that material with platinum. The most important factor to be considered when selecting a pair of materials is the "thermoelectric difference" between the two materials. A significant difference between the two materials will result in better thermocouple performance. Figure 4 illustrates the characteristics of the more commonly used materials when used with platinum.

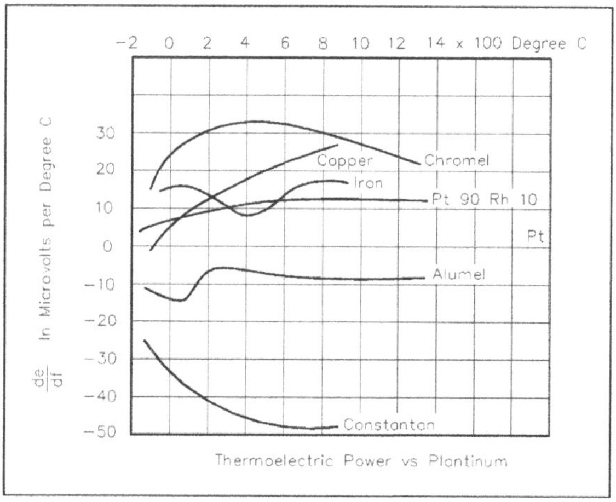

Figure 4 Thermocouple Material Characteristics When Used with Platinum

Other materials may be used in addition to those shown in Figure 4. For example: Chromel-Constantan is excellent for temperatures up to 2000°F; Nickel/Nickel-Molybdenum sometimes replaces Chromel-Alumel; and Tungsten-Rhenium is used for temperatures up to 5000°F. Some combinations used for specialized applications are Chromel-White Gold, Molybdenum-Tungsten, Tungsten-Iridium, and Iridium/Iridium-Rhodium.

Figure 5 shows the internal construction of a typical thermocouple. The leads of the thermocouple are encased in a rigid metal sheath. The measuring junction is normally formed at the bottom of the thermocouple housing. Magnesium oxide surrounds the thermocouple wires to prevent vibration that could damage the fine wires and to enhance heat transfer between the measuring junction and the medium surrounding the thermocouple.

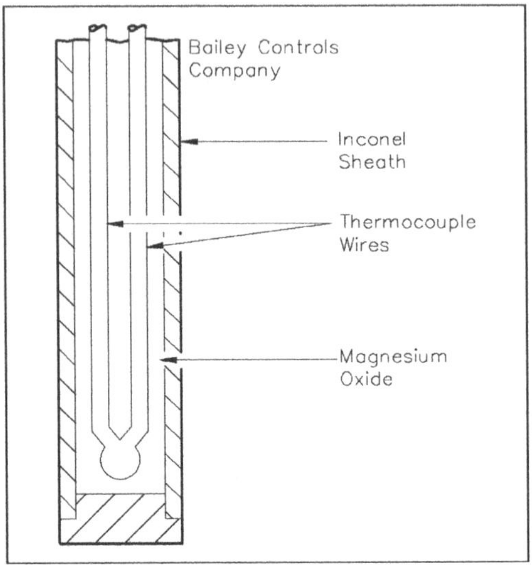

Figure 5 Internal Construction of a Typical Thermocouple

Thermocouple Operation

Thermocouples will cause an electric current to flow in the attached circuit when subjected to changes in temperature. The amount of current that will be produced is dependent on the temperature difference between the measurement and reference junction; the characteristics of the two metals used; and the characteristics of the attached circuit. Figure 6 illustrates a simple thermocouple circuit.

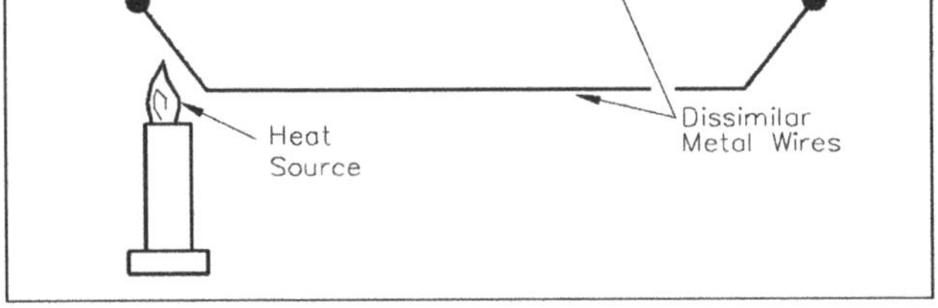

Figure 6 Simple Thermocouple Circuit

Heating the measuring junction of the thermocouple produces a voltage which is greater than the voltage across the reference junction. The difference between the two voltages is proportional to the difference in temperature and can be measured on the voltmeter (in millivolts). For ease of operator use, some voltmeters are set up to read out directly in temperature through use of electronic circuity.

Other applications provide only the millivolt readout. In order to convert the millivolt reading to its corresponding temperature, you must refer to tables like the one shown in Figure 7. These tables can be obtained from the thermocouple manufacturer, and they list the specific temperature corresponding to a series of millivolt readings.

Temperatures (°C) (IPTS 1968). Reference Junction 0°C

°C	0	10	20	30	40	50	60	70	80	90	100	°C
				Thermoelectric Voltage in Absolute Millivolts								
- 0	0.000	-0.053	-0.103	-0.150	-0.194	-0.236						- 0
+ 0	0.000	0.055	0.113	0.173	0.235	0.299	0.365	0.432	0.502	0.573	0.645	+ 0
100	0.645	0.719	0.795	0.872	0.950	1.029	1.109	1.190	1.273	1.356	1.440	100
200	1.440	1.525	1.611	1.698	1.785	1.873	1.962	2.051	2.141	2.232	2.323	200
300	2.323	2.414	2.506	2.599	2.692	2.786	2.880	2.974	3.069	3.164	3.260	300
400	3.260	3.356	3.452	3.549	3.645	3.743	3.840	3.938	4.036	4.135	4.234	400
500	4.234	4.333	4.432	4.532	4.632	4.732	4.332	4.933	5.034	5.136	5.237	500
600	5.237	5.339	5.442	5.544	5.648	5.751	5.855	5.960	6.064	6.169	6.274	600
700	6.274	6.380	6.486	6.592	6.699	6.805	6.913	7.020	7.128	7.236	7.345	700
800	7.345	7.454	7.563	7.672	7.782	7.892	8.003	8.114	8.225	8.336	8.448	800
900	8.448	8.560	8.673	8.786	8.899	9.012	9.126	9.240	9.355	9.470	9.585	900
1,000	9.585	9.700	9.816	9.932	10.048	10.165	10.282	10.400	10.517	10.635	10.754	1,000
1,100	10.754	10.872	10.991	11.110	11.229	11.348	11.467	11.587	11.707	11.827	11.947	1,100
1,200	11.947	12.067	12.188	12.308	12.429	12.550	12.671	12.792	12.913	13.034	13.155	1,200
1,300	13.155	13.276	13.397	13.519	13.640	13.761	13.883	14.004	14.125	14.247	14.368	1,300
1,400	14.368	14.489	14.610	14.731	14.852	14.973	15.094	15.215	15.336	15.456	15.576	1,400
1,500	15.576	15.697	15.817	15.937	16.057	16.176	16.296	16.415	16.534	16.653	16.771	1,500
1,600	16.771	16.890	17.008	17.125	17.243	17.360	17.477	17.594	17.711	17.826	17.942	1,600
1,700	17.942	18.058	18.170	18.282	18.394	18.504	18.612					1,700
°C	0	10	20	30	40	50	60	70	80	90	100	°C

Figure 7 Temperature-vs-Voltage Reference Table

Summary

Thermocouples are summarized below.

Thermocouple Summary

- A thermocouple is constructed of two dissimilar wires joined at one end and encased in a metal sheath.
- The other end of each wire is connected to a meter or measuring circuit.
- Heating the measuring junction of the thermocouple produces a voltage that is greater than the voltage across the reference junction.
- The difference between the two voltages is proportional to the difference in temperature and can be measured on a voltmeter.

FUNCTIONAL USES OF TEMPERATURE DETECTORS

Temperature sensing devices, such as RTDs and thermocouples, provide necessary temperature indications for the safe and continued operation of the DOE facility fluid systems. These temperature indications may include:

- *Reactor hot and cold leg temperatures*
- *Pressurizer temperature*
- *Purification demineralizer inlet temperature*
- *Cooling water to and from various components*
- *Secondary feed temperature*

EO 1.6 **STATE the three basic functions of temperature detectors.**

EO 1.7 **DESCRIBE the two alternate methods of determining temperature when the normal temperature sensing devices are inoperable.**

EO 1.8 **STATE the two environmental concerns which can affect the accuracy and reliability of temperature detection instrumentation.**

Functions of Temperature Detectors

Although the temperatures that are monitored vary slightly depending on the details of facility design, temperature detectors are used to provide three basic functions: indication, alarm, and control. The temperatures monitored may normally be displayed in a central location, such as a control room, and may have audible and visual alarms associated with them when specified preset limits are exceeded. These temperatures may have control functions associated with them so that equipment is started or stopped to support a given temperature condition or so that a protective action occurs.

Detector Problems

In the event that key temperature sensing instruments become inoperative, there are several alternate methods that may be used. Some applications utilize installed spare temperature detectors or dual-element RTDs. The dual-element RTD has two sensing elements of which only one is normally connected. If the operating element becomes faulty, the second element may be used to provide temperature indication. If an installed spare is not utilized, a contact pyrometer (portable thermocouple) may be used to obtain temperature readings on those pieces of equipment or systems that are accessible.

If the malfunction is in the circuitry and the detector itself is still functional, it may be possible to obtain temperatures by connecting an external bridge circuit to the detector. Resistance readings may then be taken and a corresponding temperature obtained from the detector calibration curves.

Environmental Concerns

Ambient temperature variations will affect the accuracy and reliability of temperature detection instrumentation. Variations in ambient temperature can directly affect the resistance of components in a bridge circuit and the resistance of the reference junction for a thermocouple. In addition, ambient temperature variations can affect the calibration of electric/electronic equipment. The effects of temperature variations are reduced by the design of the circuitry and by maintaining the temperature detection instrumentation in the proper environment.

The presence of humidity will also affect most electrical equipment, especially electronic equipment. High humidity causes moisture to collect on the equipment. This moisture can cause short circuits, grounds, and corrosion, which, in turn, may damage components. The effects due to humidity are controlled by maintaining the equipment in the proper environment.

Summary

Detector Uses Summary

- Temperature detectors are used for:
  - Indication
  - Alarm functions
  - Control functions
- If a temperature detector became inoperative:
  - A spare detector may be used (if installed)
  - A contact pyrometer can be used
- Environmental concerns:
  - Ambient temperature
  - Humidity

TEMPERATURE DETECTION CIRCUITRY

The bridge circuit is used whenever extremely accurate resistance measurements are required (such as RTD measurements).

EO 1.9 Given a simplified schematic diagram of a basic bridge circuit, STATE the purpose of the following components:
- **a. R_1 and R_2**
- **b. R_x**
- **c. Adjustable resistor**
- **d. Sensitive ammeter**

EO 1.10 DESCRIBE the bridge circuit conditions that create a balanced bridge.

EO 1.11 Given a block diagram of a basic temperature instrument detection and control system, STATE the purpose of the following blocks:
- **a. RTD**
- **b. Bridge circuit**
- **c. DC-AC converter**
- **d. Amplifier**
- **e. Balancing motor/mechanical linkage**

EO 1.12 DESCRIBE the temperature instrument indication(s) for the following circuit faults:
- **a. Short circuit**
- **b. Open circuit**

EO 1.13 EXPLAIN the three methods of bridge circuit compensation for changes in ambient temperature.

Bridge Circuit Construction

Figure 8 shows a basic bridge circuit which consists of three known resistances, R_1, R_2, and R_3 (variable), an unknown variable resistor R_X (RTD), a source of voltage, and a sensitive ammeter.

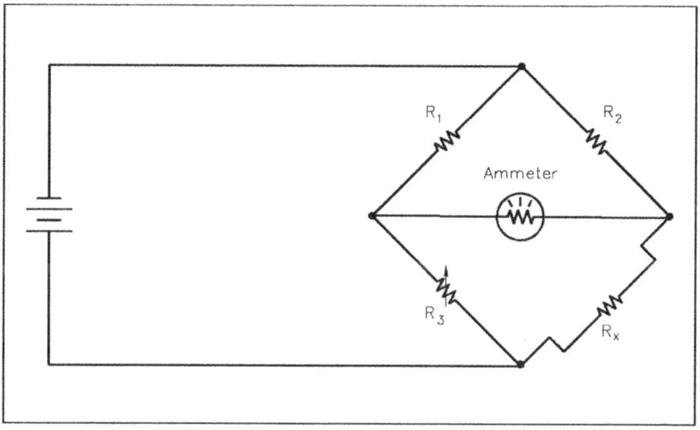

Figure 8 Bridge Circuit

Resistors R_1 and R_2 are the ratio arms of the bridge. They ratio the two variable resistances for current flow through the ammeter. R_3 is a variable resistor known as the standard arm that is adjusted to match the unknown resistor. The sensing ammeter visually displays the current that is flowing through the bridge circuit. Analysis of the circuit shows that when R_3 is adjusted so that the ammeter reads zero current, the resistance of both arms of the bridge circuit is the same. Equation 1-1 shows the relationship of the resistance between the two arms of the bridge.

$$\frac{R_1}{R_3} = \frac{R_2}{R_x} \tag{1-1}$$

Since the values of R_1, R_2, and R_3 are known values, the only unkown is R_x. The value of R_x can be calulated for the bridge during an ammeter zero current condition. Knowing this resistance value provides a baseline point for calibration of the instrument attached to the bridge circuit. The unknown resistance, R_x, is given by Equation 1-2.

$$R_x = \frac{R_2 R_3}{R_1} \tag{1-2}$$

Bridge Circuit Operation

The bridge operates by placing R_x in the circuit, as shown in Figure 8, and then adjusting R_3 so that all current flows through the arms of the bridge circuit. When this condition exists, there is no current flow through the ammeter, and the bridge is said to be balanced. When the bridge is balanced, the currents through each of the arms are exactly proportional. They are equal if $R_1 = R_2$. Most of the time the bridge is constructed so that $R_1 = R_2$. When this is the case, and the bridge is balanced, then the resistance of R_x is the same as R_3, or $R_x = R_3$.

When balance exists, R_3 will be equal to the unknown resistance, even if the voltage source is unstable or is not accurately known. A typical Wheatstone bridge has several dials used to vary the resistance. Once the bridge is balanced, the dials can be read to find the value of R_3. Bridge circuits can be used to measure resistance to tenths or even hundredths of a percent accuracy. When used to measure temperature, some Wheatstone bridges with precision resistors are accurate to about + 0.1°F.

Two types of bridge circuits (unbalanced and balanced) are utilized in resistance thermometer temperature detection circuits. The unbalanced bridge circuit (Figure 9) uses a millivoltmeter that is calibrated in units of temperature that correspond to the RTD resistance.

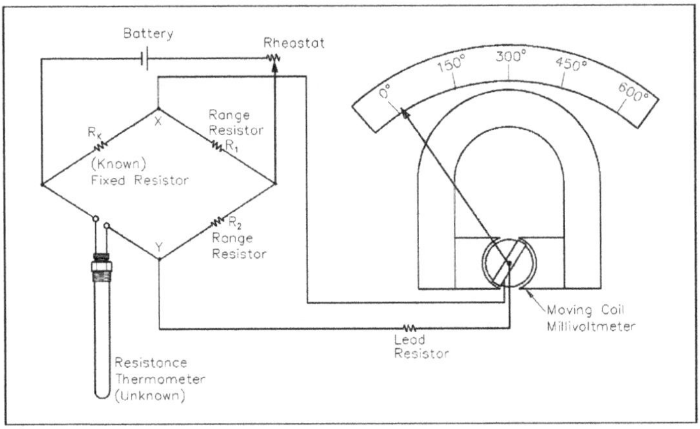

Figure 9 Unbalanced Bridge Circuit

The battery is connected to two opposite points of the bridge circuit. The millivoltmeter is connected to the two remaining points. The rheostat regulates bridge current. The regulated current is divided between the branch with the fixed resistor and range resistor R_1, and the branch with the RTD and range resistor R_2. As the electrical resistance of the RTD changes, the voltage at points X and Y changes. The millivoltmeter detects the change in voltage caused by unequal division of current in the two branches. The meter can be calibrated in units of temperature because the only changing resistance value is that of the RTD.

The balanced bridge circuit (Figure 10) uses a galvanometer to compare the RTD resistance with that of a fixed resistor. The galvanometer uses a pointer that deflects on either side of zero when the resistance of the arms is not equal. The resistance of the slide wire is adjusted until the galvanometer indicates zero. The value of the slide resistance is then used to determine the temperature of the system being monitored.

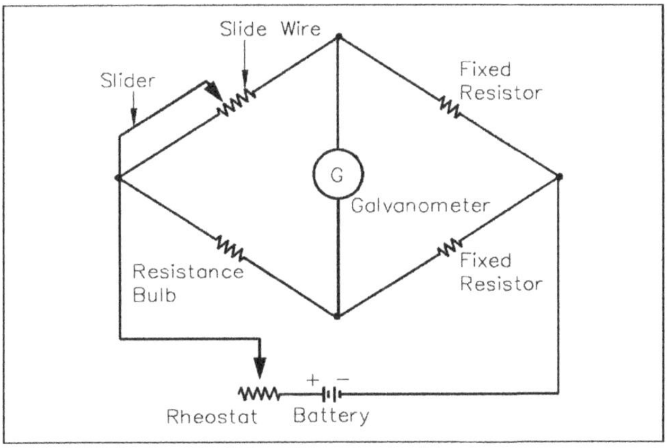

Figure 10 Balanced Bridge Circuit

A slidewire resistor is used to balance the arms of the bridge. The circuit will be in balance whenever the value of the slidewire resistance is such that no current flows through the galvanometer. For each temperature change, there is a new value; therefore, the slider must be moved to a new position to balance the circuit.

Temperature Detection Circuit

Figure 11 is a block diagram of a typical temperature detection circuit. This represents a balanced bridge temperature detection circuit that has been modified to eliminate the galvanometer.

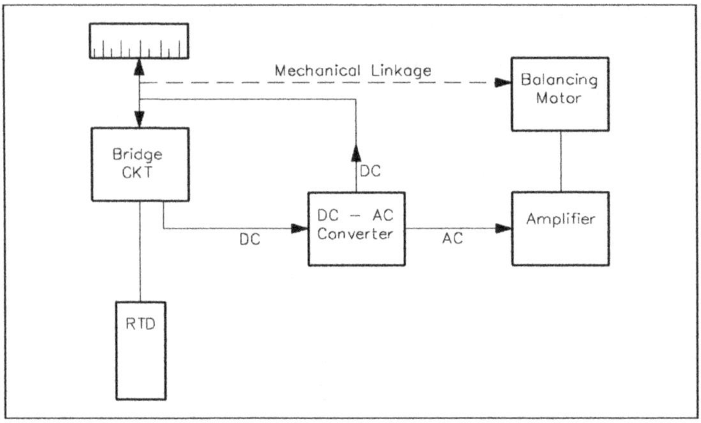

Figure 11 Block Diagram of a Typical Temperature Detection Circuit

The block consists of a temperature detector (RTD) that measures the temperature. The detector is felt as resistance to the bridge network. The bridge network converts this resistance to a DC voltage signal.

An electronic instrument has been developed in which the DC voltage of the potentiometer, or the bridge, is converted to an AC voltage. The AC voltage is then amplified to a higher (usable) voltage that is used to drive a bi-directional motor. The bi-directional motor positions the slider on the slidewire to balance the circuit resistance.

If the RTD becomes open in either the unbalanced and balanced bridge circuits, the resistance will be infinite, and the meter will indicate a very high temperature. If it becomes shorted, resistance will be zero, and the meter will indicate a very low temperature.

When calibrating the circuit, a precision resistor of known value is substituted for the resistance bulb, as shown in Figure 12.

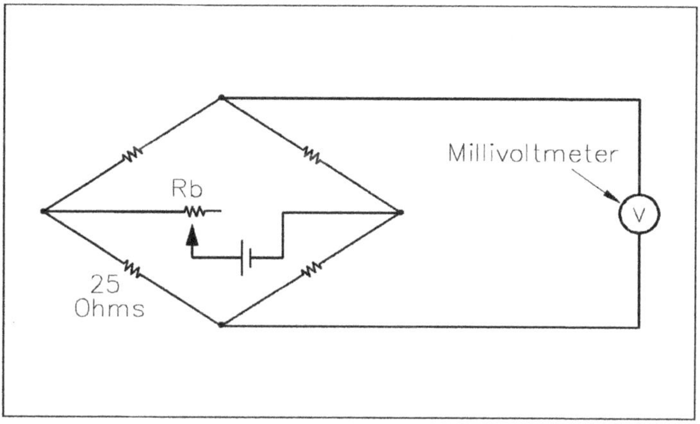

Figure 12 Resistance Thermometer Circuit with Precision Resistor in Place of Resistance Bulb

Battery voltage is then adjusted by varying R_b until the meter indication is correct for the known resistance.

Temperature Compensation

Because of changes in ambient temperature, the resistance thermometer circuitry must be compensated. The resistors that are used in the measuring circuitry are selected so that their resistance will remain constant over the range of temperature expected. Temperature compensation is also accomplished through the design of the electronic circuitry to compensate for ambient changes in the equipment cabinet. It is also possible for the resistance of the detector leads to change due to a change in ambient temperature. To compensate for this change, three and four wire RTD circuits are used. In this way, the same amount of lead wire is used in both branches of the bridge circuit, and the change in resistance will be felt on both branches, negating the effects of the change in temperature.

Summary

Temperature detection circuit operation is summarized below.

Circuit Operation Summary

- The basic bridge circuit consists of:

  - Two known resistors (R_1 and R_2) that are used for ratioing the adjustable and known resistances
  - One known variable resistor (R_3) that is used to match the unknown variable resistor
  - One unknown resistor (R_x) that is used to measure temperature
  - A sensing ammeter that indicates the current flow through the bridge circuit

- The bridge circuit is considered balanced when the sensing ammeter reads zero current.

- A basic temperature instrument is comprised of:

  - An RTD for measuring the temperature
  - A bridge network for converting resistance to voltage
  - A DC to AC voltage converter to supply an amplifiable AC signal to the amplifier
  - An AC signal amplifier to amplify the AC signal to a usable level
  - A balancing motor/mechanical linkage assembly to balance the circuit's resistance

- An open circuit in a temperature instrument is indicated by a very high temperature. A short circuit in a temperature instrument is indicated by a very low temperature.

- Temperature instrument ambient temperature compensation is accomplished by:

  - Measuring circuit resistor selection
  - Electronic circuitry design
  - Use of three or four wire RTD circuits

Department of Energy
Fundamentals Handbook

INSTRUMENTATION AND CONTROL
Module 2
Pressure Detectors

TABLE OF CONTENTS

LIST OF FIGURES ii

LIST OF TABLES iii

REFERENCES iv

OBJECTIVES v

PRESSURE DETECTORS 1

- Bellows-Type Detectors 1
- Bourdon Tube-Type Detectors 2
- Summary 3

PRESSURE DETECTOR FUNCTIONAL USES 4

- Pressure Detector Functions 4
- Detector Failure 4
- Environmental Concerns 4
- Summary 5

PRESSURE DETECTION CIRCUITRY 6

- Resistance-Type Transducers 6
- Inductance-Type Transducers 9
- Capacitive-Type Transducers 11
- Detection Circuitry 12
- Summary 13

LIST OF FIGURES

Figure 1 Basic Metallic Bellows 1

Figure 2 Bourdon Tube 2

Figure 3 Strain Gauge 7

Figure 4 Strain Gauge Pressure Transducer 7

Figure 5 Strain Gauge Used in a Bridge Circuit 8

Figure 6 Bellows Resistance Transducer 9

Figure 7 Inductance-Type Pressure Transducer Coil 9

Figure 8 Differential Transformer 10

Figure 9 Capacitive Pressure Transducer 11

Figure 10 Typical Pressure Detection Block Diagram 12

LIST OF TABLES

NONE

REFERENCES

- Kirk, Franklin W. and Rimboi, Nicholas R., Instrumentation, Third Edition, American Technical Publishers, ISBN 0-8269-3422-6.

- Academic Program for Nuclear Power Plant Personnel, Volume IV, General Physics Corporation, Library of Congress Card #A 397747, April 1982.

- Fozard, B., Instrumentation and Control of Nuclear Reactors, ILIFFE Books Ltd., London.

- Wightman, E.J., Instrumentation in Process Control, CRC Press, Cleveland, Ohio.

- Rhodes, T.J. and Carroll, G.C., Industrial Instruments for Measurement and Control, Second Edition, McGraw-Hill Book Company.

- Process Measurement Fundamentals, Volume I, General Physics Corporation, ISBN 0-87683-001-7, 1981.

TERMINAL OBJECTIVE

1.0 Given a pressure instrument, **RELATE** the fundamental principles, including possible failure modes, to that specific instrument.

ENABLING OBJECTIVES

1.1 **EXPLAIN** how a bellows-type pressure detector produces an output signal including:
   a. Method of detection
   b. Method of signal generation

1.2 **EXPLAIN** how a bourdon tube-type pressure detector produces an output signal including:
   a. Method of detection
   b. Method of signal generation

1.3 **STATE** the three functions of pressure measuring instrumentation.

1.4 **DESCRIBE** the three alternate methods of determining pressure when the normal pressure sensing devices are inoperable.

1.5 **STATE** the three environmental concerns which can affect the accuracy and reliability of pressure detection instrumentation.

1.6 **EXPLAIN** how a strain gauge pressure transducer produces an output signal including:
   a. Method of detection
   b. Method of signal generation

1.7 Given a basic block diagram of a typical pressure detection device, **STATE** the purpose of the following blocks:
   a. Sensing element
   b. Transducer
   c. Pressure detection circuitry
   d. Pressure indication

Intentionally Left Blank

PRESSURE DETECTORS

Many processes are controlled by measuring pressure. This chapter describes the detectors associated with measuring pressure.

EO 1.1 EXPLAIN how a bellows-type pressure detector produces an output signal including:
a. Method of detection
b. Method of signal generation

EO 1.2 EXPLAIN how a bourdon tube-type pressure detector produces an output signal including:
a. Method of detection
b. Method of signal generation

Bellows-Type Detectors

The need for a pressure sensing element that was extremely sensitive to low pressures and provided power for activating recording and indicating mechanisms resulted in the development of the metallic bellows pressure sensing element. The metallic bellows is most accurate when measuring pressures from 0.5 to 75 psig. However, when used in conjunction with a heavy range spring, some bellows can be used to measure pressures of over 1000 psig. Figure 1 shows a basic metallic bellows pressure sensing element.

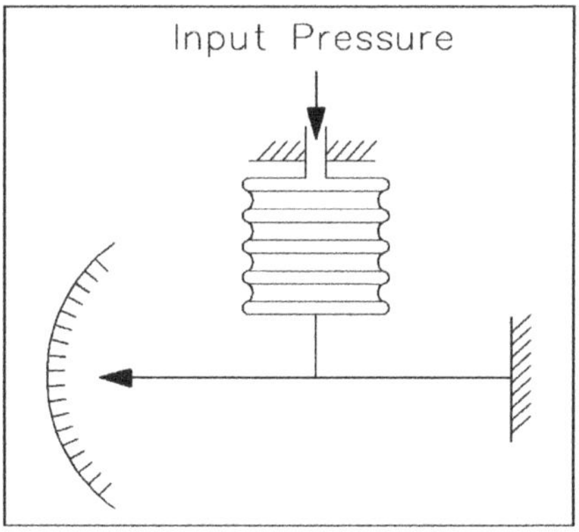

Figure 1 Basic Metallic Bellows

The bellows is a one-piece, collapsible, seamless metallic unit that has deep folds formed from very thin-walled tubing. The diameter of the bellows ranges from 0.5 to 12 in. and may have as many as 24 folds. System pressure is applied to the internal volume of the bellows. As the inlet pressure to the instrument varies, the bellows will expand or contract. The moving end of the bellows is connected to a mechanical linkage assembly. As the bellows and linkage assembly moves, either an electrical signal is generated or a direct pressure indication is provided. The flexibility of a metallic bellows is similar in character to that of a helical, coiled compression spring. Up to the elastic limit of the bellows, the relation between increments of load and deflection is linear. However, this relationship exists only when the bellows is under compression. It is necessary to construct the bellows such that all of the travel occurs on the compression side of the point of equilibrium. Therefore, in practice, the bellows must always be opposed by a spring, and the deflection characteristics will be the resulting force of the spring and bellows.

Bourdon Tube-Type Detectors

The bourdon tube pressure instrument is one of the oldest pressure sensing instruments in use today. The bourdon tube (refer to Figure 2) consists of a thin-walled tube that is flattened diametrically on opposite sides to produce a cross-sectional area elliptical in shape, having two long flat sides and two short round sides. The tube is bent lengthwise into an arc of a circle of 270 to 300 degrees. Pressure applied to the inside of the tube causes distention of the flat sections and tends to restore its original round cross-section. This change in cross-section causes the tube to straighten slightly. Since the tube is permanently fastened at one end, the tip of the tube traces a curve that is the result of the change in angular position with respect to the center. Within limits, the movement of the tip of the tube can then be used to position a pointer or to develop an equivalent electrical signal (which is discussed later in the text) to indicate the value of the applied internal pressure.

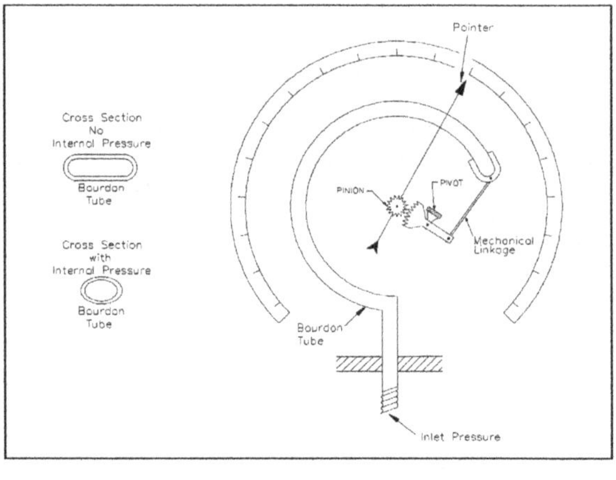

Figure 2 Bourdon Tube

Summary

The operation of bellows-type and bourdon tube-type pressure detectors is summarized below.

Bellows and Bourdon Tube Pressure Detectors Summary

- In a bellows-type detector:
  - System pressure is applied to the internal volume of a bellows and mechanical linkage assembly.
  - As pressure changes, the bellows and linkage assembly move to cause an electrical signal to be produced or to cause a gauge pointer to move.

- In a bourdon tube-type detector:
  - System pressure is applied to the inside of a slightly flattened arc-shaped tube. As pressure increases, the tube tends to restore to its original round cross-section. This change in cross-section causes the tube to straighten.

  - Since the tube is permanently fastened at one end, the tip of the tube traces a curve that is the result of the change in angular position with respect to the center. The tip movement can then be used to position a pointer or to develop an electrical signal.

PRESSURE DETECTOR FUNCTIONAL USES

Pressure measurement is a necessary function in the safe and efficient operation of DOE nuclear facilities.

EO 1.3 **STATE the three functions of pressure measuring instrumentation.**

EO 1.4 **DESCRIBE the three alternate methods of determining pressure when the normal pressure sensing devices are inoperable.**

EO 1.5 **STATE the three environmental concerns which can affect the accuracy and reliability of pressure detection instrumentation.**

Pressure Detector Functions

Although the pressures that are monitored vary slightly depending on the details of facility design, all pressure detectors are used to provide up to three basic functions: indication, alarm, and control. Since the fluid system may operate at both saturation and subcooled conditions, accurate pressure indication must be available to maintain proper cooling. Some pressure detectors have audible and visual alarms associated with them when specified preset limits are exceeded. Some pressure detector applications are used as inputs to protective features and control functions.

Detector Failure

If a pressure instrument fails, spare detector elements may be utilized if installed. If spare detectors are not installed, the pressure may be read at an independent local mechanical gauge, if available, or a precision pressure gauge may be installed in the system at a convenient point. If the detector is functional, it may be possible to obtain pressure readings by measuring voltage or current values across the detector leads and comparing this reading with calibration curves.

Environmental Concerns

Pressure instruments are sensitive to variations in the atmospheric pressure surrounding the detector. This is especially apparent when the detector is located within an enclosed space. Variations in the pressure surrounding the detector will cause the indicated pressure from the detector to change. This will greatly reduce the accuracy of the pressure instrument and should be considered when installing and maintaining these instruments.

Ambient temperature variations will affect the accuracy and reliability of pressure detection instrumentation. Variations in ambient temperature can directly affect the resistance of components in the instrumentation circuitry, and, therefore, affect the calibration of electric/electronic equipment. The effects of temperature variations are reduced by the design of the circuitry and by maintaining the pressure detection instrumentation in the proper environment.

The presence of humidity will also affect most electrical equipment, especially electronic equipment. High humidity causes moisture to collect on the equipment. This moisture can cause short circuits, grounds, and corrosion, which, in turn, may damage components. The effects due to humidity are controlled by maintaining the equipment in the proper environment.

Summary

The three functions of pressure monitoring instrumentation and alternate methods of monitoring pressure are summarized below.

Functional Uses Summary

- Pressure detectors perform the following basic functions:

  - Indication
  - Alarm
  - Control

- If a pressure detector becomes inoperative:

  - A spare detector element may be used (if installed).
  - A local mechanical pressure gauge can be used (if available).
  - A precision pressure gauge may be installed in the system.

- Environmental concerns:

  - Atmospheric pressure
  - Ambient temperature
  - Humidity

PRESSURE DETECTION CIRCUITRY

Any of the pressure detectors previously discussed can be joined to an electrical device to form a pressure transducer. Transducers can produce a change in resistance, inductance, or capacitance.

EO 1.6 EXPLAIN how a strain gauge pressure transducer produces an output signal including:

a. Method of detection

b. Method of signal generation

EO 1.7 Given a basic block diagram of a typical pressure detection device, STATE the purpose of the following blocks:

a. Sensing element

b. Transducer

c. Pressure detection circuitry

d. Pressure indication

Resistance-Type Transducers

Included in this category of transducers are strain gauges and moving contacts (slidewire variable resistors). Figure 3 illustrates a simple strain gauge. A strain gauge measures the external force (pressure) applied to a fine wire. The fine wire is usually arranged in the form of a grid. The pressure change causes a resistance change due to the distortion of the wire. The value of the pressure can be found by measuring the change in resistance of the wire grid. Equation 2-1 shows the pressure to resistance relationship.

$$R = K\frac{L}{A} \qquad (2\text{-}1)$$

where

R = resistance of the wire grid in ohms
K = resistivity constant for the particular type of wire grid
L = length of wire grid
A = cross sectional area of wire grid

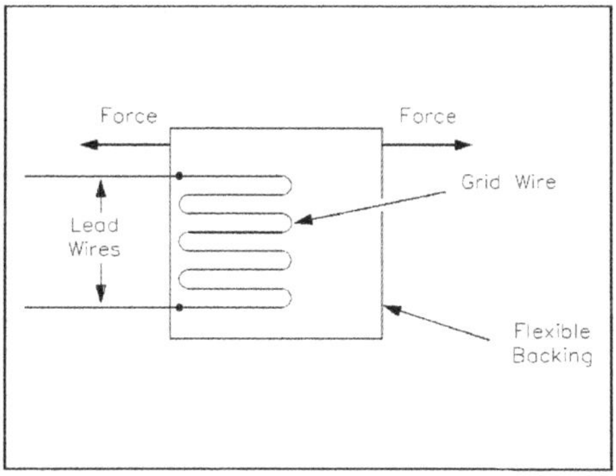

Figure 3 Strain Gauge

As the wire grid is distorted by elastic deformation, its length is increased, and its cross-sectional area decreases. These changes cause an increase in the resistance of the wire of the strain gauge. This change in resistance is used as the variable resistance in a bridge circuit that provides an electrical signal for indication of pressure. Figure 4 illustrates a strain gauge pressure transducer.

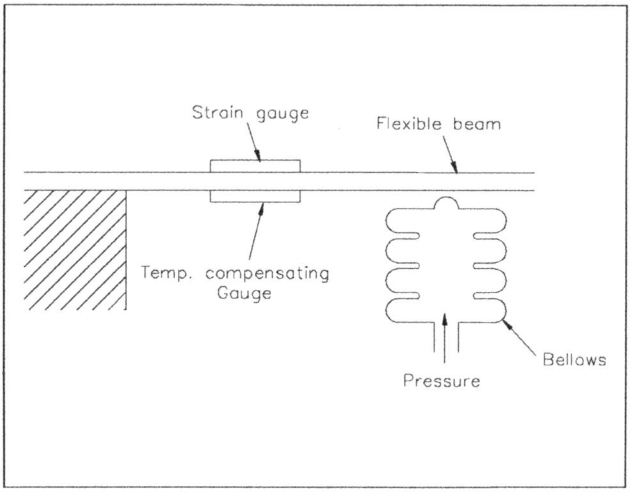

Figure 4 Strain Gauge Pressure Transducer

An increase in pressure at the inlet of the bellows causes the bellows to expand. The expansion of the bellows moves a flexible beam to which a strain gauge has been attached. The movement of the beam causes the resistance of the strain gauge to change. The temperature compensating gauge compensates for the heat produced by current flowing through the fine wire of the strain gauge. Strain gauges, which are nothing more than resistors, are used with bridge circuits as shown in Figure 5.

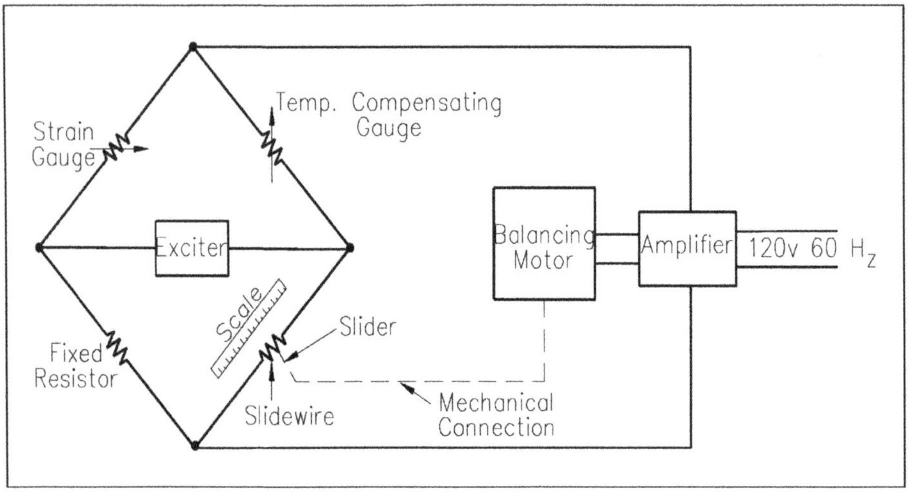

Figure 5 Strain Gauge Used in a Bridge Circuit

Alternating current is provided by an exciter that is used in place of a battery to eliminate the need for a galvanometer. When a change in resistance in the strain gauge causes an unbalanced condition, an error signal enters the amplifier and actuates the balancing motor. The balancing motor moves the slider along the slidewire, restoring the bridge to a balanced condition. The slider's position is noted on a scale marked in units of pressure.

Other resistance-type transducers combine a bellows or a bourdon tube with a variable resistor, as shown in Figure 6. As pressure changes, the bellows will either expand or contract. This expansion and contraction causes the attached slider to move along the slidewire, increasing or decreasing the resistance, and thereby indicating an increase or decrease in pressure.

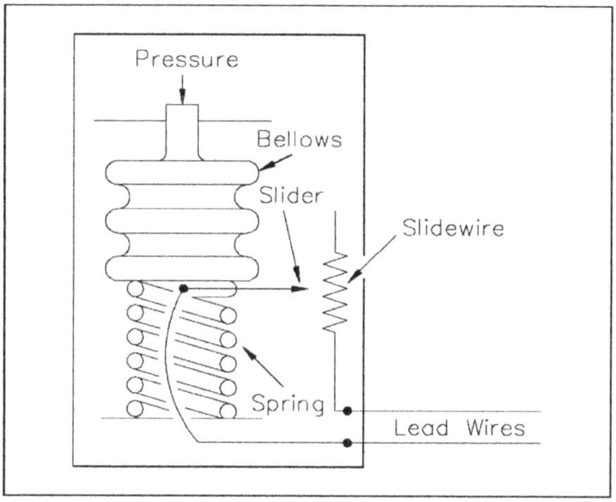

Figure 6 Bellows Resistance Transducer

Inductance-Type Transducers

The inductance-type transducer consists of three parts: a coil, a movable magnetic core, and a pressure sensing element. The element is attached to the core, and, as pressure varies, the element causes the core to move inside the coil. An AC voltage is applied to the coil, and, as the core moves, the inductance of the coil changes. The current through the coil will increase as the inductance decreases. For increased sensitivity, the coil can be separated into two coils by utilizing a center tap, as shown in Figure 7. As the core moves within the coils, the inductance of one coil will increase, while the other will decrease.

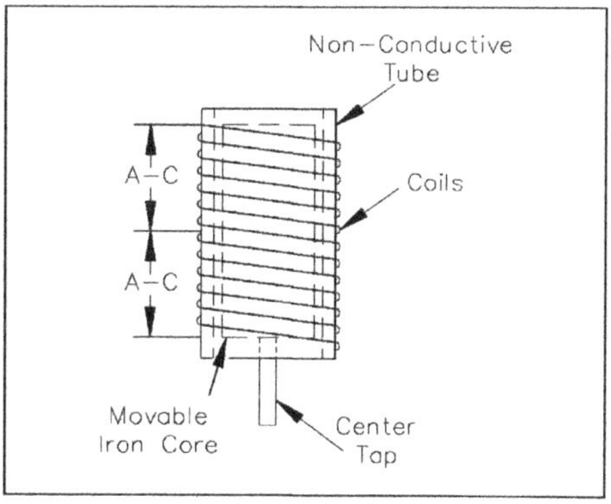

Figure 7 Inductance-Type Pressure Transducer Coil

Another type of inductance transducer, illustrated in Figure 8, utilizes two coils wound on a single tube and is commonly referred to as a Differential Transformer.

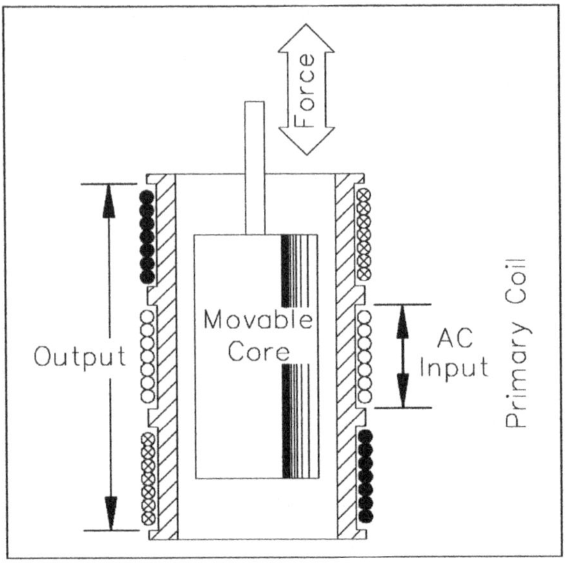

Figure 8 Differential Transformer

The primary coil is wound around the center of the tube. The secondary coil is divided with one half wound around each end of the tube. Each end is wound in the opposite direction, which causes the voltages induced to oppose one another. A core, positioned by a pressure element, is movable within the tube. When the core is in the lower position, the lower half of the secondary coil provides the output. When the core is in the upper position, the upper half of the secondary coil provides the output. The magnitude and direction of the output depends on the amount the core is displaced from its center position. When the core is in the mid-position, there is no secondary output.

Capacitive-Type Transducers

Capacitive-type transducers, illustrated in Figure 9, consist of two flexible conductive plates and a dielectric. In this case, the dielectric is the fluid.

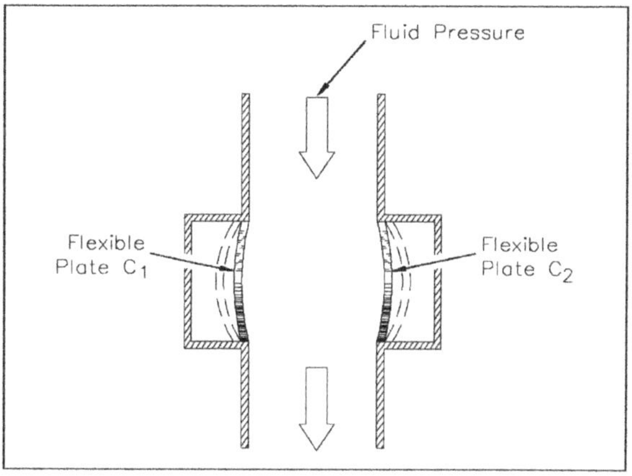

Figure 9 Capacitive Pressure Transducer

As pressure increases, the flexible conductive plates will move farther apart, changing the capacitance of the transducer. This change in capacitance is measurable and is proportional to the change in pressure.

Detection Circuitry

Figure 10 shows a block diagram of a typical pressure detection circuit.

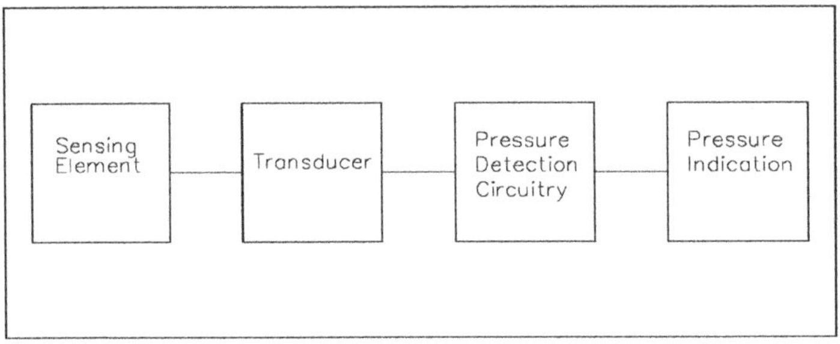

Figure 10 Typical Pressure Detection Block Diagram

The sensing element senses the pressure of the monitored system and converts the pressure to a mechanical signal. The sensing element supplies the mechanical signal to a transducer, as discussed above. The transducer converts the mechanical signal to an electrical signal that is proportional to system pressure. If the mechanical signal from the sensing element is used directly, a transducer is not required and therefore not used. The detector circuitry will amplify and/or transmit this signal to the pressure indicator. The electrical signal generated by the detection circuitry is proportional to system pressure. The exact operation of detector circuitry depends upon the type of transducer used. The pressure indicator provides remote indication of the system pressure being measured.

Summary

The operation of a strain guage and a typical pressure detection device is summarized below.

Circuit Operation Summary

- The operation of a strain gauge is as follows:
  - A strain gauge measures the pressure applied to a fine wire. The fine wire is usually arranged in the form of a grid. The pressure change causes a resistance change due to the distortion of the wire.
  - This change in resistance is used as the variable resistance in a bridge circuit that provides an electrical signal for indication of pressure.
- The operation of a typical pressure detection device is as follows:
  - The detector senses the pressure of the monitored system and converts this pressure to a mechanical signal. The mechanical signal from the detector is supplied to the transducer.
  - The transducer will convert this signal to a usable electrical signal and send a signal proportional to the detected pressure to the detection circuitry.
  - The detector circuitry will amplify and/or transmit this signal to the pressure indicator.
  - The pressure indicator will provide remote indication of the system pressure being measured.

Intentionally Left Blank

Department of Energy
Fundamentals Handbook

INSTRUMENTATION AND CONTROL
Module 3
Level Detectors

TABLE OF CONTENTS

LIST OF FIGURES ii

LIST OF TABLES iii

REFERENCES iv

OBJECTIVES v

LEVEL DETECTORS 1

Gauge Glass 1
Ball Float 4
Chain Float 5
Magnetic Bond Method 6
Conductivity Probe Method 6
Differential Pressure Level Detectors 7
Summary 10

DENSITY COMPENSATION 11

Specific Volume 11
Reference Leg Temperature Considerations 12
Pressurizer Level Instruments 13
Steam Generator Level Instrument 13
Summary 14

LEVEL DETECTION CIRCUITRY 15

Remote Indication 15
Environmental Concerns 16
Summary 17

LIST OF FIGURES

Figure 1 Transparent Tube 1

Figure 2 Gauge Glass 2

Figure 3 Reflex Gauge Glass 3

Figure 4 Refraction Gauge Glass (overhead view) 4

Figure 5 Ball Float Level Mechanism 5

Figure 6 Chain Float Gauge 5

Figure 7 Magnetic Bond Detector 6

Figure 8 Conductivity Probe Level Detection System 6

Figure 9 Open Tank Differential Pressure Detector 7

Figure 10 Closed Tank, Dry Reference Leg 8

Figure 11 Closed Tank, Wet Reference Leg 9

Figure 12 Effects of Fluid Density 12

Figure 13 Pressurizer Level System 13

Figure 14 Steam Generator Level System 13

Figure 15 Block Diagram of a Differential Pressure
Level Detection Circuit 15

LIST OF TABLES

NONE

REFERENCES

- Kirk, Franklin W. and Rimboi, Nicholas R., Instrumentation, Third Edition, American Technical Publishers, ISBN 0-8269-3422-6.
- Academic Program for Nuclear Power Plant Personnel, Volume IV, General Physics Corporation, Library of Congress Card #A 397747, April 1982.
- Fozard, B., Instrumentation and Control of Nuclear Reactors, ILIFFE Books Ltd., London.
- Wightman, E.J., Instrumentation in Process Control, CRC Press, Cleveland, Ohio.
- Rhodes, T.J. and Carroll, G.C., Industrial Instruments for Measurement and Control, Second Edition, McGraw-Hill Book Company.
- Process Measurement Fundamentals, Volume I, General Physics Corporation, ISBN 0-87683-001-7, 1981.

TERMINAL OBJECTIVE

1.0 Given a level instrument, **RELATE** the associated fundamental principles, including possible failure modes, to that instrument.

ENABLING OBJECTIVES

1.1 **IDENTIFY** the principle of operation of the following types of level instrumentation:
- a. Gauge glass
- b. Ball float
- c. Chain float
- d. Magnetic bond
- e. Conductivity probe
- f. Differential pressure (ΔP)

1.2 **EXPLAIN** the process of density compensation in level detection systems to include:
- a. Why needed
- b. How accomplished

1.3 **STATE** the three reasons for using remote level indicators.

1.4 Given a basic block diagram of a differential pressure detector-type level instrument, **STATE** the purpose of the following blocks:
- a. Differential pressure (D/P) transmitter
- b. Amplifier
- c. Indication

1.5 **STATE** the three environmental concerns which can affect the accuracy and reliability of level detection instrumentation.

Intentionally Left Blank

LEVEL DETECTORS

Liquid level measuring devices are classified into two groups: (a) direct method, and (b) inferred method. An example of the direct method is the dipstick in your car which measures the height of the oil in the oil pan. An example of the inferred method is a pressure gauge at the bottom of a tank which measures the hydrostatic head pressure from the height of the liquid.

EO 1.1 IDENTIFY the principle of operation of the following types of level instrumentation:
a. Gauge glass
b. Ball float
c. Chain float
d. Magnetic bond
e. Conductivity probe
f. Differential pressure (ΔP)

Gauge Glass

A very simple means by which liquid level is measured in a vessel is by the gauge glass method (Figure 1). In the gauge glass method, a transparent tube is attached to the bottom and top (top connection not needed in a tank open to atmosphere) of the tank that is monitored. The height of the liquid in the tube will be equal to the height of water in the tank.

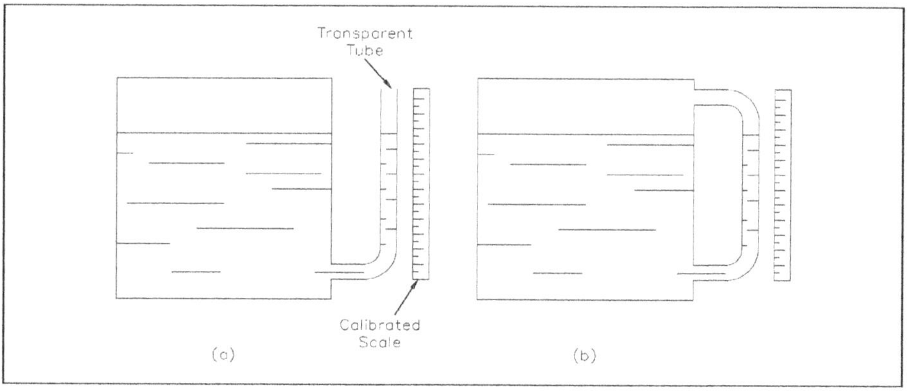

Figure 1 Transparent Tube

Figure 1 (a) shows a gauge glass which is used for vessels where the liquid is at ambient temperature and pressure conditions. Figure 1 (b) shows a gauge glass which is used for vessels where the liquid is at an elevated pressure or a partial vacuum. Notice that the gauge glasses in Figure 1 effectively form a "U" tube manometer where the liquid seeks its own level due to the pressure of the liquid in the vessel.

Gauge glasses made from tubular glass or plastic are used for service up to 450 psig and 400°F. If it is desired to measure the level of a vessel at higher temperatures and pressures, a different type of gauge glass is used. The type of gauge glass utilized in this instance has a body made of metal with a heavy glass or quartz section for visual observation of the liquid level. The glass section is usually flat to provide strength and safety. Figure 2 illustrates a typical transparent gauge glass.

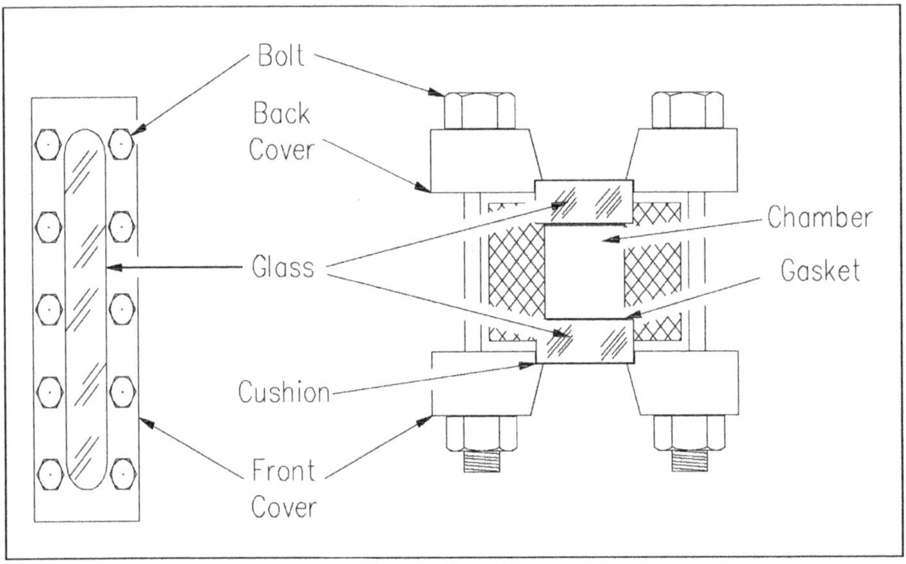

Figure 2 Gauge Glass

Another type of gauge glass is the reflex gauge glass (Figure 3). In this type, one side of the glass section is prism-shaped. The glass is molded such that one side has 90-degree angles which run lengthwise. Light rays strike the outer surface of the glass at a 90-degree angle. The light rays travel through the glass striking the inner side of the glass at a 45-degree angle. The presence or absence of liquid in the chamber determines if the light rays are refracted into the chamber or reflected back to the outer surface of the glass.

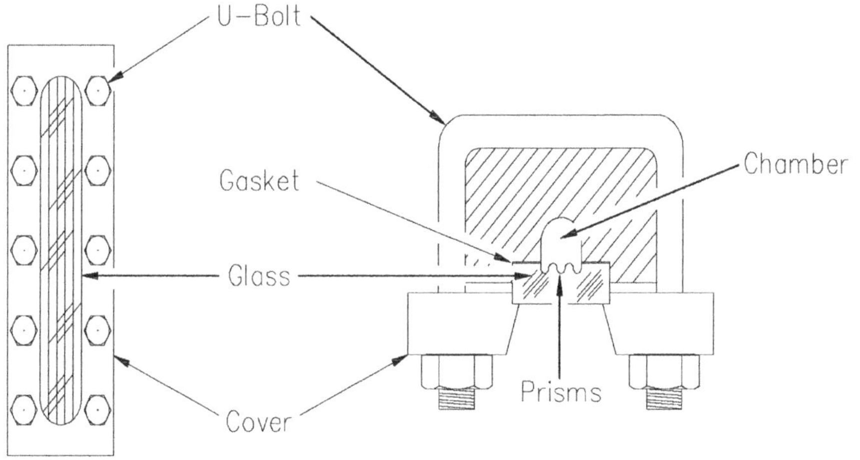

Figure 3 Reflex Gauge Glass

When the liquid is at an intermediate level in the gauge glass, the light rays encounter an air-glass interface in one portion of the chamber and a water-glass interface in the other portion of the chamber. Where an air-glass interface exists, the light rays are reflected back to the outer surface of the glass since the critical angle for light to pass from air to glass is 42 degrees. This causes the gauge glass to appear silvery-white. In the portion of the chamber with the water-glass interface, the light is refracted into the chamber by the prisms. Reflection of the light back to the outer surface of the gauge glass does not occur because the critical angle for light to pass from glass to water is 62-degrees. This results in the glass appearing black, since it is possible to see through the water to the walls of the chamber which are painted black.

A third type of gauge glass is the refraction type (Figure 4). This type is especially useful in areas of reduced lighting; lights are usually attached to the gauge glass. Operation is based on the principle that the bending of light, or refraction, will be different as light passes through various media. Light is bent, or refracted, to a greater extent in water than in steam. For the portion of the chamber that contains steam, the light rays travel relatively straight, and the red lens is illuminated. For the portion of the chamber that contains water, the light rays are bent, causing the green lens to be illuminated. The portion of the gauge containing water appears green; the portion of the gauge from that level upward appears red.

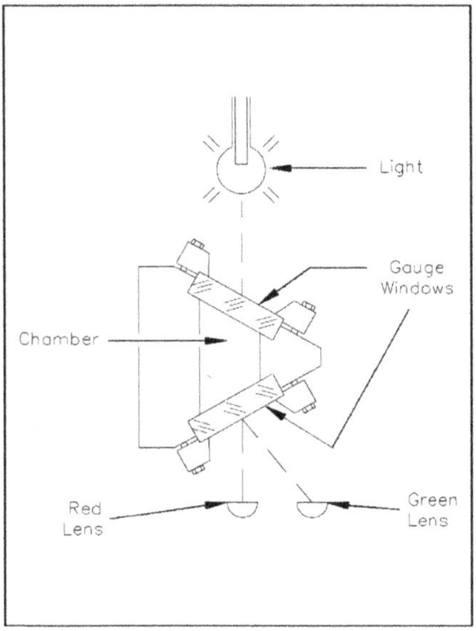

Figure 4 Refraction Gauge Glass
(overhead view)

Ball Float

The ball float method is a direct reading liquid level mechanism. The most practical design for the float is a hollow metal ball or sphere. However, there are no restrictions to the size, shape, or material used. The design consists of a ball float attached to a rod, which in turn is connected to a rotating shaft which indicates level on a calibrated scale (Figure 5). The operation of the ball float is simple. The ball floats on top of the liquid in the tank. If the liquid level changes, the float will follow and change the position of the pointer attached to the rotating shaft.

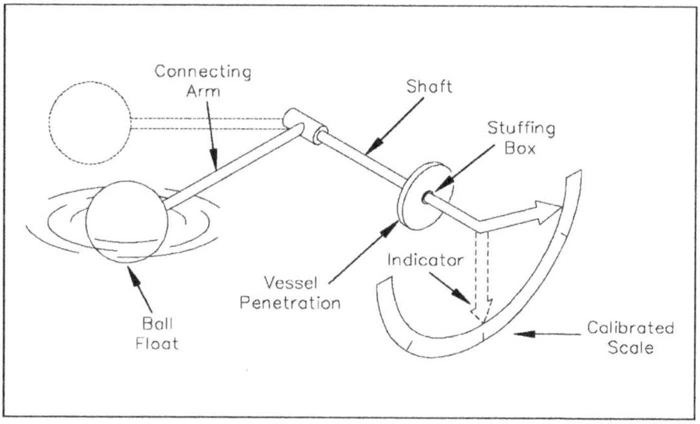

Figure 5 Ball Float Level Mechanism

The travel of the ball float is limited by its design to be within ±30 degrees from the horizontal plane which results in optimum response and performance. The actual level range is determined by the length of the connecting arm.

The stuffing box is incorporated to form a water-tight seal around the shaft to prevent leakage from the vessel.

Chain Float

This type of float gauge has a float ranging in size up to 12 inches in diameter and is used where small level limitations imposed by ball floats must be exceeded. The range of level measured will be limited only by the size of the vessel. The operation of the chain float is similiar to the ball float except in the method of positioning the pointer and in its connection to the position indication. The float is connected to a rotating element by a chain with a weight attached to the other end to provide a means of keeping the chain taut during changes in level (Figure 6).

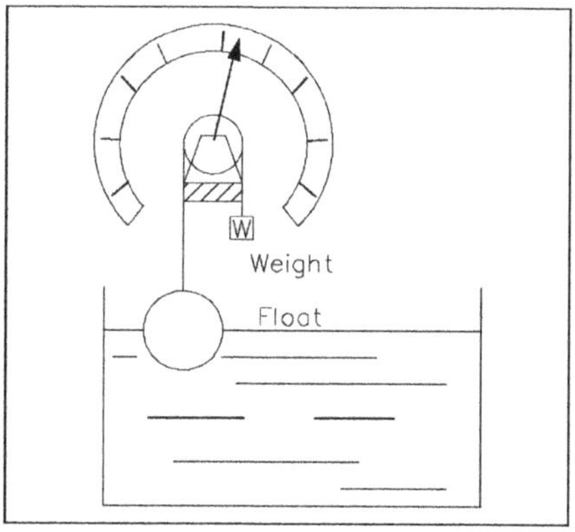

Figure 6 Chain Float Gauge

Magnetic Bond Method

The magnetic bond method was developed to overcome the problems of cages and stuffing boxes. The magnetic bond mechanism consists of a magnetic float which rises and falls with changes in level. The float travels outside of a non-magnetic tube which houses an inner magnet connected to a level indicator. When the float rises and falls, the outer magnet will attract the inner magnet, causing the inner magnet to follow the level within the vessel (Figure 7).

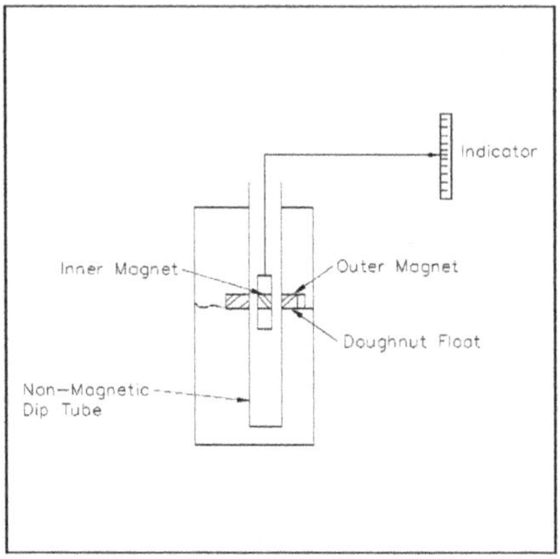

Figure 7 Magnetic Bond Detector

Conductivity Probe Method

Figure 8 illustrates a conductivity probe level detection system. It consists of one or more level detectors, an operating relay, and a controller. When the liquid makes contact with any of the electrodes, an electric current will flow between the electrode and ground. The current energizes a relay which causes the relay contacts to open or close depending on the state of the process involved. The relay in turn will actuate an alarm, a pump, a control valve, or all three. A typical system has three probes: a low level probe, a high level probe, and a high level alarm probe.

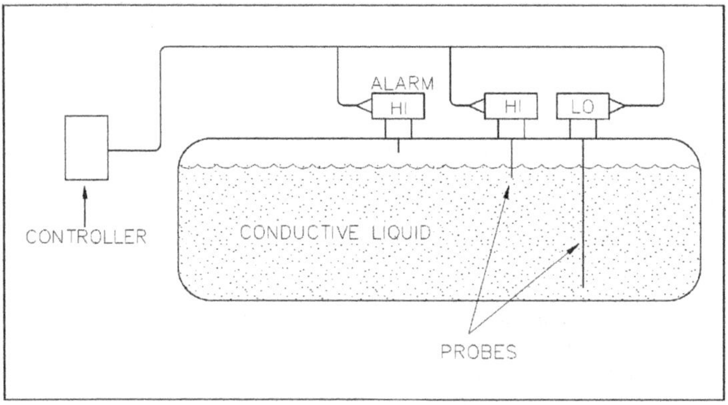

Figure 8 Conductivity Probe Level Detection System

Differential Pressure Level Detectors

The differential pressure (ΔP) detector method of liquid level measurement uses a ΔP detector connected to the bottom of the tank being monitored. The higher pressure, caused by the fluid in the tank, is compared to a lower reference pressure (usually atmospheric). This comparison takes place in the ΔP detector. Figure 9 illustrates a typical differential pressure detector attached to an open tank.

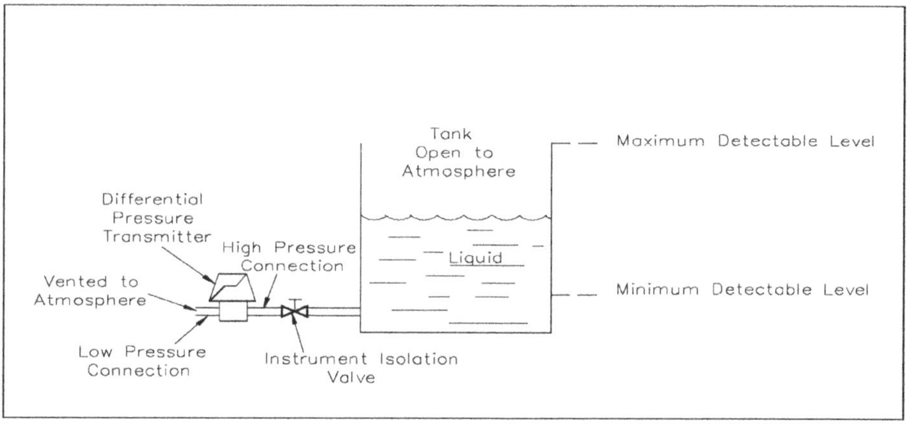

Figure 9 Open Tank Differential Pressure Detector

The tank is open to the atmosphere; therefore, it is necessary to use only the high pressure (HP) connection on the ΔP transmitter. The low pressure (LP) side is vented to the atmosphere; therefore, the pressure differential is the hydrostatic head, or weight, of the liquid in the tank. The maximum level that can be measured by the ΔP transmitter is determined by the maximum height of liquid above the transmitter. The minimum level that can be measured is determined by the point where the transmitter is connected to the tank.

Not all tanks or vessels are open to the atmosphere. Many are totally enclosed to prevent vapors or steam from escaping, or to allow pressurizing the contents of the tank. When measuring the level in a tank that is pressurized, or the level that can become pressurized by vapor pressure from the liquid, both the high pressure and low pressure sides of the ΔP transmitter must be connected (Figure 10).

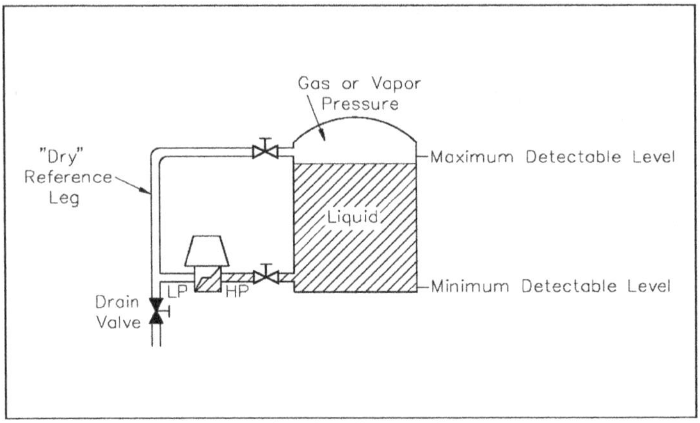

Figure 10 Closed Tank, Dry Reference Leg

The high pressure connection is connected to the tank at or below the lower range value to be measured. The low pressure side is connected to a "reference leg" that is connected at or above the upper range value to be measured. The reference leg is pressurized by the gas or vapor pressure, but no liquid is permitted to remain in the reference leg. The reference leg must be maintained dry so that there is no liquid head pressure on the low pressure side of the transmitter. The high pressure side is exposed to the hydrostatic head of the liquid plus the gas or vapor pressure exerted on the liquid's surface. The gas or vapor pressure is equally applied to the low and high pressure sides. Therefore, the output of the ΔP transmitter is directly proportional to the hydrostatic head pressure, that is, the level in the tank.

Where the tank contains a condensible fluid, such as steam, a slightly different arrangement is used. In applications with condensible fluids, condensation is greatly increased in the reference leg. To compensate for this effect, the reference leg is filled with the same fluid as the tank. The liquid in the reference leg applies a hydrostatic head to the high pressure side of the transmitter, and the value of this level is constant as long as the reference leg is maintained full. If this pressure remains constant, any change in ΔP is due to a change on the low pressure side of the transmitter (Figure 11).

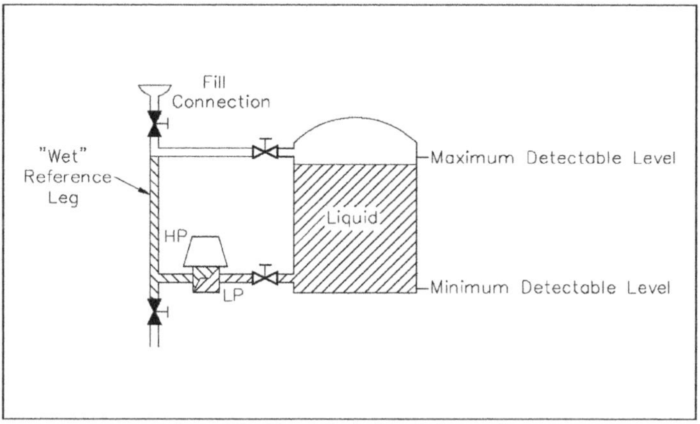

Figure 11 Closed Tank, Wet Reference Leg

The filled reference leg applies a hydrostatic pressure to the high pressure side of the transmitter, which is equal to the maximum level to be measured. The ΔP transmitter is exposed to equal pressure on the high and low pressure sides when the liquid level is at its maximum; therefore, the differential pressure is zero. As the tank level goes down, the pressure applied to the low pressure side goes down also, and the differential pressure increases. As a result, the differential pressure and the transmitter output are inversely proportional to the tank level.

Summary

The different types of level instruments presented in this chapter are summarized below.

Level Instrumentation Summary

- In the gauge glass method, a transparent tube is attached to the bottom and top (top connection not needed in a tank open to atmosphere) of the tank that is monitored. The height of the liquid in the tube will be equal to the height of water in the tank.
- The operation of the ball float is simple. The ball floats on top of the liquid in the tank. If the liquid level changes, the float will follow and change the position of the pointer attached to the rotating shaft.
- The operation of the chain float is similar to the ball float except in its method of positioning the pointer and its connection to the position indication. The float is connected to a rotating element by a chain with a weight attached to the other end to provide a means of keeping the chain taut during changes in level.
- The magnetic bond mechanism consists of a magnetic float that rises and falls with changes in level. The float travels outside of a non-magnetic tube which houses an inner magnet connected to a level indicator. When the float rises and falls, the outer magnet will attract the inner magnet, causing the inner magnet to follow the level within the vessel.
- The conductivity probe consists of one or more level detectors, an operating relay, and a controller. When the liquid makes contact with any of the electrodes, an electric current will flow between the electrode and ground. The current energizes a relay which causes the relay contacts to open or close depending on the state of the process involved. The relay in turn will actuate an alarm, a pump, a control valve, or all three.
- The differential pressure (ΔP) detector uses a ΔP detector connected to the bottom of the tank that is being monitored. The higher pressure in the tank is compared to a lower reference pressure (usually atmospheric). This comparison takes place in the ΔP detector.

DENSITY COMPENSATION

If a vapor with a significant density exists above the liquid, the hydrostatic pressure added needs to be considered if accurate transmitter output is required.

EO 1.2 EXPLAIN the process of density compensation in level detection systems to include:
a. Why needed
b. How accomplished

Specific Volume

Before examining an example which shows the effects of density, the unit "specific volume" must be defined. Specific volume is defined as volume per unit mass as shown in Equation 3-1.

$$\text{Specific Volume} = \text{Volume/Mass} \tag{3-1}$$

Specific volume is the reciprocal of density as shown in Equation 3-2.

$$\text{Specific Volume} = \frac{1}{\text{density}} \tag{3-2}$$

Specific volume is the standard unit used when working with vapors and steam that have low values of density.

For the applications that involve water and steam, specific volume can be found using "Saturated Steam Tables," which list the specific volumes for water and saturated steam at different pressures and temperatures.

The density of steam (or vapor) above the liquid level will have an effect on the weight of the steam or vapor bubble and the hydrostatic head pressure. As the density of the steam or vapor increases, the weight increases and causes an increase in hydrostatic head even though the actual level of the tank has not changed. The larger the steam bubble, the greater the change in hydrostatic head pressure.

Figure 12 illustrates a vessel in which the water is at saturated boiling conditions.

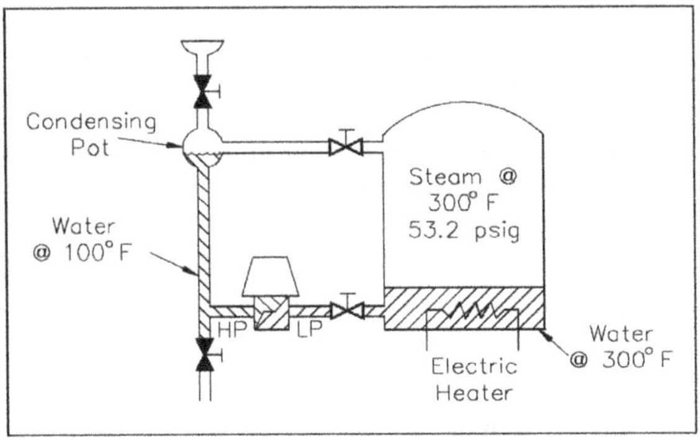

Figure 12 Effects of Fluid Density

A condensing pot at the top of the reference leg is incorporated to condense the steam and maintain the reference leg filled. As previously stated, the effect of the steam vapor pressure is cancelled at the ΔP transmitter due to the fact that this pressure is equally applied to both the low and high pressure sides of the transmitter. The differential pressure to the transmitter is due only to hydrostatic head pressure, as stated in Equation 3-3.

$$\text{Hydrostatic Head Pressure} = \text{Density} \times \text{Height} \tag{3-3}$$

Reference Leg Temperature Considerations

When the level to be measured is in a pressurized tank at elevated temperatures, a number of additional consequences must be considered. As the temperature of the fluid in the tank is increased, the density of the fluid decreases. As the fluid's density decreases, the fluid expands, occupying more volume. Even though the density is less, the mass of the fluid in the tank is the same. The problem encountered is that, as the fluid in the tank is heated and cooled, the density of the fluid changes, but the reference leg density remains relatively constant, which causes the indicated level to remain constant. The density of the fluid in the reference leg is dependent upon the ambient temperature of the room in which the tank is located; therefore, it is relatively constant and independent of tank temperature. If the fluid in the tank changes temperature, and therefore density, some means of density compensation must be incorporated in order to have an accurate indication of tank level. This is the problem encountered when measuring pressurizer water level or steam generator water level in pressurized water reactors, and when measuring reactor vessel water level in boiling water reactors.

Pressurizer Level Instruments

Figure 13 shows a typical pressurizer level system. Pressurizer temperature is held fairly constant during normal operation. The ΔP detector for level is calibrated with the pressurizer hot, and the effects of density changes do not occur. The pressurizer will not always be hot. It may be cooled down for non-operating maintenance conditions, in which case a second ΔP detector, calibrated for level measurement at low temperatures, replaces the normal ΔP detector. The density has not really been compensated for; it has actually been aligned out of the instrument by calibration.

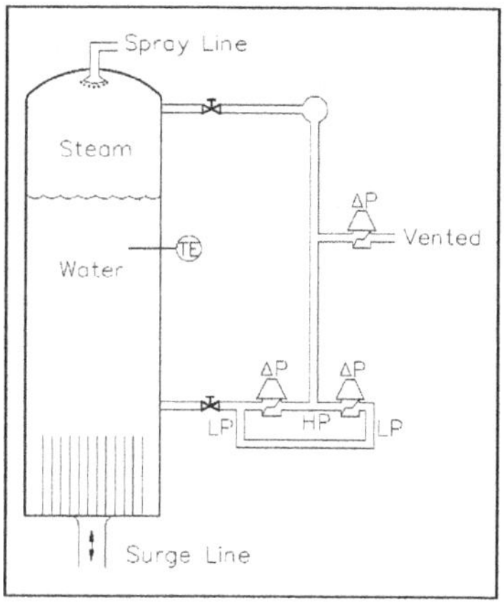

Figure 13 Pressurizer Level System

Density compensation may also be accomplished through electronic circuitry. Some systems compensate for density changes automatically through the design of the level detection circuitry. Other applications compensate for density by manually adjusting inputs to the circuit as the pressurizer cools down and depressurizes, or during heatup and pressurization. Calibration charts are also available to correct indications for changes in reference leg temperature.

Steam Generator Level Instrument

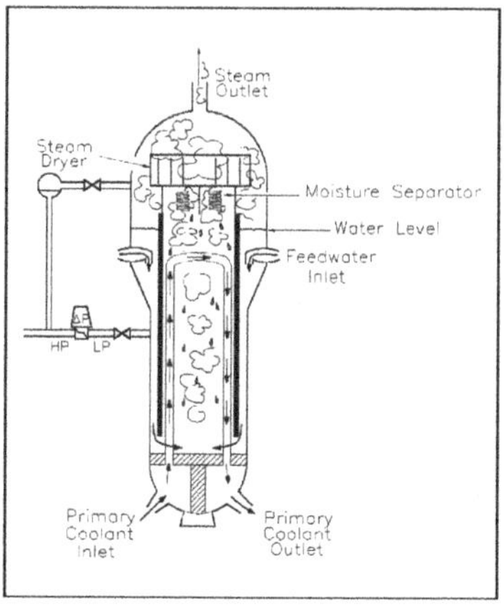

Figure 14 Steam Generator Level System

Figure 14 illustrates a typical steam generator level detection arrangement. The ΔP detector measures actual differential pressure. A separate pressure detector measures the pressure of the saturated steam. Since saturation pressure is proportional to saturation temperature, a pressure signal can be used to correct the differential pressure for density. An electronic circuit uses the pressure signal to compensate for the difference in density between the reference leg water and the steam generator fluid.

As the saturation temperature and pressure increase, the density of the steam generator water will decrease. The ΔP detector should now indicate a higher level, even though the actual ΔP has not changed. The increase in pressure is used to increase the output of the ΔP level detector in proportion to saturation pressure to reflect the change in actual level.

Summary

Density compensation is summarized below.

Density Compensation Summary

- If a vapor with a significant density exists above the liquid, the hydrostatic pressure that it will add may need to be considered if accurate transmitter output is required.
- Density compensation is accomplished by using either:
    - Electronic circuitry
    - Pressure detector input
    - Instrument calibration

LEVEL DETECTION CIRCUITRY

Remote indication provides vital level information to a central location.

EO 1.3 STATE the three reasons for using remote level indicators.

EO 1.4 Given a basic block diagram of a differential pressure detector-type level instrument, STATE the purpose of the following blocks:
a. Differential pressure (D/P) transmitter
b. Amplifier
c. Indication

EO 1.5 State the three environmental concerns which can affect the accuracy and reliability of level detection instrumentation.

Remote Indication

Remote indication is necessary to provide transmittal of vital level information to a central location, such as the control room, where all level information can be coordinated and evaluated. There are three major reasons for utilizing remote level indication:

- Level measurements may be taken at locations far from the main facility
- The level to be controlled may be a long distance from the point of control
- The level being measured may be in an unsafe/radioactive area.

Figure 15 illustrates a block diagram of a typical differential pressure detector. It consists of a differential pressure (D/P) transmitter (transducer), an amplifier, and level indication. The D/P transmitter consists of a diaphragm with the high pressure (H/P) and low pressure (L/P) inputs on opposite sides. As the differential pressure changes, the diaphragm will move. The transducer changes this mechanical motion into an electrical signal. The electrical signal generated by the transducer is then amplified and passed on to the level indicator for level indication at a remote

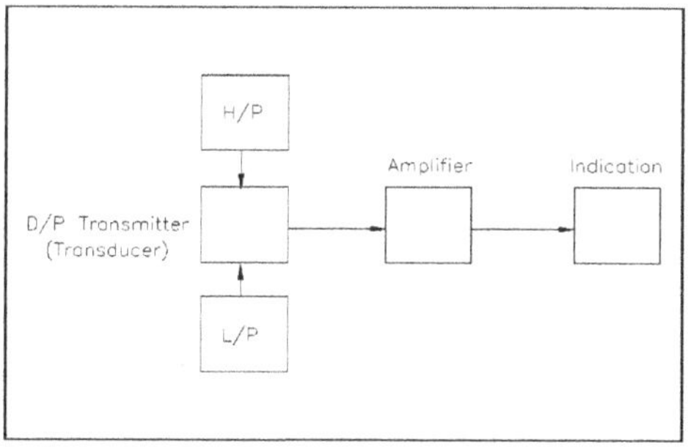

Figure 15 Block Diagram of a Differential Pressure Level Detection Circuit

location. Using relays, this system provides alarms on high and low level. It may also provide control functions such as repositioning a valve and protective features such as tripping a pump.

Environmental Concerns

Density of the fluid whose level is to be measured can have a large effect on level detection instrumentation. It primarily affects level sensing instruments which utilize a wet reference leg. In these instruments, it is possible for the reference leg temperature to be different from the temperature of the fluid whose level is to be measured. An example of this is the level detection instrumentation for a boiler steam drum. The water in the reference leg is at a lower temperature than the water in the steam drum. Therefore, it is more dense, and must be compensated for to ensure the indicated steam drum level is accurately indicated.

Ambient temperature variations will affect the accuracy and reliability of level detection instrumentation. Variations in ambient temperature can directly affect the resistance of components in the instrumentation circuitry, and, therefore, affect the calibration of electric/electronic equipment. The effects of temperature variations are reduced by the design of the circuitry and by maintaining the level detection instrumentation in the proper environment.

The presence of humidity will also affect most electrical equipment, especially electronic equipment. High humidity causes moisture to collect on the equipment. This moisture can cause short circuits, grounds, and corrosion, which, in turn, may damage components. The effects due to humidity are controlled by maintaining the equipment in the proper environment.

Summary

The density of the fluid, ambient temperature changes, and humidity are three factors which can affect the accuracy and reliability of level detection instrumentation. Level detection circuit operation is summarized below.

Circuit Operation Summary

- There are three major reasons for utilizing remote level indication:
  - Level measurements may be taken at locations far from the main facility.
  - The level to be controlled may be a long distance from the point of control.
  - The level being measured may be in an unsafe/radioactive area.
- The basic block diagram of a differential pressure level instrument are:
  - A differential pressure (D/P) transmitter which consists of a diaphragm with the high pressure (H/P) and low pressure (L/P) inputs on opposite sides. As the differential pressure changes, the diaphragm will move. The transducer changes this mechanical motion into an electrical signal.
  - An amplifier amplifies the electrical signal generated by the transducer and sends it to the level indicator.
  - A level indicator displays the level indication at a remote location.

Intentionally Left Blank

Department of Energy
Fundamentals Handbook

INSTRUMENTATION AND CONTROL
Module 4
Flow Detectors

www.KnowledgePublications.com

TABLE OF CONTENTS

LIST OF FIGURES ii

LIST OF TABLES iii

REFERENCES iv

OBJECTIVES v

HEAD FLOW METERS 1

Orifice Plate 3
Venturi Tube 4
Dall Flow Tube 5
Pitot Tube 6
Summary 7

OTHER FLOW METERS 8

Area Flow Meter 8
Displacement Meter 9
Hot-Wire Anemometer 10
Electromagnetic Flowmeter 10
Ultrasonic Flow Equipment 10
Summary 11

STEAM FLOW DETECTION 12

Summary 16

FLOW CIRCUITRY 17

Circuitry 17
Use of Flow Indication 18
Environmental Concerns 18
Summary 19

LIST OF FIGURES

Figure 1 Head Flow Meter 1

Figure 2 Orifice Plates 3

Figure 3 Venturi Tube 4

Figure 4 Dall Flow Tube 5

Figure 5 Pitot Tube 6

Figure 6 Rotameter 8

Figure 7 Nutating Disk 9

Figure 8 Flow Nozzle 12

Figure 9 Simple Mass Flow Detection System 14

Figure 10 Gas Flow Computer 15

Figure 11 Differential Pressure Flow Detection
Block Diagram 17

LIST OF TABLES

NONE

REFERENCES

- Kirk, Franklin W. and Rimboi, Nicholas R., Instrumentation, Third Edition, American Technical Publishers, ISBN 0-8269-3422-6.
- Academic Program for Nuclear Power Plant Personnel, Volume IV, General Physics Corporation, Library of Congress Card #A 397747, April 1982.
- Fozard, B., Instrumentation and Control of Nuclear Reactors, ILIFFE Books Ltd., London.
- Wightman, E.J., Instrumentation in Process Control, CRC Press, Cleveland, Ohio.
- Rhodes, T.J. and Carroll, G.C., Industrial Instruments for Measurement and Control, Second Edition, McGraw-Hill Book Company.
- Process Measurement Fundamentals, Volume I, General Physics Corporation, ISBN 0-87683-001-7, 1981.

TERMINAL OBJECTIVE

1.0 Given a flow instrument, **RELATE** the associated fundamental principles, including possible failure modes, to that instrument.

ENABLING OBJECTIVES

1.1 **EXPLAIN** the theory of operation of a basic head flow meter.

1.2 **DESCRIBE** the basic construction of the following types of head flow detectors:
- a. Orifice plates
- b. Venturi tube
- c. Dall flow tube
- d. Pitot tube

1.3 **DESCRIBE** the following types of mechanical flow detectors, including the basic construction and theory of operation.
- a. Rotameter
- b. Nutating Disk

1.4 **DESCRIBE** density compensation of a steam flow instrument to include the reason density compensation is required and the parameters used.

1.5 Given a block diagram of a typical flow detection device, **STATE** the purpose of the following blocks:
- a. Differential pressure (ΔP) transmitter
- b. Extractor
- c. Indicator

1.6 **STATE** the three environmental concerns which can affect the accuracy and reliability of flow sensing instrumentation.

Intentionally Left Blank

HEAD FLOW METERS

Flow measurement is an important process measurement to be considered in operating a facility's fluid systems. For efficient and economic operation of these fluid systems, flow measurement is necessary.

EO 1.1 EXPLAIN the theory of operation of a basic head flow meter.

EO 1.2 DESCRIBE the basic construction of the following types of head flow detectors:
- **a. Orifice plates**
- **b. Venturi tube**
- **c. Dall flow tube**
- **d. Pitot tube**

Head flow meters operate on the principle of placing a restriction in the line to cause a differential pressure head. The differential pressure, which is caused by the head, is measured and converted to a flow measurement. Industrial applications of head flow meters incorporate a pneumatic or electrical transmitting system for remote readout of flow rate. Generally, the indicating instrument extracts the square root of the differential pressure and displays the flow rate on a linear indicator.

There are two elements in a head flow meter; the primary element is the restriction in the line, and the secondary element is the differential pressure measuring device. Figure 1 shows the basic operating characteristics of a head flow meter.

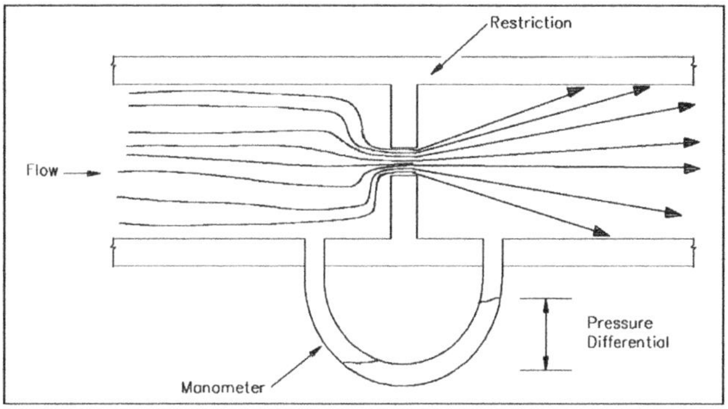

Figure 1 Head Flow Meter

The flowpath restriction, such as an orifice, causes a differential pressure across the orifice. This pressure differential is measured by a mercury manometer or a differential pressure detector. From this measurement, flow rate is determined from known physical laws.

The head flow meter actually measures volume flow rate rather than mass flow rate. Mass flow rate is easily calculated or computed from volumetric flow rate by knowing or sensing temperature and/or pressure. Temperature and pressure affect the density of the fluid and, therefore, the mass of fluid flowing past a certain point. If the volumetric flow rate signal is compensated for changes in temperature and/or pressure, a true mass flow rate signal can be obtained. In Thermodynamics it is described that temperature and density are inversely proportional, while pressure and density are directly proportional. To show the relationship between temperature or pressure, the mass flow rate equation is often written as either Equation 4-1 or 4-2.

$$\dot{m} - KA\sqrt{\Delta P(P)} \qquad (4\text{-}1)$$

$$\dot{m} - KA\sqrt{\Delta P(1/T)} \qquad (4\text{-}2)$$

where

$\dot{m}$ = mass flow rate (lbm/sec)
A = area (ft^2)
ΔP = differential pressure (lbf/ft^2)
P = pressure (lbf/ft^2)
T = temperature (°F)
K = flow coefficient

The flow coefficient is constant for the system based mainly on the construction characteristics of the pipe and type of fluid flowing through the pipe. The flow coefficient in each equation contains the appropriate units to balance the equation and provide the proper units for the resulting mass flow rate. The area of the pipe and differential pressure are used to calculate volumetric flow rate. As stated above, this volumetric flow rate is converted to mass flow rate by compensating for system temperature or pressure.

Orifice Plate

The orifice plate is the simplest of the flowpath restrictions used in flow detection, as well as the most economical. Orifice plates are flat plates 1/16 to 1/4 inch thick. They are normally mounted between a pair of flanges and are installed in a straight run of smooth pipe to avoid disturbance of flow patterns from fittings and valves.

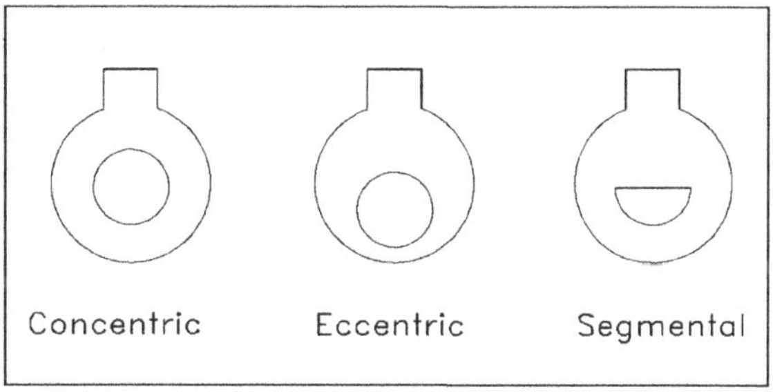

Figure 2 Orifice Plates

Three kinds of orifice plates are used: concentric, eccentric, and segmental (as shown in Figure 2).

The concentric orifice plate is the most common of the three types. As shown, the orifice is equidistant (concentric) to the inside diameter of the pipe. Flow through a sharp-edged orifice plate is characterized by a change in velocity. As the fluid passes through the orifice, the fluid converges, and the velocity of the fluid increases to a maximum value. At this point, the pressure is at a minimum value. As the fluid diverges to fill the entire pipe area, the velocity decreases back to the original value. The pressure increases to about 60% to 80% of the original input value. The pressure loss is irrecoverable; therefore, the output pressure will always be less than the input pressure. The pressures on both sides of the orifice are measured, resulting in a differential pressure which is proportional to the flow rate.

Segmental and eccentric orifice plates are functionally identical to the concentric orifice. The circular section of the segmental orifice is concentric with the pipe. The segmental portion of the orifice eliminates damming of foreign materials on the upstream side of the orifice when mounted in a horizontal pipe. Depending on the type of fluid, the segmental section is placed on either the top or bottom of the horizontal pipe to increase the accuracy of the measurement.

Eccentric orifice plates shift the edge of the orifice to the inside of the pipe wall. This design also prevents upstream damming and is used in the same way as the segmental orifice plate.

Orifice plates have two distinct disadvantages; they cause a high permanent pressure drop (outlet pressure will be 60% to 80% of inlet pressure), and they are subject to erosion, which will eventually cause inaccuracies in the measured differential pressure.

Venturi Tube

The venturi tube, illustrated in Figure 3, is the most accurate flow-sensing element when properly calibrated. The venturi tube has a converging conical inlet, a cylindrical throat, and a diverging recovery cone. It has no projections into the fluid, no sharp corners, and no sudden changes in contour.

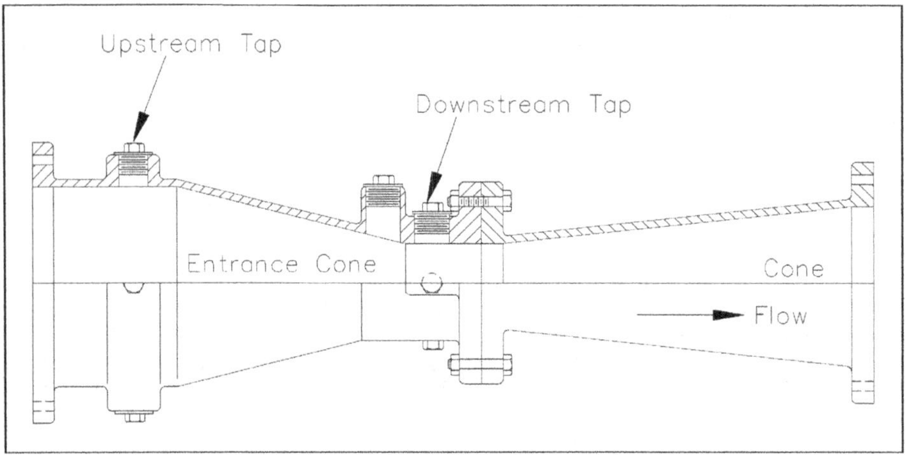

Figure 3 Venturi Tube

The inlet section decreases the area of the fluid stream, causing the velocity to increase and the pressure to decrease. The low pressure is measured in the center of the cylindrical throat since the pressure will be at its lowest value, and neither the pressure nor the velocity is changing. The recovery cone allows for the recovery of pressure such that total pressure loss is only 10% to 25%. The high pressure is measured upstream of the entrance cone. The major disadvantages of this type of flow detection are the high initial costs for installation and difficulty in installation and inspection.

Dall Flow Tube

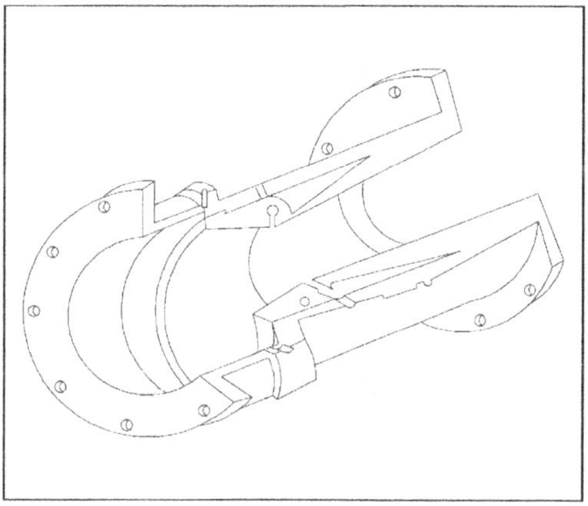

Figure 4 Dall Flow Tube

The dall flow tube, illustrated in Figure 4, has a higher ratio of pressure developed to pressure lost than the venturi flow tube. It is more compact and is commonly used in large flow applications. The tube consists of a short, straight inlet section followed by an abrupt decrease in the inside diameter of the tube. This section, called the inlet shoulder, is followed by the converging inlet cone and a diverging exit cone. The two cones are separated by a slot or gap between the two cones. The low pressure is measured at the slotted throat (area between the two cones). The high pressure is measured at the upstream edge of the inlet shoulder.

The dall flow tube is available in medium to very large sizes. In the large sizes, the cost is normally less than that of a venturi flow tube. This type of flow tube has a pressure loss of about 5%. Flow rate and pressure drop are related as shown in Equation 4-3.

$$\dot{V} = K\sqrt{\Delta P} \tag{4-3}$$

where

$\dot{V}$ = volumetric flow rate
K = constant derived from the mechanical parameters of the primary elements
ΔP = differential pressure

Pitot Tube

The pitot tube, illustrated in Figure 5, is another primary flow element used to produce a differential pressure for flow detection. In its simplest form, it consists of a tube with an opening at the end. The small hole in the end is positioned such that it faces the flowing fluid. The velocity of the fluid at the opening of the tube decreases to zero. This provides for the high pressure input to a differential pressure detector. A pressure tap provides the low pressure input.

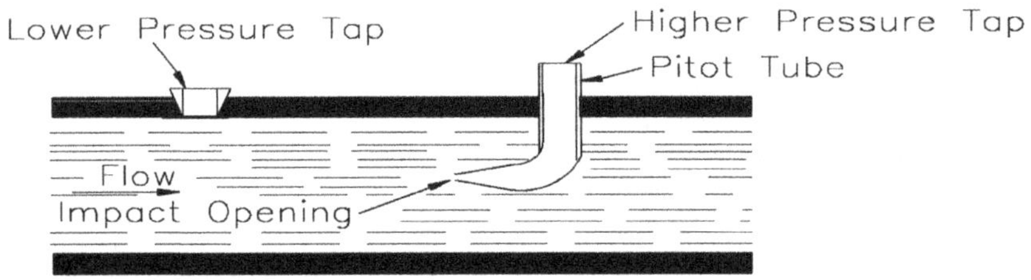

Figure 5 Pitot Tube

The pitot tube actually measures fluid velocity instead of fluid flow rate. However, volumetric flow rate can be obtained using Equation 4-4.

$$\dot{V} = KAV \tag{4-4}$$

where

$\dot{V}$ = volumetric flow rate (ft^3/sec.)
A = area of flow cross-section (ft^2)
V = velocity of flowing fluid (ft/sec.)
K = flow coefficient (normally about 0.8)

Pitot tubes must be calibrated for each specific application, as there is no standardization. This type of instrument can be used even when the fluid is not enclosed in a pipe or duct.

Summary

Head flow meters operate on the principle of placing a restriction in the line to cause a pressure drop. The differential pressure which is caused by the head is measured and converted to a flow measurement. The basic construction of various types of head flow detectors is summarized below.

Head Flow Meter Construction Summary

Orifice plates

- Flat plates 1/16 to 1/4 in. thick
- Mounted between a pair of flanges
- Installed in a straight run of smooth pipe to avoid disturbance of flow patterns due to fittings and valves

Venturi tube

- Converging conical inlet, a cylindrical throat, and a diverging recovery cone
- No projections into the fluid, no sharp corners, and no sudden changes in contour

Dall flow tube

- Consists of a short, straight inlet section followed by an abrupt decrease in the inside diameter of the tube
- Inlet shoulder followed by the converging inlet cone and a diverging exit cone
- Two cones separated by a slot or gap between the two cones

Pitot tube

- Consists of a tube with an opening at the end
- Small hole in the end positioned so that it faces the flowing fluid

OTHER FLOW METERS

Two other types of mechanical flow meters which can be used are the area flow and displacement meters. In addition, there exists much more sophisticated techniques for measurement of flow rate than use of differential pressure devices, such as anemometry, magnetic, and ultrasonic.

EO 1.3 DESCRIBE the following types of mechanical flow detectors, including the basic construction and theory of operation.
- **a. Rotameter**
- **b. Nutating Disk**

Area Flow Meter

The head causing the flow through an area meter is relatively constant such that the rate of flow is directly proportional to the metering area. The variation in area is produced by the rise and fall of a floating element. This type of flow meter must be mounted so that the floating element moves vertically and friction is minimal.

Rotameter

The rotameter, illustrated in Figure 6, is an area flow meter so named because a rotating float is the indicating element.

The rotameter consists of a metal float and a conical glass tube, constructed such that the diameter increases with height. When there is no fluid passing through the rotameter, the float rests at the bottom of the tube. As fluid enters the tube, the higher density of the float will cause the float to remain on the bottom. The space between the float and the tube allows for flow past the float. As flow increases in the tube, the pressure drop increases. When the pressure drop is sufficient, the float will rise to indicate the amount of flow. The higher the flow rate the greater the pressure drop. The higher the pressure drop the farther up the tube the float rises.

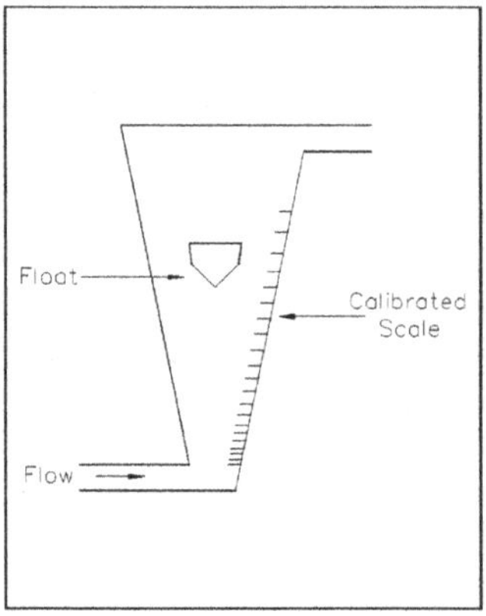

Figure 6 Rotameter

The float should stay at a constant position at a constant flow rate. With a smooth float, fluctuations appear even when flow is constant. By using a float with slanted slots cut in the head, the float maintains a constant position with respect to flow rate. This type of flow meter is usually used to measure low flow rates.

Displacement Meter

In a displacement flow meter, all of the fluid passes through the meter in almost completely isolated quantities. The number of these quantities is counted and indicated in terms of volume or weight units by a register.

Nutating Disk

The most common type of displacement flow meter is the nutating disk, or wobble plate meter. A typical nutating disk is shown in Figure 7.

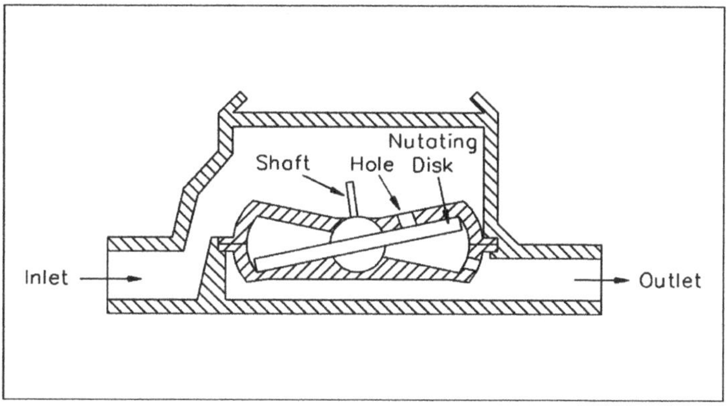

Figure 7 Nutating Disk

This type of flow meter is normally used for water service, such as raw water supply and evaporator feed. The movable element is a circular disk which is attached to a central ball. A shaft is fastened to the ball and held in an inclined position by a cam or roller. The disk is mounted in a chamber which has spherical side walls and conical top and bottom surfaces. The fluid enters an opening in the spherical wall on one side of the partition and leaves through the other side. As the fluid flows through the chamber, the disk wobbles, or executes a nutating motion. Since the volume of fluid required to make the disc complete one revolution is known, the total flow through a nutating disc can be calculated by multiplying the number of disc rotations by the known volume of fluid.

To measure this flow, the motion of the shaft generates a cone with the point, or apex, down. The top of the shaft operates a revolution counter, through a crank and set of gears, which is calibrated to indicate total system flow. A variety of accessories, such as automatic count resetting devices, can be added to the fundamental mechanism, which perform functions in addition to measuring the flow.

Hot-Wire Anemometer

The hot-wire anemometer, principally used in gas flow measurement, consists of an electrically heated, fine platinum wire which is immersed into the flow. As the fluid velocity increases, the rate of heat flow from the heated wire to the flow stream increases. Thus, a cooling effect on the wire electrode occurs, causing its electrical resistance to change. In a constant-current anemometer, the fluid velocity is determined from a measurement of the resulting change in wire resistance. In a constant-resistance anemometer, fluid velocity is determined from the current needed to maintain a constant wire temperature and, thus, the resistance constant.

Electromagnetic Flowmeter

The electromagnetic flowmeter is similar in principle to the generator. The rotor of the generator is replaced by a pipe placed between the poles of a magnet so that the flow of the fluid in the pipe is normal to the magnetic field. As the fluid flows through this magnetic field, an electromotive force is induced in it that will be mutually normal (perpendicular) to both the magnetic field and the motion of the fluid. This electromotive force may be measured with the aid of electrodes attached to the pipe and connected to a galvanometer or an equivalent. For a given magnetic field, the induced voltage will be proportional to the average velocity of the fluid. However, the fluid should have some degree of electrical conductivity.

Ultrasonic Flow Equipment

Devices such as ultrasonic flow equipment use the Doppler frequency shift of ultrasonic signals reflected from discontinuities in the fluid stream to obtain flow measurements. These discontinuities can be suspended solids, bubbles, or interfaces generated by turbulent eddies in the flow stream. The sensor is mounted on the outside of the pipe, and an ultrasonic beam from a piezoelectric crystal is transmitted through the pipe wall into the fluid at an angle to the flow stream. Signals reflected off flow disturbances are detected by a second piezoelectric crystal located in the same sensor. Transmitted and reflected signals are compared in an electrical circuit, and the corresponding frequency shift is proportional to the flow velocity.

Summary

The basic construction and theory of operation of rotameters, nutating disks, anemometers, electromagnetic flow meters, and ultrasonic flow equipment are summarized below.

Other Flow Meters Summary

Rotameter

- Consists of a metal float and a conical glass tube
- Tube diameter increases with height
- High density float will remain on the bottom of tube with no flow
- Space between the float and the tube allows for flow past the float
- As flow increases, the pressure drop increases, when the pressure drop is sufficient, the float rises to indicate the amount of flow

Nutating Disc

- Circular disk which is attached to a central ball
- A shaft is fastened to the ball and held in an inclined position by a cam, or roller
- Fluid enters an opening in the spherical wall on one side of the partition and leaves through the other side
- As the fluid flows through the chamber, the disk wobbles, or executes a nutating motion

Hot-Wire Anemometer

- Electrically heated, fine platinum wire immersed in flow
- Wire is cooled as flow is increased
- Measure either change in wire resistance or heating current to determine flow

Electromagnetic Flowmeter

- Magnetic field established around system pipe
- Electromotive force induced in fluid as it flows through magnetic field
- Electromotive force measured with electrodes and is proportional to flow rate

Ultrasonic Flow equipment

- Uses Doppler frequency shift of ultrasonic signals reflected off discontinuities in fluid

STEAM FLOW DETECTION

Steam flow detection is normally accomplished through the use of a steam flow nozzle.

EO 1.4 DESCRIBE density compensation of a steam flow instrument to include the reason density compensation is required and the parameters used.

The flow nozzle is commonly used for the measurement of steam flow and other high velocity fluid flow measurements where erosion may occur. It is capable of measuring approximately 60% higher flow rates than an orifice plate with the same diameter. This is due to the streamlined contour of the throat, which is a distinct advantage for the measurement of high velocity fluids. The flow nozzle requires less straight run piping than an orifice plate. However, the pressure drop is about the same for both. A typical flow nozzle is shown in Figure 8.

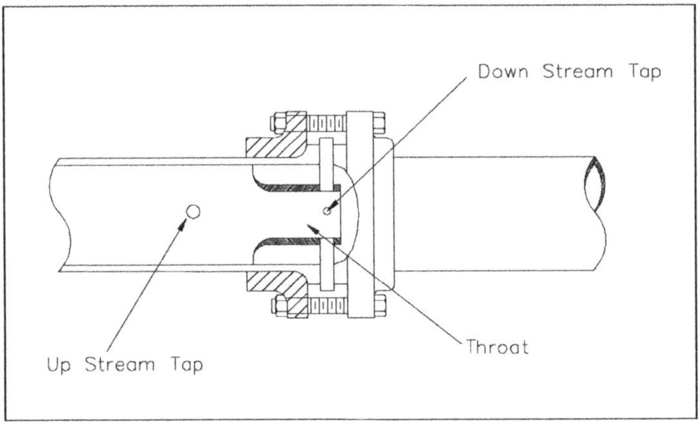

Figure 8 Flow Nozzle

Since steam is considered to be a gas, changes in pressure and temperature greatly affect its density. Equations 4-5 and 4-6 list the fundamental relationship for volumetric flow and mass flow.

$$\dot{V} = K\sqrt{\frac{\text{head loss}}{\rho}h} \tag{4-5}$$

and

$$\dot{m} = \dot{V}\rho \tag{4-6}$$

where

$\dot{V}$ = volumetric flow
K = constant relating to the ratio of pipe to orifice
h = differential pressure
ρ = density
$\dot{m}$ = mass flow

It is possible to substitute for density in the relationship using Equation 4-7.

$$\rho = \frac{pm}{R\theta} \tag{4-7}$$

where

ρ = density
p = upstream pressure
m = molecular weight of the gas
θ = absolute temperature
R = gas constant

By substituting for density, the values are used by the electronic circuit to calculate the density automatically. Since steam temperature is relatively constant in most steam systems, upstream pressure is the only variable in the above equation that changes as the system operates. If the other variables are hardwired, measuring the system pressure is all that is required for the electronics to calculate the fluid's density.

As the previous equations demonstrate, temperature and pressure values can be used to electronically compensate flow for changes in density. A simple mass flow detection system is illustrated by Figure 9 where measurements of temperature and pressure are made with commonly used instruments.

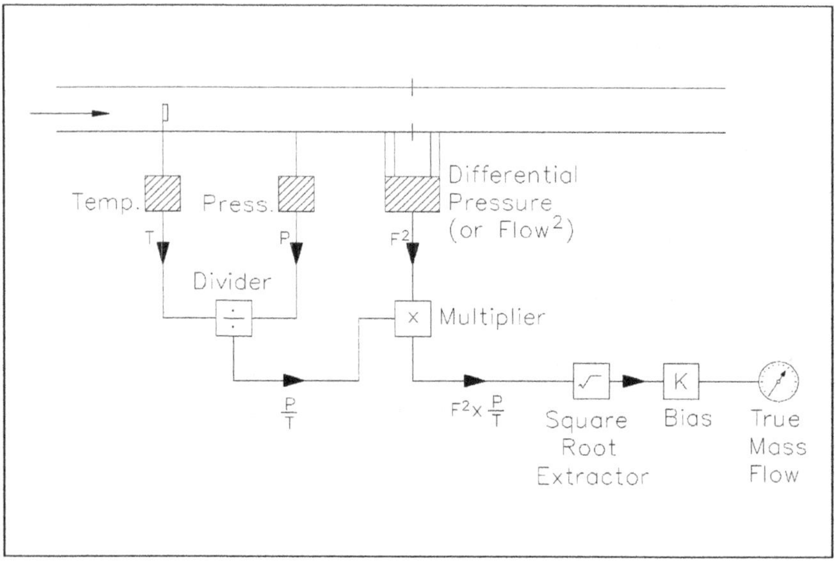

Figure 9 Simple Mass Flow Detection System

For the precise measurement of gas flow (steam) at varying pressures and temperatures, it is necessary to determine the density, which is pressure and temperature dependent, and from this value to calculate the actual flow. The use of a computer is essential to measure flow with changing pressure or temperature. Figure 10 illustrates an example of a computer specifically designed for the measurement of gas flow. The computer is designed to accept input signals from commonly used differential pressure detectors, or from density or pressure plus temperature sensors, and to provide an output which is proportional to the actual rate of flow. The computer has an accuracy better than $\pm$0.1% at flow rates of 10% to 100%.

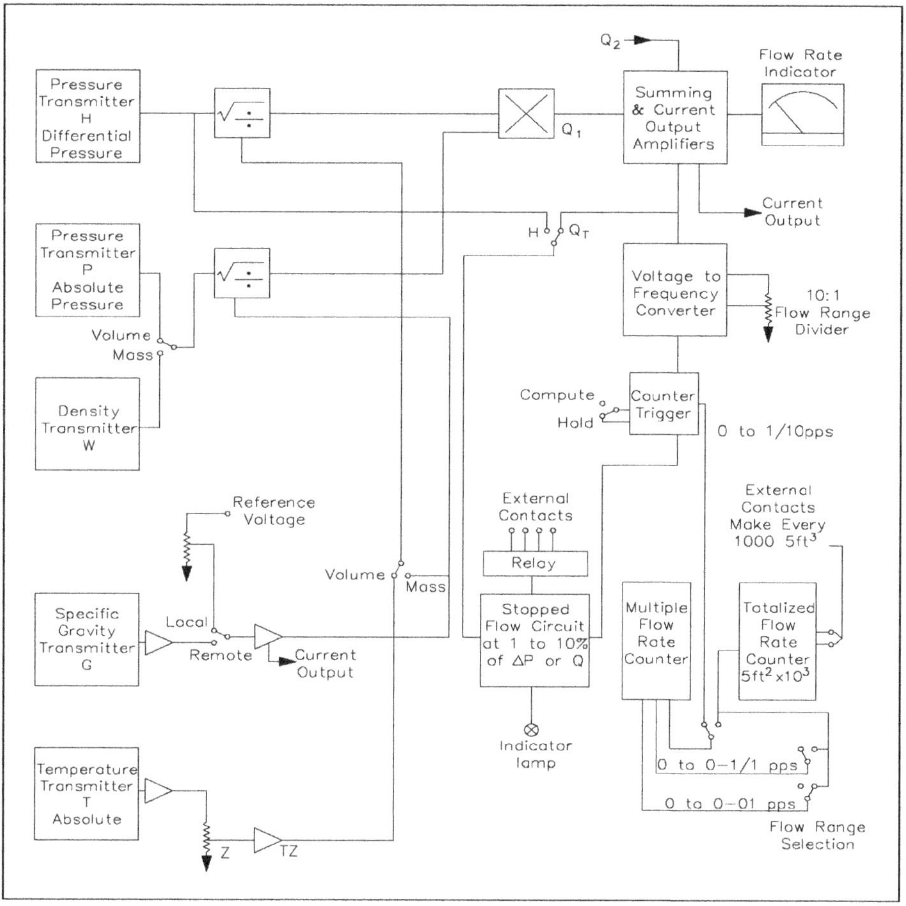

Figure 10 Gas Flow Computer

Summary

Density compensation is summarized below.

Density Compensation Summary

- Changes in temperature and pressure greatly affect indicated steam flow.
- By measuring temperature and pressure, a computerized system can be used to electronically compensate a steam or gas flow indication for changes in fluid density.

FLOW CIRCUITRY

The primary elements provide the input to the secondary element which provides for indications, alarms, and controls.

EO 1.5 **Given a block diagram of a typical flow detection device, STATE the purpose of the following blocks:**
- **a. Differential pressure (DP) transmitter**
- **b. Extractor**
- **c. Indicator**

EO 1.6 **STATE the three environmental concerns which can affect the accuracy and reliability of flow sensing instrumentation.**

Circuitry

Figure 11 shows a block diagram of a typical differential pressure flow detection circuit. The DP transmitter operation is dependent on the pressure difference across an orifice, venturi, or flow tube. This differential pressure is used to position a mechanical device such as a bellows. The bellows acts against spring pressure to reposition the core of a differential transformer. The transformer's output voltage on each of two secondary windings varies with a change in flow.

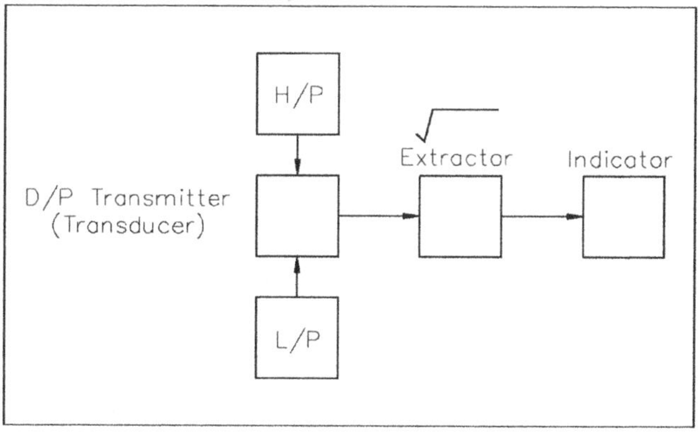

Figure 11 Differential Pressure Flow Detection Block Diagram

A loss of differential pressure integrity of the secondary element, the DP transmitter, will introduce an error into the indicated flow. This loss of integrity implies an impaired or degraded pressure boundary between the high-pressure and low-pressure sides of the transmitter. A loss of differential pressure boundary is caused by anything that results in the high- and low-pressure sides of the DP transmitter being allowed to equalize pressure.

As previously discussed, flow rate is proportional to the square root of the differential pressure. The extractor is used to electronically calculate the square root of the differential pressure and provide an output proportional to system flow. The constants are determined by selection of the appropriate electronic components.

The extractor output is amplified and sent to an indicator. The indicator provides either a local or a remote indication of system flow.

Use of Flow Indication

The flow of liquids and gases carries energy through the piping system. In many situations, it is very important to know whether there is flow and the rate at which the flow is occurring. An example of flow that is important to a facility operator is equipment cooling flow. The flow of coolant is essential in removing the heat generated by the system, thereby preventing damage to the equipment. Typically, flow indication is used in protection systems and control systems that help maintain system temperature.

Another method of determining system coolant flow is by using pump differential pressure. If all means of flow indication are lost, flow can be approximated using pump differential pressure. Pump differential pressure is proportional to the square of pump flow.

Environmental Concerns

As previously discussed, the density of the fluid whose flow is to be measured can have a large effect on flow sensing instrumentation. The effect of density is most important when the flow sensing instrumentation is measuring gas flows, such as steam. Since the density of a gas is directly affected by temperature and pressure, any changes in either of these parameters will have a direct effect on the measured flow. Therefore, any changes in fluid temperature or pressure must be compensated for to achieve an accurate measurement of flow.

Ambient temperature variations will affect the accuracy and reliability of flow sensing instrumentation. Variations in ambient temperature can directly affect the resistance of components in the instrumentation circuitry, and, therefore, affect the calibration of electric/electronic equipment. The effects of temperature variations are reduced by the design of the circuitry and by maintaining the flow sensing instrumentation in the proper environment.

The presence of humidity will also affect most electrical equipment, especially electronic equipment. High humidity causes moisture to collect on the equipment. This moisture can cause short circuits, grounds, and corrosion, which, in turn, may damage components. The effects due to humidity are controlled by maintaining the equipment in the proper environment.

Summary

The density of the fluid, ambient temperature, and humidity are the three factors which can affect the accuracy and reliability of flow sensing instrumentation. The purpose of each block of a typical differential pressure flow detection circuit is summarized below.

Flow Circuitry Summary

- The differential pressure is used by the DP transmitter to provide an output proportional to the flow.
- The extractor is used to electronically calculate the square root of the differential pressure and to provide an output proportional to system flow.
- The indicator provides either a local or a remote indication of system flow.

Intentionally Left Blank

Department of Energy
Fundamentals Handbook

INSTRUMENTATION AND CONTROL
Module 5
Position Indicators

www.KnowledgePublications.com

TABLE OF CONTENTS

LIST OF FIGURES ii

LIST OF TABLES iii

REFERENCES iv

OBJECTIVES v

SYNCHRO EQUIPMENT 1

Synchro Equipment 1
Summary 4

SWITCHES 5

Limit Switches 5
Reed Switches 6
Summary 7

VARIABLE OUTPUT DEVICES 8

Potentiometer 8
Linear Variable Differential Transformers (LVDT) 9
Summary 10

POSITION INDICATION CIRCUITRY 11

Environmental Concerns 13
Summary 13

LIST OF FIGURES

Figure 1 Synchro Schematics 2

Figure 2 Simple Synchro System 3

Figure 3 Limit Switches 5

Figure 4 Reed Switches 6

Figure 5 Potentiometer Valve Position Indicator 8

Figure 6 Linear Variable Differential Transformer 9

Figure 7 Position Indicators 12

LIST OF TABLES

NONE

REFERENCES

- Kirk, Franklin W. and Rimboi, Nicholas R., Instrumentation, Third Edition, American Technical Publishers, ISBN 0-8269-3422-6.
- Academic Program for Nuclear Power Plant Personnel, Volume IV, General Physics Corporation, Library of Congress Card #A 397747, April 1982.
- Fozard, B., Instrumentation and Control of Nuclear Reactors, ILIFFE Books Ltd., London.
- Wightman, E.J., Instrumentation in Process Control, CRC Press, Cleveland, Ohio.
- Rhodes, T.J. and Carroll, G.C., Industrial Instruments for Measurement and Control, Second Edition, McGraw-Hill Book Company.
- Process Measurement Fundamentals, Volume I, General Physics Corporation, ISBN 0-87683-001-7, 1981.

TERMINAL OBJECTIVE

1.0 Given a position indicating instrument, **RELATE** the associated fundamental principles, including possible failure modes, to that instrument.

ENABLING OBJECTIVES

1.1 **DESCRIBE** the synchro position indicators to include the basic construction and theory of operation.

1.2 **DESCRIBE** the following switch position indicators to include basic construction and theory of operation.
- a. Limit switches
- b. Reed switches

1.3 **DESCRIBE** the following variable output position indicators to include basic construction and theory of operation.
- a. Potentiometer
- b. Linear variable differential transformers (LVDT)

1.4 Given a diagram of a position indicator, **STATE** the purpose of the following components:
- a. Detection device
- b. Indicator and control circuits

1.5 **STATE** the two environmental concerns that can affect the accuracy and reliabiltity of position indication equipment.

Intentionally Left Blank

SYNCHRO EQUIPMENT

Position indicating instrumentation is used in DOE nuclear facilities to provide remote indication of equipment positions including control rods and major valves.

EO 1.1 DESCRIBE the synchro position indicators to include the basic construction and theory of operation.

Position indicating instrumentation is used in nuclear facilities to provide remote indication of control rod position with respect to the fully inserted position, and remote indication of the open or shut condition of important valves. This remote indication is necessary for the monitoring of vital components located within inaccessible or remote areas. Remote position indication can be used at any DOE facility, not only nuclear facilities, where valve position indication is required for safety.

Synchro Equipment

Remote indication or control may be obtained by the use of self-synchronizing motors, called synchro equipment. Synchro equipment consists of synchro units which electrically govern or follow the position of a mechanical indicator or device. An electrical synchro has two distinct advantages over mechanical indicators: (1) greater accuracy, and (2) simpler routing of remote indication.

There are five basic types of synchros which are designated according to their function. The basic types are: transmitters, differential transmitters, receivers, differential receivers, and control transformers. Figure 1 illustrates schematic diagrams used to show external connections and the relative positions of synchro windings. If the power required to operate a device is higher than the power available from a synchro, power amplification is required. Servomechanism is a term which refers to a variety of power-amplifiers. These devices are incorporated into synchro systems for automatic control rod positioning in some reactor facilities.

The transmitter, or synchro generator, consists of a rotor with a single winding and a stator with three windings placed 120 degrees apart. When the mechanical device moves, the mechanically attached rotor moves. The rotor induces a voltage in each of the stator windings based on the rotor's angular position. Since the rotor is attached to the mechanical device, the induced voltage represents the position of the attached mechanical device. The voltage produced by each of the windings is utilized to control the receiving synchro position.

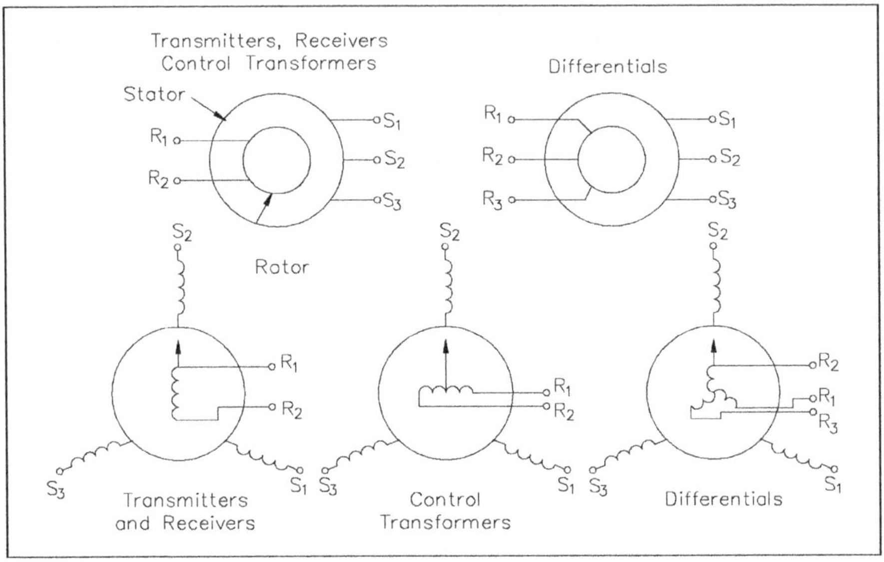

Figure 1 Synchro Schematics

The receiver, or synchro motor, is electrically similar to the synchro generator. The synchro receiver uses the voltage generated by each of the synchro generator windings to position the receiver rotor. Since the transmitter and receiver are electrically similar, the angular position of the receiver rotor corresponds to that of the synchro transmitter rotor. The receiver differs mechanically from the transmitter in that it incorporates a damping device to prevent hunting. Hunting refers to the overshoot and undershoot that occur as the receiving device tries to match the sending device. Without the damping device, the receiver would go past the desired point slightly, then return past the desired point slightly in the other direction. This would continue, by smaller amounts each time, until the receiver came to rest at the desired position. The damper prevents hunting by feeding some of the signal back, thus slowing down the approach to the desired point.

Differential synchros are used with transmitter and receiver synchros to insert a second signal. The angular positions of the transmitter and the differential synchros are compared, and the difference or sum is transmitted to the receiver. This setup can be used to provide a feedback signal to slow the response time of the receiver, thus providing a smooth receiver motion.

Control transformer synchros are used when only a voltage indication of angular position is desired. It is similar in construction to an ordinary synchro except that the rotor windings are used only to generate a voltage which is known as an error voltage. The rotor windings of a control transformer synchro are wound with many turns of fine wire to produce a high impedance. Since the rotor is not fed excitation voltage, the current drawn by the stator windings would be high if they were the same as an ordinary synchro; therefore, they are also wound with many turns of fine wire to prevent excessive current.

During normal operation, the output of a control transformer synchro is nearly zero (nulled) when its angular position is the same as that of the transmitter.

A simple synchro system, consisting of one synchro transmitter (or generator) connected to one synchro receiver (or motor), is shown in Figure 2.

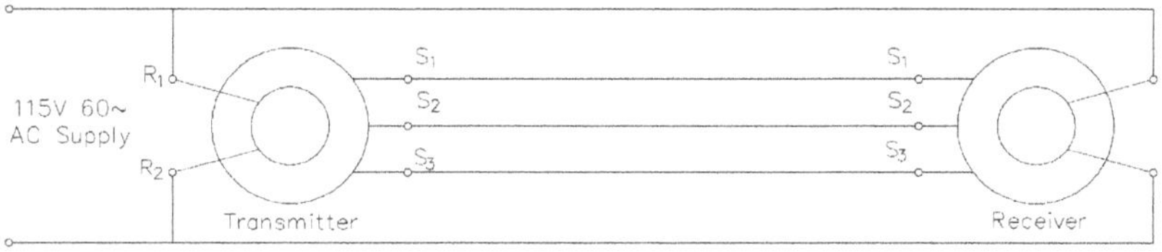

Figure 2 Simple Synchro System

When the transmitter's shaft is turned, the synchro receiver's shaft turns such that its "electrical position" is the same as the transmitter's. What this means is that when the transmitter is turned to electrical zero, the synchro receiver also turns to zero. If the transmitter is disconnected from the synchro receiver and then reconnected, its shaft will turn to correspond to the position of the transmitter shaft.

Summary

Synchro equipment is summarized below.

Synchro Equipment Summary

- A basic synchro system consists of a transmitter (synchro generator) and receiver (synchro motor).
- When the transmitter's shaft is turned, the synchro motor's shaft turns such that its "electrical position" is the same as the transmitter's.

SWITCHES

Mechanical limit switches and reed switches provide valve open and shut indications. They also are used to determine the physical position of equipment.

EO 1.2 DESCRIBE the following switch position indicators to include basic construction and theory of operation.
a. Limit switches
b. Reed switches

Limit Switches

A limit switch is a mechanical device which can be used to determine the physical position of equipment. For example, an extension on a valve shaft mechanically trips a limit switch as it moves from open to shut or shut to open. The limit switch gives ON/OFF output that corresponds to valve position. Normally, limit switches are used to provide full open or full shut indications as illustrated in Figure 3.

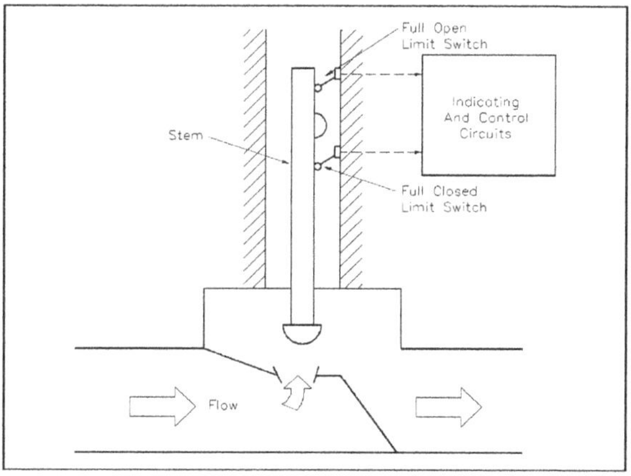

Figure 3 Limit Switches

Many limit switches are the push-button variety. When the valve extension comes in contact with the limit switch, the switch depresses to complete, or turn on, the electrical circuit. As the valve extension moves away from the limit switches, spring pressure opens the switch, turning off the circuit.

Limit switch failures are normally mechanical in nature. If the proper indication or control function is not achieved, the limit switch is probably faulty. In this case, local position indication should be used to verify equipment position.

Reed Switches

Reed switches, illustrated in Figure 4, are more reliable than limit switches, due to their simplified construction. The switches are constructed of flexible ferrous strips (reeds) and are placed near the intended travel of the valve stem or control rod extension.

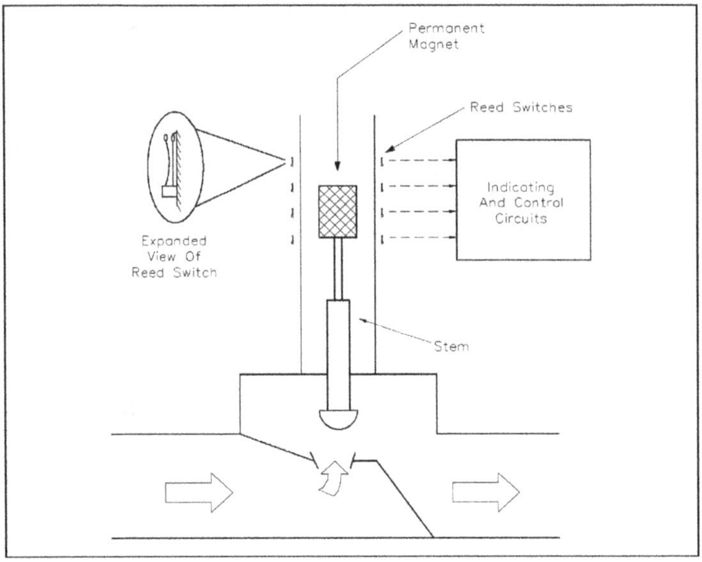

Figure 4 Reed Switches

When using reed switches, the extension used is a permanent magnet. As the magnet approaches the reed switch, the switch shuts. When the magnet moves away, the reed switch opens. This ON/OFF indicator is similar to mechanical limit switches. By using a large number of magnetic reed switches, incremental position can be measured. This technique is sometimes used in monitoring a reactor's control rod position.

Failures are normally limited to a reed switch which is stuck open or stuck shut. If a reed switch is stuck shut, the open (closed) indication will be continuously illuminated. If a reed switch is stuck open, the position indication for that switch remains extinguished regardless of valve position.

Summary

Switch position indicators are summarized below.

Switch Position Indicators Summary

- A limit switch is a mechanical device used to determine the physical position of valves. An extension on a valve shaft mechanically trips the switch as it moves from open to shut or shut to open. The limit switch gives ON/OFF output which corresponds to the valve position.

- Reed switches are constructed of flexible ferrous strips placed near the intended travel of the valve stem or control rod extension. The extension used is a permanent magnet. As the magnet approaches the reed switch, the switch shuts. When the magnet moves away, the reed switch opens.

VARIABLE OUTPUT DEVICES

Variable output devices provide an accurate position indication of a valve or control rod.

EO 1.3 DESCRIBE the following variable output position indicators to include basic construction and theory of operation.

a. Potentiometer

b. Linear variable differential transformers (LVDT)

Potentiometer

Potentiometer valve position indicators (Figure 5) provide an accurate indication of position throughout the travel of a valve or control rod. The extension is physically attached to a variable resistor. As the extension moves up or down, the resistance of the attached circuit changes, changing the amount of current flow in the circuit. The amount of current is proportional to the valve position.

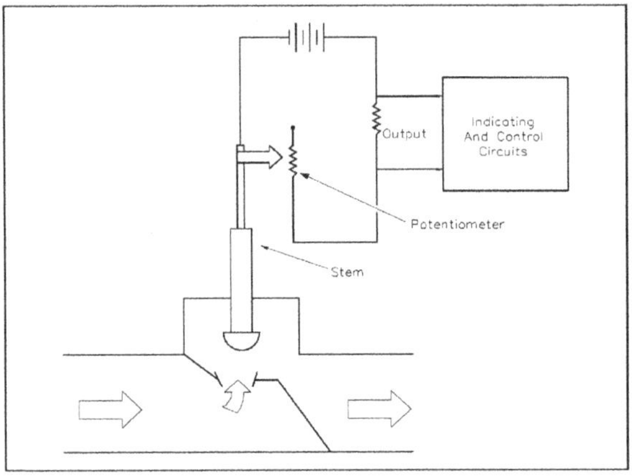

Figure 5 Potentiometer Valve Position Indicator

Potentiometer valve position indicator failures are normally electrical in nature. An electrical short or open will cause the indication to fail at one extreme or the other. If an increase or decrease in the potentiometer resistance occurs, erratic indicated valve position occurs.

Linear Variable Differential Transformers (LVDT)

A device which provides accurate position indication throughout the range of valve or control rod travel is a linear variable differential transformer (LVDT), illustrated in Figure 6. Unlike the potentiometer position indicator, no physical connection to the extension is required.

The extension valve shaft, or control rod, is made of a metal suitable for acting as the movable core of a transformer. Moving the extension between the primary and secondary windings of a transformer causes the inductance between the two windings to vary, thereby varying the output voltage proportional to the position of the valve or control rod extension. Figure 6 illustrates a valve whose position is indicated by an LVDT. If the open and shut position is all that is desired, two small secondary coils could be utilized at each end of the extension's travel.

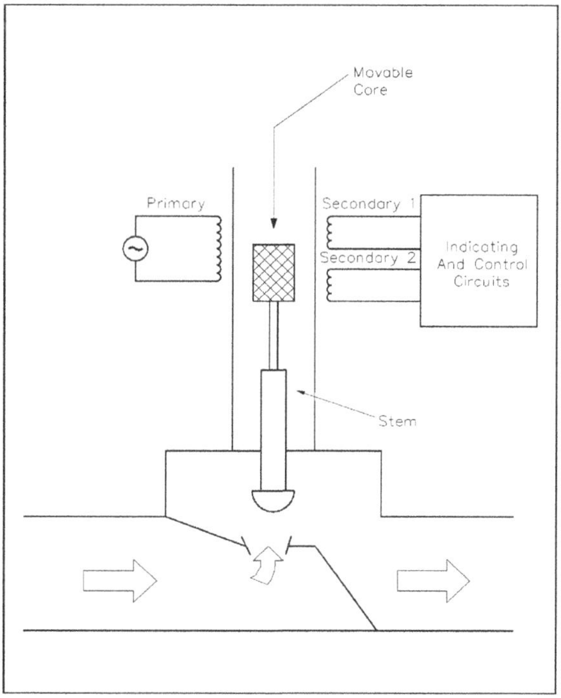

Figure 6 Linear Variable Differential Transformer

LVDTs are extremely reliable. As a rule, failures are limited to rare electrical faults which cause erratic or erroneous indications. An open primary winding will cause the indication to fail to some predetermined value equal to zero differential voltage. This normally corresponds to mid-stroke of the valve. A failure of either secondary winding will cause the output to indicate either full open or full closed.

Summary

Variable output position indicators are summarized below.

Variable Position Indicator Summary

- Potentiometer valve position indicators use an extension which is physically attached to a variable resistor. As the extension moves up or down, the resistance of the attached circuit changes, changing the amount of current flow in the circuit.

- An LVDT uses the extension shaft or control rod as a movable core of a transformer. Moving the extension between the primary and secondary windings of a transformer causes the inductance between the two windings to vary, thereby varying the output voltage proportional to the position of the valve or control rod extension.

POSITION INDICATION CIRCUITRY

Valve position circuitry provides indication and control functions.

EO 1.4 **Given a diagram of a position indicator, STATE the purpose of the following components:**
a. Detection device
b. Indicator and control circuits

EO 1.5 **STATE the two environmental concerns which can affect the accuracy and reliability of position indication equipment.**

As described above, position detection devices provide a method to determine the position of a valve or control rod. The four types of position indicators discussed were limit switches, reed switches, potentiometer valve position indicators, and LVDTs (Figure 7). Reed and limit switches act as ON/OFF indicators to provide open and closed indications and control functions. Reed switches can also be used to provide coarse, incremental position indication.

Potentiometer and LVDT position indicators provide accurate indication of valve and rod position throughout their travel. In some applications, LVDTs can be used to indicate open and closed positions when small secondary windings are used at either end of the valve stem stroke.

The indicating and control circuitry provides for remote indication of valve or rod position and/or various control functions. Position indications vary from simple indications such as a light to meter indications showing exact position.

Control functions are usually in the form of interlocks. Pump isolation valves are sometimes interlocked with the pump. In some applications, these interlocks act to prevent the pump from being started with the valves shut. The pump/valve interlocks can also be used to automatically turn off the pump if one of its isolation valves go shut or to open a discharge valve at some time interval after the pump starts.

Valves are sometimes interlocked with each other. In some systems, two valves may be interlocked to prevent both of the valves from being opened at the same time. This feature is used to prevent undesirable system flowpaths.

Control rod interlocks are normally used to prevent outward motion of certain rods unless certain conditions are met. One such interlock does not allow outward motion of control rods until the rods used to scram the reactor have been withdrawn to a predetermined height. This and all other rod interlocks ensure that the safety of the reactor remains intact.

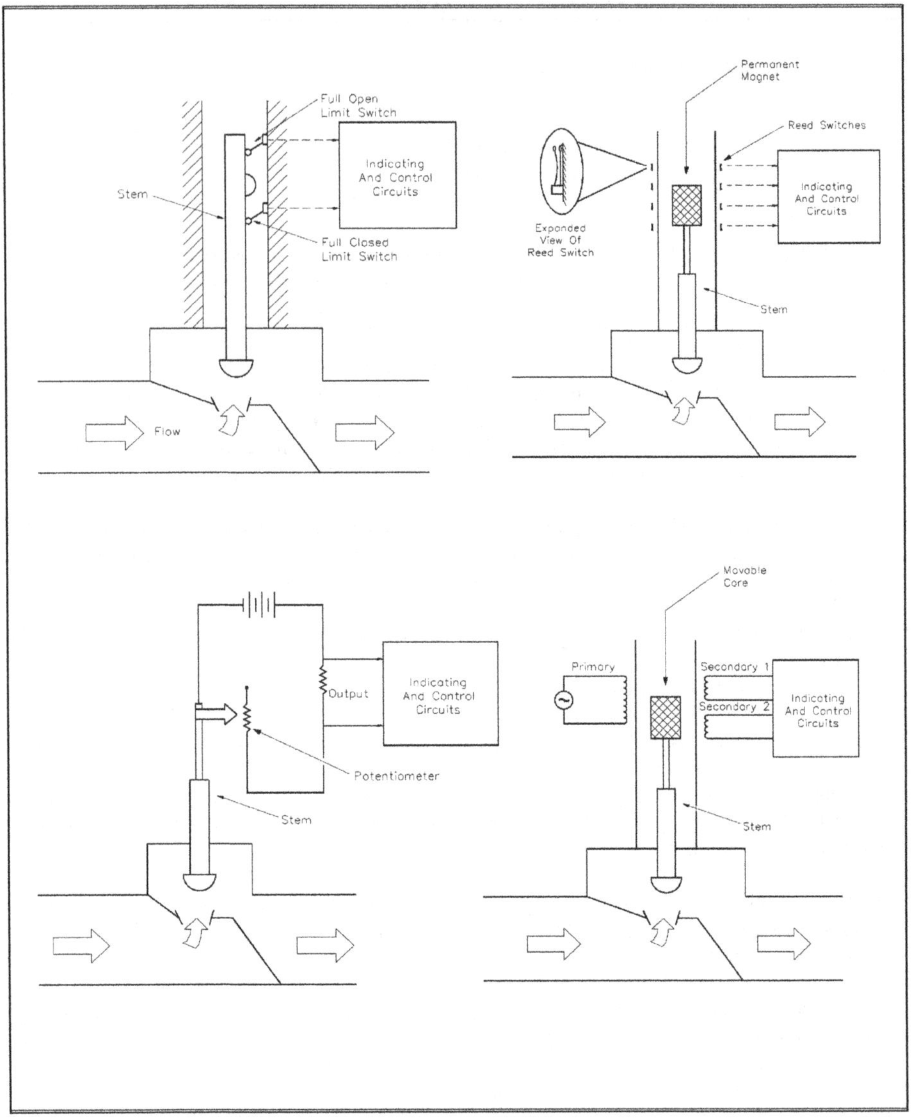

Figure 7 Position Indicators

Environmental Concerns

Ambient temperature variations can affect the accuracy and reliability of certain types of position indication instrumentation. Variations in ambient temperature can directly affect the resistance of components in the instrumentation circuitry, and, therefore, affect the calibration of electric/electronic equipment. The effects of temperature variations are reduced by the design of the circuitry and by maintaining the position indication instrumentation in the proper environment, where possible.

The presence of humidity will also affect most electrical equipment, especially electronic equipment. High humidity causes moisture to collect on the equipment. This moisture can cause short circuits, grounds, and corrosion, which, in turn, may damage components. The effects due to humidity are controlled by maintaining the equipment in the proper environment, where possible.

Summary

The accuracy and reliability of position indication instrumentation can be affected by ambient temperature and humidity. The purposes of position indicator components are summarized below.

Position Indicator Components Summary

- Detection devices provide a method to determine the position of a valve or control rod.
- The indicating and control circuitry provides for remote indication of valve or rod position and/or various control functions.

Intentionally Left Blank

DOE-HDBK-1013/2-92
JUNE 1992

DOE FUNDAMENTALS HANDBOOK
INSTRUMENTATION AND CONTROL
Volume 2 of 2

U.S. Department of Energy **FSC-6910**
Washington, D.C. 20585

This document has been reproduced directly from the best available copy.

Available to DOE and DOE contractors from the Office of Scientific and Technical Information. P. O. Box 62, Oak Ridge, TN 37831;(615) 576-8401.

Available to the public from the National Technical Information Service, U.S. Department of Commerce, 5285 Port Royal Rd., Springfield, VA 22161.

Order No. DE92019793

ABSTRACT

The *Instrumentation and Control Fundamentals Handbook* was developed to assist nuclear facility operating contractors provide operators, maintenance personnel, and the technical staff with the necessary fundamentals training to ensure a basic understanding of instrumentation and control systems. The handbook includes information on temperature, pressure, flow, and level detection systems; position indication systems; process control systems; and radiation detection principles. This information will provide personnel with an understanding of the basic operation of various types of DOE nuclear facility instrumentation and control systems.

Key Words: Training Material, Temperature Detection, Pressure Detection, Level Detection, Flow Detection, Position Indication, Radiation Detection, Process Control

FOREWORD

The *Department of Energy (DOE) Fundamentals Handbooks* consist of ten academic subjects, which include Mathematics; Classical Physics; Thermodynamics, Heat Transfer, and Fluid Flow; Instrumentation and Control; Electrical Science; Material Science; Mechanical Science; Chemistry; Engineering Symbology, Prints, and Drawings; and Nuclear Physics and Reactor Theory. The handbooks are provided as an aid to DOE nuclear facility contractors.

These handbooks were first published as Reactor Operator Fundamentals Manuals in 1985 for use by DOE Category A reactors. The subject areas, subject matter content, and level of detail of the Reactor Operator Fundamentals Manuals was determined from several sources. DOE Category A reactor training managers determined which materials should be included, and served as a primary reference in the initial development phase. Training guidelines from the commercial nuclear power industry, results of job and task analyses, and independent input from contractors and operations-oriented personnel were all considered and included to some degree in developing the text material and learning objectives.

The *DOE Fundamentals Handbooks* represent the needs of various DOE nuclear facilities' fundamentals training requirements. To increase their applicability to nonreactor nuclear facilities, the Reactor Operator Fundamentals Manual learning objectives were distributed to the Nuclear Facility Training Coordination Program Steering Committee for review and comment. To update their reactor-specific content, DOE Category A reactor training managers also reviewed and commented on the content. On the basis of feedback from these sources, information that applied to two or more DOE nuclear facilities was considered generic and was included. The final draft of each of these handbooks was then reviewed by these two groups. This approach has resulted in revised modular handbooks that contain sufficient detail such that each facility may adjust the content to fit their specific needs.

Each handbook contains an abstract, a foreword, an overview, learning objectives, and text material, and is divided into modules so that content and order may be modified by individual DOE contractors to suit their specific training needs. Each subject area is supported by a separate examination bank with an answer key.

The *DOE Fundamentals Handbooks* have been prepared for the Assistant Secretary for Nuclear Energy, Office of Nuclear Safety Policy and Standards, by the DOE Training Coordination Program. This program is managed by EG&G Idaho, Inc.

OVERVIEW

The *Department of Energy Fundamentals Handbook* entitled *Instrumentation and Control* was prepared as an information resource for personnel who are responsible for the operation of the Department's nuclear facilities. A basic understanding of instrumentation and control is necessary for DOE nuclear facility operators, maintenance personnel, and the technical staff to safely operate and maintain the facility and facility support systems. The information in the handbook is presented to provide a foundation for applying engineering concepts to the job. This knowledge will help personnel more fully understand the impact that their actions may have on the safe and reliable operation of facility components and systems.

The *Instrumentation and Control* handbook consists of seven modules that are contained in two volumes. The following is a brief description of the information presented in each module of the handbook.

Volume 1 of 2

Module 1 - Temperature Detectors

This module describes the construction, operation, and failure modes for various types of temperature detectors and indication circuits.

Module 2 - Pressure Detectors

This module describes the construction, operation, and failure modes for various types of pressure detectors and indication circuits.

Module 3 - Level Detectors

This module describes the construction, operation, and failure modes for various types of level detectors and indication circuits.

Module 4 - Flow Detectors

This module describes the construction, operation, and failure modes for various types of flow detectors and indication circuits.

Module 5 - Position Indicators

This module describes the construction, operation, and failure modes for various types of position indicators and control circuits.

Volume 2 of 2

Module 6 - Radiation Detectors

This module describes the principles of radiation detection, detector operation, circuit operation, and specific radiation detector applications.

Module 7 - Principles of Control Systems

This module describes the principles of operation for control systems used in evaluating and regulating changing conditions in a process.

The information contained in this handbook is by no means all encompassing. An attempt to present the entire subject of instrumentation and control would be impractical. However, the *Instrumentation and Control* handbook does present enough information to provide the reader with a fundamental knowledge level sufficient to understand the advanced theoretical concepts presented in other subject areas, and to better understand basic system and equipment operations.

Department of Energy
Fundamentals Handbook

INSTRUMENTATION AND CONTROL
Module 6
Radiation Detectors

TABLE OF CONTENTS

LIST OF FIGURES iv

LIST OF TABLES vi

REFERENCES vii

OBJECTIVES viii

RADIATION DETECTION TERMINOLOGY 1

Electron-Ion Pair 1
Specific Ionization 1
Stopping Power 2
Summary 3

RADIATION TYPES 4

Alpha Particle 4
Beta Particle 5
Gamma Ray 6
Neutron 8
Summary 10

GAS-FILLED DETECTOR 11

Summary 13

DETECTOR VOLTAGE 14

Applied Voltage 14
Summary 18

PROPORTIONAL COUNTER 19

Summary 22

TABLE OF CONTENTS (Cont.)

PROPORTIONAL COUNTER CIRCUITRY 23

Summary 27

IONIZATION CHAMBER 28

Summary 34

COMPENSATED ION CHAMBER 35

Summary 39

ELECTROSCOPE IONIZATION CHAMBER 40

Summary 41

GEIGER-M LLER DETECTOR 42

Summary 44

SCINTILLATION COUNTER 45

Summary 48

GAMMA SPECTROSCOPY 49

Summary 50

MISCELLANEOUS DETECTORS 51

Self-Powered Neutron Detector 51
Wide Range Fission Chamber 52
Activation Foils and Flux Wires 53
Photographic Film 53
Summary 54

TABLE OF CONTENTS (Cont.)

CIRCUITRY AND CIRCUIT ELEMENTS 55

Terminology 55
Components 57
Summary 62

SOURCE RANGE NUCLEAR INSTRUMENTATION 63

Summary 65

INTERMEDIATE RANGE NUCLEAR INSTRUMENTATION 66

Summary 68

POWER RANGE NUCLEAR INSTRUMENTATION 69

Summary 71

LIST OF FIGURES

Figure 1 Alpha Particle Specific Ionization -vs- Distance Traveled in Air 5

Figure 2 Photoelectric Effect 6

Figure 3 Compton Scattering 6

Figure 4 Pair Production 7

Figure 5 Schematic Diagram of a Gas-Filled Detector 11

Figure 6 Ion Pairs Collected -vs- Applied Voltage 15

Figure 7 Proportional Counter 19

Figure 8 Gas Ionization Curve 20

Figure 9 Proportional Counter Circuit 23

Figure 10 Single Channel Analyzer Operation 24

Figure 11 Single Channel Analyzer Output 25

Figure 12 Discriminator 26

Figure 13 BF_3 Proportional Counter Circuit 26

Figure 14 Simple Ionization Circuit 29

Figure 15 Recombination and Ionization Regions 30

Figure 16 Ionization Chamber 31

Figure 17 Minimizing Gamma Influence by Size and Volume 32

Figure 18 Minimizing Gamma Influence with Boron Coating Area 33

Figure 19 Compensated Ion Chamber 35

LIST OF FIGURES (Cont.)

Figure 20 Compensated Ion Chamber with Concentric Cylinders 36

Figure 21 Typical Compensation Curve 38

Figure 22 Quartz Fiber Electroscope 40

Figure 23 Gas Ionization Curve 42

Figure 24 Electronic Energy Band of an Ionic Crystal 45

Figure 25 Scintillation Counter 46

Figure 26 Photomultiplier Tube Schematic Diagram 47

Figure 27 Gamma Spectrometer Block Diagram 49

Figure 28 Multichannel Analyzer Output 50

Figure 29 Self-Powered Neutron Detector 51

Figure 30 Analog and Digital Displays 56

Figure 31 Single and Two-Stage Amplifier Circuits 58

Figure 32 Biased Diode Discriminator 59

Figure 33 Log Count Rate Meter 60

Figure 34 Period Meter Circuit 61

Figure 35 Source Range Channel 64

Figure 36 Intermediate Range Channel 67

Figure 37 Power Range Channel 70

LIST OF TABLES

NONE

REFERENCES

- Kirk, Franklin W. and Rimboi, Nicholas R., Instrumentation, Third Edition, American Technical Publishers, ISBN 0-8269-3422-6.
- Gollnick, D.A., Basic Radiation Protection Technology, Pacific Radiation Press, Temple City, California.
- Cember, H., Introduction to Health Physics, Pergamon Press Inc., Library of Congress Card #68-8528, 1985.
- Academic Program for Nuclear Power Plant Personnel, Volume IV, General Physics Corporation, Library of Congress Card #A 397747, April 1982.
- Knief, R.A., Nuclear Energy Technology, McGraw-Hill Book Company.
- Cork, James M., Radioactivity and Nuclear Physics, Third Edition, D. Van Nostrand Company, Inc.
- Fozard, B., Instrumentation and Control of Nuclear Reactors, ILIFFE Books Ltd., London.
- Wightman, E.J., Instrumentation in Process Control, CRC Press, Cleveland, Ohio.
- Rhodes, T.J. and Carroll, G.C., Industrial Instruments for Measurement and Control, Second Edition, McGraw-Hill Book Company.
- Process Measurement Fundamentals, Volume I, General Physics Corporation, ISBN 0-87683-001-7, 1981.
- B. Fozard, Instrumentation and Control of Nuclear Reactors, ILIFFE Books Ltd., London.
- Knoll, Glenn F., Radiation Detection and Measurement, John Wiley and Sons, ISBN 0-471-49545-X, 1979.

TERMINAL OBJECTIVE

1.0 **SUMMARIZE** radiation protection principles to include definition of terms, types of radiation, and the basic operation of a gas-filled detector.

ENABLING OBJECTIVES

1.1 **DEFINE** the following radiation detection terms:
- a. Electron-ion pair
- b. Specific ionization
- c. Stopping power

1.2 **EXPLAIN** the relationship between stopping power and specific ionization.

1.3 **DESCRIBE** the following types of radiation to include the definition and interactions with matter.
- a. Alpha (α)
- b. Beta (β)
- c. Gamma (γ)
- d. Neutron (n)

1.4 **DESCRIBE** the principles of operation of a gas-filled detector to include:
- a. How the electric field affects ion pairs
- b. How gas amplification occurs

1.5 Given a diagram of an ion pairs collected -vs- detector voltage curve, **DESCRIBE** the regions of the curve to include:
- a. The name of the region
- b. Interactions taking place within the gas of the detector
- c. Difference between the alpha and beta curves, where applicable

TERMINAL OBJECTIVE

2.0 **SUMMARIZE** the principles of operation of various types of radiation detectors.

ENABLING OBJECTIVES

2.1 **DESCRIBE** the operation of a proportional counter to include:
- a. Radiation detection
- b. Quenching
- c. Voltage variations

2.2 Given a block diagram of a proportional counter circuit, **STATE** the purpose of the following major blocks:
- a. Proportional counter
- b. Preamplifier/amplifier
- c. Single channel analyzer/discriminator
- d. Scaler
- e. Timer

2.3 **DESCRIBE** the operation of an ionization chamber to include:
- a. Radiation detection
- b. Voltage variations
- c. Gamma sensitivity reduction

2.4 **DESCRIBE** how a compensated ion chamber compensates for gamma radiation.

2.5 **DESCRIBE** the operation of an electroscope ionization chamber.

2.6 **DESCRIBE** the operation of a Geiger-M ller (G-M) detector to include:
- a. Radiation detection
- b. Quenching
- c. Positive ion sheath

2.7 **DESCRIBE** the operation of a scintillation counter to include:
- a. Radiation detection
- b. Three classes of phosphors
- c. Photomultiplier tube operation

ENABLING OBJECTIVES (Cont.)

2.8 **DESCRIBE** the operation of a gamma spectrometer to include:
   a. Type of detector used
   b. Multichannel analyzer operation

2.9 **DESCRIBE** how the following detect neutrons:
   a. Self-powered neutron detector
   b. Wide range fission chamber
   c. Flux wire

2.10 **DESCRIBE** how a photographic film is used to measure the following:
   a. Total radiation dose
   b. Neutron dose

TERMINAL OBJECTIVE

3.0 **SUMMARIZE** the operation of typical source, intermediate, and power range nuclear instruments.

ENABLING OBJECTIVES

3.1 **DEFINE** the following terms:
- a. Signal-to-noise ratio
- b. Discriminator
- c. Analog
- d. Logarithm
- e. Period
- f. Decades per minute (DPM)
- g. Scalar

3.2 **LIST** the type of detector used in each of the following nuclear instruments:
- a. Source range
- b. Intermediate range
- c. Power range

3.3 Given a block diagram of a typical source range instrument, **STATE** the purpose of major components.
- a. Linear amplifier
- b. Discriminator
- c. Pulse integrator
- d. Log count rate amplifier
- e. Differentiator

3.4 Given a block diagram of a typical intermediate range instrument, **STATE** the purpose of major components.
- a. Log n amplifier
- b. Differentiator
- c. Reactor protection interface

3.5 **STATE** the reason gamma compensation is NOT required in the power range.

3.6 Given a block diagram of a typical power range instrument, **STATE** the purpose of major components.
- a. Linear amplifier
- b. Reactor protection interface

Intentionally Left Blank

RADIATION DETECTION TERMINOLOGY

Understanding how radiation detection occurs requires a working knowledge of basic terminology.

EO 1.1 **DEFINE the following radiation detection terms:**
- **a. Electron-ion pair**
- **b. Specific ionization**
- **c. Stopping power**

EO 1.2 **EXPLAIN the relationship between stopping power and specific ionization.**

Electron-Ion Pair

Ionization is the process of removing one or more electrons from a neutral atom. This results in the loss of units of negative charge by the affected atom. The atom becomes electrically positive (a positive ion). The products of a single ionizing event are called an electron-ion pair.

Specific Ionization

Specific ionization is that number of ion pairs produced per centimeter of travel through matter. Equation 6-1 expresses this relationship.

$$\text{Specific Ionization} = \frac{\text{ion pairs produced}}{\text{path length}} \qquad (6\text{-}1)$$

Specific ionization is dependent on the mass, charge, energy of the particle, and the electron density of matter. The greater the mass of a particle, the more interactions it produces in a given distance. A larger number of interactions results in the production of more ion pairs and a higher specific ionization.

A particle's charge has the greatest effect on specific ionization. A higher charge increases the number of interactions which occur in a given distance. Increasing the number of interactions produces more ion pairs, therefore increasing the specific ionization.

As the energy of a particle decreases, it produces more ion pairs for the same amount of distance traveled. Think of the particle as a magnet. As a magnet is passed over a pile of paper clips, the magnet attracts the clips. Maintain the same distance from the pile and vary the speed of the magnet. Notice that the slower the magnet is passed over the pile of paper clips, the more clips become attached to the magnet. The same is true of a particle passing by a group of atoms at a given distance. The slower a particle travels, the more atoms it affects.

Stopping Power

Stopping power or linear energy transfer (LET) is the energy lost per unit path length. Equation 6-2 expresses this relationship.

$$S = LET = \frac{\Delta E}{\Delta X} \tag{6-2}$$

where

S = stopping power
LET = linear energy transfer
ΔE = energy lost
ΔX = path length of travel

Specific ionization times the energy per ion pair yields the stopping power (LET), as shown in Equation 6-3.

$$\begin{aligned} S &= \left(\frac{\text{ion pairs}}{\text{path length}}\right)\left(\frac{\text{energy}}{\text{ion pairs}}\right) \\ &= \frac{\text{energy}}{\text{path length}} \end{aligned} \tag{6-3}$$

Stopping power, or LET, is proportional to the specific ionization.

Summary

Stopping power is proportional to specific ionization. Radiation detection terms discussed in this chapter are summarized below.

Radiation Detection Terms Summary

- An electron-ion pair is the product of a single ionizing event.
- Specific ionization is that number of ion pairs produced per centimeter of travel through matter.
- Stopping power is the energy lost per unit path length.

RADIATION TYPES

The four types of radiation discussed in this chapter are alpha, beta, gamma, and neutron.

EO 1.3 DESCRIBE the following types of radiation to include the definition and interactions with matter.

a. Alpha (α)
b. Beta (β)
c. Gamma (γ)
d. Neutron (n)

Alpha Particle

The alpha particle is a helium nucleus produced from the radioactive decay of heavy metals and some nuclear reactions. Alpha decay often occurs among nuclei that have a favorable neutron/proton ratio, but contain too many nucleons for stability. The alpha particle is a massive particle consisting of an assembly of two protons and two neutrons and a resultant charge of +2.

Alpha particles are the least penetrating radiation. The major energy loss for alpha particles is due to electrical excitation and ionization. As an alpha particle passes through air or soft tissue, it loses, on the average, 35 eV per ion pair created. Due to its highly charged state, large mass, and low velocity, the specific ionization of an alpha particle is very high.

Figure 1 illustrates the specific ionization of an alpha particle, on the order of tens of thousands of ion pairs per centimeter in air. An alpha particle travels a relatively straight path over a short distance.

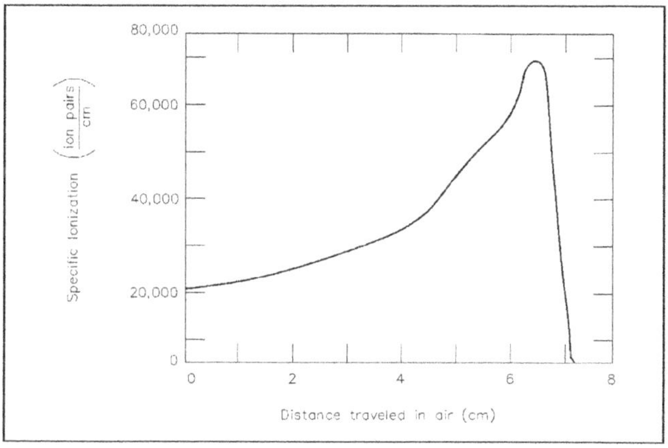

Figure 1 Alpha Particle Specific Ionization -vs- Distance Traveled in Air

Beta Particle

The beta particle is an ordinary electron or positron ejected from the nucleus of a beta-unstable radioactive atom. The beta has a single negative or positive electrical charge and a very small mass.

The interaction of a beta particle and an orbital electron leads to electrical excitation and ionization of the orbital electron. These interactions cause the beta particle to lose energy in overcoming the electrical forces of the orbital electron. The electrical forces act over long distances; therefore, the two particles do not have to come into direct contact for ionization to occur.

The amount of energy lost by the beta particle depends upon both its distance of approach to the electron and its kinetic energy. Beta particles and orbital electrons have the same mass; therefore, they are easily deflected by collision. Because of this fact, the beta particle follows a tortuous path as it passes through absorbing material. The specific ionization of a beta particle is low due to its small mass, small charge, and relatively high speed of travel.

Gamma Ray

The gamma ray is a photon of electromagnetic radiation with a very short wavelength and high energy. It is emitted from an unstable atomic nucleus and has high penetrating power.

There are three methods of attenuating (reducing the energy level of) gamma-rays: photoelectric effect, compton scattering, and pair production.

The photoelectric effect occurs when a low energy gamma strikes an orbital electron, as shown in Figure 2. The total energy of the gamma is expended in ejecting the electron from its orbit. The result is ionization of the atom and expulsion of a high energy electron.

The photoelectric effect is most predominant with low energy gammas and rarely occurs with gammas having an energy above 1 MeV (million electron volts).

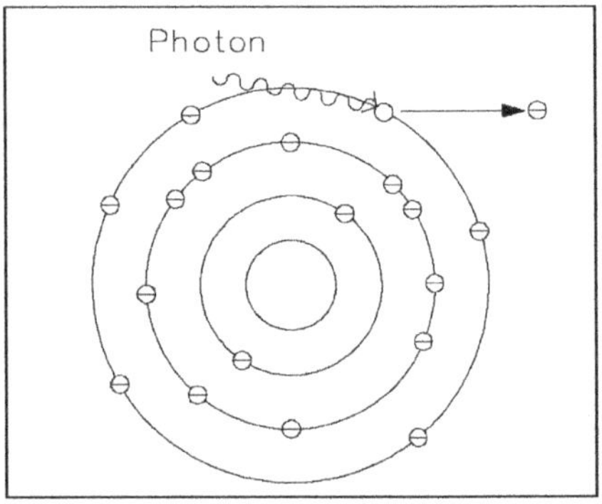

Figure 2 Photoelectric Effect

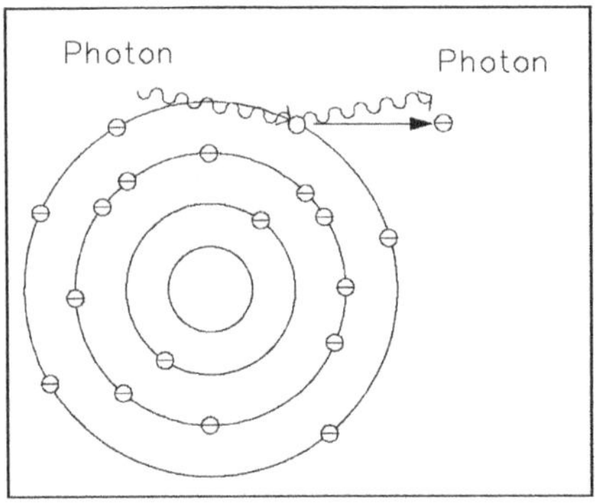

Figure 3 Compton Scattering

Compton scattering is an elastic collision between an electron and a photon, as shown in Figure 3. In this case, the photon has more energy than is required to eject the electron from orbit, or it cannot give up all of its energy in a collision with a free electron. Since all of the energy from the photon cannot be transferred, the photon must be scattered; the scattered photon must have less energy, or a longer wavelength. The result is ionization of the atom, a high energy beta, and a gamma at a lower energy level than the original.

Compton scattering is most predominant with gammas at an energy level in the 1.0 to 2.0 MeV range.

At higher energy levels, pair production is predominate. When a high energy gamma passes close enough to a heavy nucleus, the gamma disappears, and its energy reappears in the form of an electron and a positron (same mass as an electron, but has a positive charge), as shown in Figure 4. This transformation of energy into mass must take place near a particle, such as a nucleus, to conserve momentum. The kinetic energy of the recoiling nucleus is very small; therefore, all of the photon's energy that is in excess of that needed to supply the mass of the pair appears as kinetic energy of the pair. For this reaction to take place, the original gamma must have at least 1.02 MeV energy.

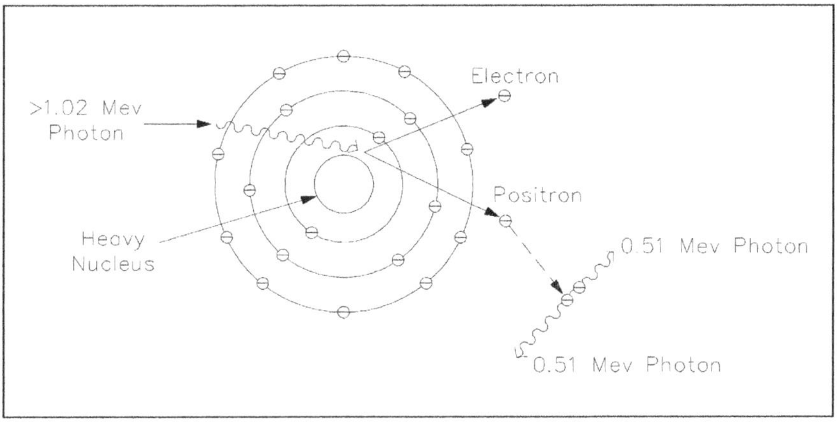

Figure 4 Pair Production

The electron loses energy by ionization. The positron interacts with other electrons and loses energy by ionizing them. If the energy of the positron is low enough, it will combine with an electron (mutual annihilation occurs), and the energy is released as a gamma. The probability of pair production increases significantly for higher energy gammas.

Gamma radiation has a very high penetrating power. A small fraction of the original stream will pass through several feet of concrete or several meters of air. The specific ionization of a gamma is low compared to that of an alpha particle, but is higher than that of a beta particle.

Neutron

Neutrons have no electrical charge and have nearly the same mass as a proton (a hydrogen atom nucleus). A neutron is hundreds of times larger than an electron, but one quarter the size of an alpha particle. The source of neutrons is primarily nuclear reactions, such as fission, but they are also produced from the decay of radioactive elements. Because of its size and lack of charge, the neutron is fairly difficult to stop, and has a relatively high penetrating power.

Neutrons may collide with nuclei causing one of the following reactions: inelastic scattering, elastic scattering, radiative capture, or fission.

Inelastic scattering causes some of the neutron's kinetic energy to be transferred to the target nucleus in the form of kinetic energy and some internal energy. This transfer of energy slows the neutron, but leaves the nucleus in an excited state. The excitation energy is emitted as a gamma ray photon. The interaction between the neutron and the nucleus is best described by the compound nucleus mode; the neutron is captured, then re-emitted from the nucleus along with a gamma ray photon. This re-emission is considered the threshold phenomenon. The neutron threshold energy varies from infinity for hydrogen, (inelastic scatter cannot occur) to about 6 MeV for oxygen, to less than 1 MeV for uranium.

Elastic scattering is the most likely interaction between fast neutrons and low atomic mass number absorbers. The interaction is sometimes referred to as the "billiard ball effect." The neutron shares its kinetic energy with the target nucleus without exciting the nucleus.

Radiative capture (n, γ) takes place when a neutron is absorbed to produce an excited nucleus. The excited nucleus regains stability by emitting a gamma ray.

The fission process for uranium (U^{235} or U^{238}) is a nuclear reaction whereby a neutron is absorbed by the uranium nucleus to form the intermediate (compound) uranium nucleus (U^{236} or U^{239}). The compound nucleus fissions into two nuclei (fission fragments) with the simultaneous emission of one to several neutrons. The fission fragments produced have a combined kinetic energy of about 168 MeV for U^{235} and 200 MeV for U^{238}, which is dissipated, causing ionization. The fission reaction can occur with either fast or thermal neutrons.

The distance that a fast neutron will travel, between its introduction into the slowing-down medium (moderator) and thermalization, is dependent on the number of collisions and the distance between collisions. Though the actual path of the neutron slowing down is tortuous because of collisions, the average straight-line distance can be determined; this distance is called the fast diffusion length or slowing-down length. The distance traveled, once thermalized, until the neutron is absorbed, is called the thermal diffusion length.

Fast neutrons rapidly degrade in energy by elastic collisions when they interact with low atomic number materials. As neutrons reach thermal energy, or near thermal energies, the likelihood of capture increases. In present day reactor facilities the thermalized neutron continues to scatter elastically with the moderator until it is absorbed by fuel or non-fuel material, or until it leaks from the core.

Secondary ionization caused by the capture of neutrons is important in the detection of neutrons. Neutrons will interact with B-10 to produce Li-7 and He-4.

$$^{10}_{5}B + ^{1}_{0}n \rightarrow ^{7}_{3}Li^{+++} + ^{4}_{2}He^{++} + 5e^{-}$$

The lithium and alpha particles share the energy and produce "secondary ionizations" which are easily detectable.

Summary

Alpha, beta, gamma, and neutron radiation are summarized below.

Radiation Types Summary

Alpha particles

- The alpha particle is a helium nucleus produced from the radioactive decay of heavy metals and some nuclear reactions.
- The high positive charge of an alpha particle causes electrical excitation and ionization of surrounding atoms.

Beta particles

- The beta particle is an ordinary electron or positron ejected from the nucleus of a beta-unstable radioactive atom.
- The interaction of a beta particle and an orbital electron leads to electrical excitation and ionization of the orbital electron.

Gamma rays

- The gamma ray is a photon of electromagnetic radiation with a very short wavelength and high energy.
- The three methods of attenuating gamma-rays are: photoelectric effect, compton scattering, and pair production.

Neutrons

- Neutrons have no electrical charge and have nearly the same mass as a proton (a hydrogen atom nucleus).
- Neutrons collide with nuclei, causing one of the following reactions: inelastic scattering, elastic scattering, radiative capture, or fission.

GAS-FILLED DETECTOR

A gas-filled detector is used to detect incident radiation.

EO 1.4 DESCRIBE the principles of operation of a gas-filled detector to include:
a. How the electric field affects ion pairs
b. How gas amplification occurs

The pulsed operation of the gas-filled detector illustrates the principles of basic radiation detection. Gases are used in radiation detectors since their ionized particles can travel more freely than those of a liquid or a solid. Typical gases used in detectors are argon and helium, although boron-triflouride is utilized when the detector is to be used to measure neutrons. Figure 5 shows a schematic diagram of a gas-filled chamber with a central electrode.

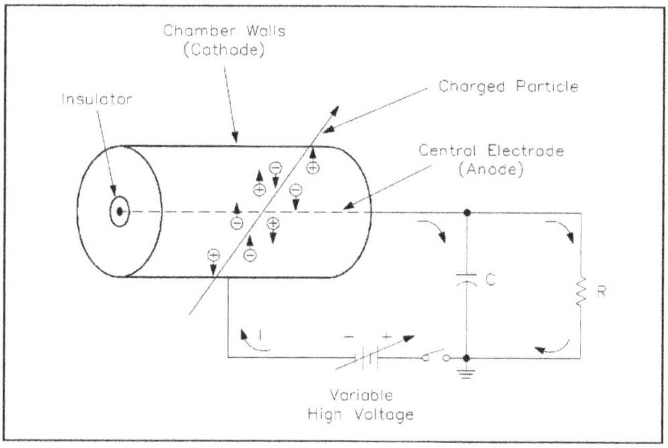

Figure 5 Schematic Diagram of a Gas-Filled Detector

The central electrode, or anode, collects negative charges. The anode is insulated from the chamber walls and the cathode, which collects positive charges. A voltage is applied to the anode and the chamber walls. The resistor in the circuit is shunted by a capacitor in parallel, so that the anode is at a positive voltage with respect to the detector wall. As a charged particle passes through the gas-filled chamber, it ionizes some of the gas (air) along its path of travel. The positive anode attracts the electrons, or negative particles. The detector wall, or cathode, attracts the positive charges. The collection of these charges reduces the voltage across the capacitor, causing a pulse across the resistor that is recorded by an electronic circuit. The voltage applied to the anode and cathode determines the electric field and its strength.

As detector voltage is increased, the electric field has more influence upon electrons produced. Sufficient voltage causes a cascade effect that releases more electrons from the cathode. Forces on the electron are greater, and its mean-free path between collisions is reduced at this threshold. Calculating the change in the capacitor's charge yields the height of the resulting pulse. Initial capacitor charge (Q), with an applied voltage (V), and capacitance (C), is given by Equation 6-4.

$$Q = CV \tag{6-4}$$

A change of charge (ΔQ) is proportional to the change in voltage (ΔV) and equals the height of the pulse, as given by Equation 6-5 or 6-6.

$$\Delta Q = C\Delta V \tag{6-5}$$

$$\Delta V = \frac{\Delta Q}{C} \tag{6-6}$$

The total number of electrons collected by the anode determines the change in the charge of the capacitor (ΔQ). The change in charge is directly related to the total ionizing events which occur in the gas. The ion pairs (n) initially formed by the incident radiation attain a great enough velocity to cause secondary ionization of other atoms or molecules in the gas. The resultant electrons cause further ionizations. This multiplication of electrons is termed gas amplification. The gas amplification factor (A) designates the increase in ion pairs when the initial ion pairs create additional ion pairs. Therefore, the height of the pulse is given by Equation 6-7.

$$\Delta V = \frac{Ane}{C} \tag{6-7}$$

where

ΔV = pulse height (volts)
A = gas amplification factor
n = initial ionizing events
e = charge of the electron (1.602 x 10^{-19} coulombs)
C = detector capacitance (farads)

The pulse height can be computed if the capacitance, detector characteristics, and radiation are known. The capacitance is normally about 10^{-4} farads. The number of ionizing events may be calculated if the detector size and specific ionization, or range of the charged particle, are known. The only variable is the gas amplification factor that is dependent on applied voltage.

Summary

The operation of gas-filled detectors is summarized below.

Gas-Filled Detectors Summary

- The central electrode, or anode, attracts and collects the electron of the ion-pair.
- The chamber walls attract and collect the positive ion.
- When the applied voltage is high enough, the ion pairs initially formed accelerate to a high enough velocity to cause secondary ionizations. The resultant ions cause further ionizations. This multiplication of electrons is called gas amplification.

DETECTOR VOLTAGE

Different ranges of applied voltage result in unique detection characteristics.

EO 1.5 **Given a diagram of an ion pairs collected -vs- detector voltage curve, DESCRIBE the regions of the curve to include:**
- **a. The name of the region**
- **b. Interactions taking place within the gas of the detector**
- **c. Difference between the alpha and beta curves, where applicable**

Applied Voltage

The relationship between the applied voltage and pulse height in a detector is very complex. Pulse height and the number of ion pairs collected are directly related. Figure 6 illustrates ion pairs collected -vs- applied voltage. Two curves are shown: one curve for alpha particles and one curve for beta particles; each curve is divided into several voltage regions. The alpha curve is higher than the beta curve from Region I to part of Region IV due to the larger number of ion pairs produced by the initial reaction of the incident radiation. An alpha particle will create more ion pairs than a beta since the alpha has a much greater mass. The difference in mass is negated once the detector voltage is increased to Region IV since the detector completely discharges with each initiating event.

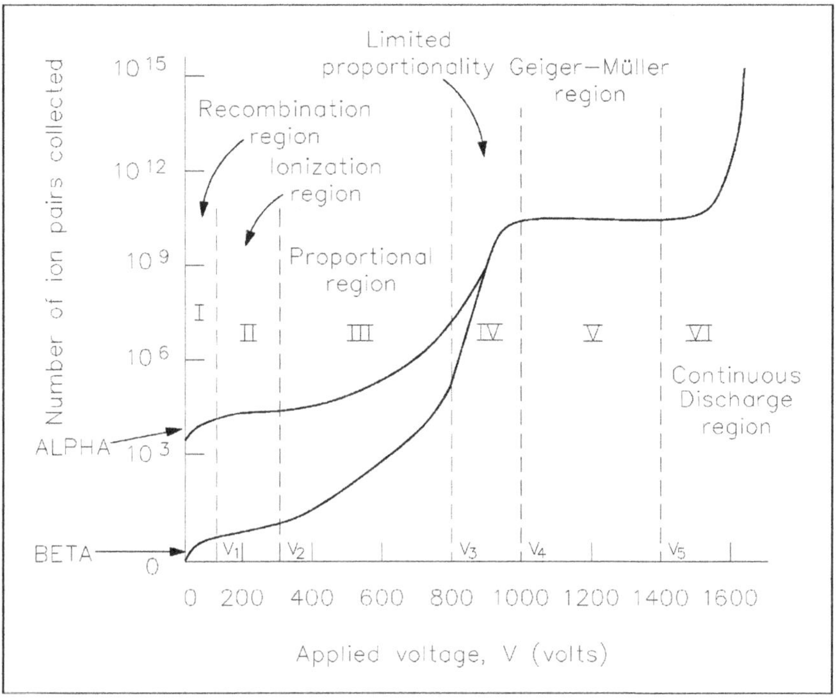

Figure 6 Ion Pairs Collected -vs- Applied Voltage

Recombination Region

In the recombination region (Region I), as voltage increases to V_1, the pulse height increases until it reaches a saturation value. At V_1, the field strength between the cathode and anode is sufficient for collection of all ions produced within the detector. At voltages less than V_1, ions move slowly toward the electrodes, and the ions tend to recombine to form neutral atoms or molecules. In this case, the pulse height is less than it would have been if all the ions originally formed reached the electrodes. Gas ionization instruments are, therefore, not operated in this region of response.

Ionization Region

As voltage is increased in the ionization region (Region II), there is no appreciable increase in the pulse height. The field strength is more than adequate to ensure collection of all ions produced; however, it is insufficient to cause any increase in ion pairs due to gas amplification. This region is called the ionization chamber region.

Proportional Region

As voltage increases to the proportional region (Region III), the pulse height increases smoothly. The voltage is sufficient to produce a large potential gradient near the anode, and it imparts a very high velocity to the electrons produced through ionization of the gas by charged radiation particles. The velocity of these electrons is sufficient to cause ionization of other atoms or molecules in the gas. This multiplication of electrons is called gas amplification and is referred to as Townsend avalanche. The gas amplification factor (A) varies from 10^3 to 10^4. This region is called the proportional region since the gas amplification factor (A) is proportional to applied voltage.

Limited Proportional Region

In the limited proportional region (Region IV), as voltage increases, additional processes occur leading to increased ionization. The strong field causes increased electron velocity, which results in excited states of higher energies capable of releasing more electrons from the cathode. These events cause the Townsend avalanche to spread along the anode. The positive ions remain near where they were originated and reduce the electric field to a point where further avalanches are impossible. For this reason, Region IV is called the limited proportional region, and it is not used for detector operation.

Geiger-M ller Region

The pulse height in the Geiger-M ller region (Region V) is independent of the type of radiation causing the initial ionizations. The pulse height obtained is on the order of several volts. The field strength is so great that the discharge, once ignited, continues to spread until amplification cannot occur, due to a dense positive ion sheath surrounding the central wire (anode). V_4 is termed the threshold voltage. This is where the number of ion pairs level off and remain relatively independent of the applied voltage. This leveling off is called the Geiger plateau which extends over a region of 200 to 300 volts. The threshold is normally about 1000 volts. In the G-M region, the gas amplification factor (A) depends on the specific ionization of the radiation to be detected.

Continuous Discharge Region

In the continuous discharge region (Region VI), a steady discharge current flows. The applied voltage is so high that, once ionization takes place in the gas, there is a continuous discharge of electricity, so that the detector cannot be used for radiation detection.

Radiation detectors are normally designed to respond to a certain type of radiation. Since the detector response can be sensitive to both energy and intensity of the radiation, each type of detector has defined operating limits based on the characteristics of the radiation to be measured. A large variety of detectors are in use in DOE facilities to detect alpha and beta particles, gamma rays, or neutrons. Some types of detectors are capable of distinguishing between the types of radiation; others are not. Some detectors only count the number of particles that enter the detector, while others are used to determine both the number and energy of the incident particles. Most detectors used in DOE facilities have one thing in common: they respond only to electrons produced in the detector. In order to detect the different types of incident particles, the particle's energy must be converted to electrons in the detector.

Gas-filled detectors are used, for the most part, to measure alpha and beta particles, neutrons, and gamma rays. The detectors operate in the ionization, proportional, and G-M regions with an arrangement most sensitive to the type of radiation being measured. Neutron detectors utilize ionization chambers or proportional counters of appropriate design. Compensated ion chambers, BF_3 counters, fission counters, and proton recoil counters are examples of neutron detectors.

Summary

The alpha curve is higher than the beta curve from Region I to part of Region IV due to the larger number of ion pairs produced by the initial reaction of the incident radiation. Detector voltage principles are summarized below.

Gas Amplification Region Summary

Recombination Region

- The voltage is such a low value that recombination takes place before most of the negative ions are collected by the electrode.

Ionization Region

- The voltage is sufficient to ensure all ion pairs produced by the incident radiation are collected.
- No gas amplification takes place.

Proportional Region

- The voltage is sufficient to ensure all ion pairs produced by the incident radiation are collected.
- Amount of gas amplification is proportional to the applied voltage.

Limited Proportional Region

- As voltage increases, additional processes occur leading to increased ionizations.
- Since positive ions remain near their point of origin, further avalanches are impossible.

Geiger-M ller Region

- The ion pair production is independent of the radiation, causing the initial ionization.
- The field strength is so great that the discharge continues to spread until amplification cannot occur, due to a dense positive ion sheath surrounding the central wire.

Continuous Discharge Region

- The applied voltage is so high that, once ionization takes place, there is a continuous discharge of electricity.

PROPORTIONAL COUNTER

A proportional counter is a detector that operates in the proportional region.

EO 2.1 DESCRIBE the operation of a proportional counter to include:
- **a. Radiation detection**
- **b. Quenching**
- **c. Voltage variations**

A proportional counter is a detector which operates in the proportional region, as shown in Figure 6. Figure 7 illustrates a simplified proportional counter circuit.

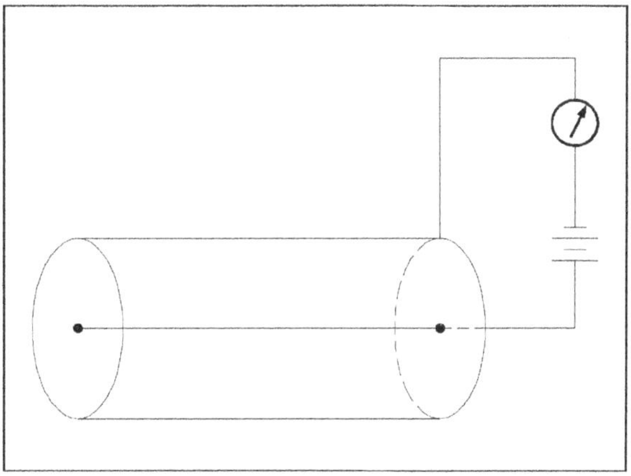

Figure 7 Proportional Counter

To be able to detect a single particle, the number of ions produced must be increased. As voltage is increased into the proportional region, the primary ions acquire enough energy to cause secondary ionizations (gas amplification) and increase the charge collected. These secondary ionizations may cause further ionization.

In this region, there is a linear relationship between the number of ion pairs collected and applied voltage. A charge amplification of 10^4 can be obtained in the proportional region. By proper functional arrangements, modifications, and biasing, the proportional counter can be used to detect alpha, beta, gamma, or neutron radiation in mixed radiation fields.

To a limited degree, the fill-gas will determine what type of radiation the proportional counter will be able to detect. Argon and helium are the most frequently used fill gases and allow for the detection of alpha, beta, and gamma radiation. When detection of neutrons is necessary, the detectors are usually filled with boron-triflouride gas.

The simplified circuit, illustrated in Figure 7, shows that the detector wall acts as one electrode, while the other electrode is a fine wire in the center of the chamber with a positive voltage applied.

Figure 8 illustrates how the number of electrons collected varies with the applied voltage.

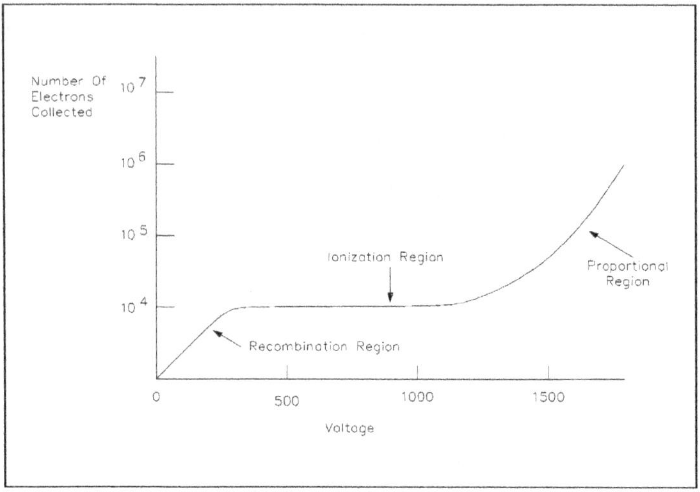

Figure 8 Gas Ionization Curve

When a single gamma ray interacts with the gas in the chamber, it produces a rapidly moving electron which produces secondary electrons. About 10,000 electrons may be formed depending on the gas used in the chamber. The applied voltage can be increased until the amount of recombination is very low. However, further increases do not appreciably increase the number of electrons collected. This region in which all 10,000 electrons are collected is the ionization region.

As applied voltage is increased above 1000 V, the number of electrons becomes greater than the initial 10,000. The additional electrons which are collected are due to gas amplification. As voltage is increased, the velocity of the 10,000 electrons produced increases. However, beyond a certain voltage, the 10,000 electrons are accelerated to such speeds that they have enough energy to cause more ionization. This phenomenon is called gas amplification.

As an example, if the 10,000 electrons produced by the gamma ray are increased to 40,000 by gas amplification, the amplification factor would be 4. Gas amplification factors can range from unity in the ionization region to 10^3 or 10^4 in the proportional region. The high amplification factor of the proportional counter is the major advantage over the ionization chamber. The internal amplification of the proportional counter is such that low energy particles (< 10 KeV) can be registered, whereas the ion chamber is limited by amplifier noise to particles of > 10 KeV energy.

Proportional counters are extremely sensitive, and the voltages are large enough so that all of the electrons are collected within a few tenths of a microsecond. Each pulse corresponds to one gamma ray or neutron interaction. The amount of charge in each pulse is proportional to the number of original electrons produced. The proportionality factor in this case is the gas amplification factor. The number of electrons produced is proportional to the energy of the incident particle.

For each electron collected in the chamber, there is a positively charged gas ion left over. These gas ions are heavy compared to an electron and move much more slowly. Eventually the positive ions move away from the positively charged central wire to the negatively charged wall and are neutralized by gaining an electron. In the process, some energy is given off, which causes additional ionization of the gas atoms. The electrons produced by this ionization move toward the central wire and are multiplied en route. This pulse of charge is unrelated to the radiation to be detected and can set off a series of pulses. These pulses must be eliminated or "quenched."

One method for quenching these discharges is to add a small amount (≈ 10%) of an organic gas, such as methane, in the chamber. The quenching gas molecules have a weaker affinity for electrons than the chamber gas does; therefore, the ionized atoms of the chamber gas readily take electrons from the quenching gas molecules. Thus, the ionized molecules of quenching gas reach the chamber wall instead of the chamber gas. The ionized molecules of the quenching gas are neutralized by gaining an electron, and the energy liberated does not cause further ionization, but causes dissociation of the molecule. This dissociation quenches multiple discharges. The quenching gas molecules are eventually consumed, thus limiting the lifetime of the proportional counter. There are, however, some proportional counters that have an indefinite lifetime because the quenching gas is constantly replenished. These counters are referred to as gas flow counters.

Summary

Proportional counters are summarized below.

Proportional Counters Summary

- When radiation enters a proportional counter, the detector gas, at the point of incident radiation, becomes ionized.
- The detector voltage is set so that the electrons cause secondary ionizations as they accelerate toward the electrode.
- The electrons produced from the secondary ionizations cause additional ionizations.
- This multiplication of electrons is called gas amplification.
- Varying the detector voltage within the proportional region increases or decreases the gas amplification factor.
- A quenching gas is added to give up electrons to the chamber gas so that inaccuracies are NOT introduced due to ionizations caused by the positive ion.

PROPORTIONAL COUNTER CIRCUITRY

Proportional counters measure different types of radiation.

EO 2.2 **Given a block diagram of a proportional counter circuit, STATE the purpose of the following major blocks:**

a. Proportional counter
b. Preamplifier/amplifier
c. Single channel analyzer/discriminator
d. Scaler
e. Timer

Proportional counters measure the charge produced by each particle of radiation. To make full use of the counter's capabilities, it is necessary to measure the number of pulses and the charge in each pulse. Figure 9 shows a typical circuit used to make such measurements.

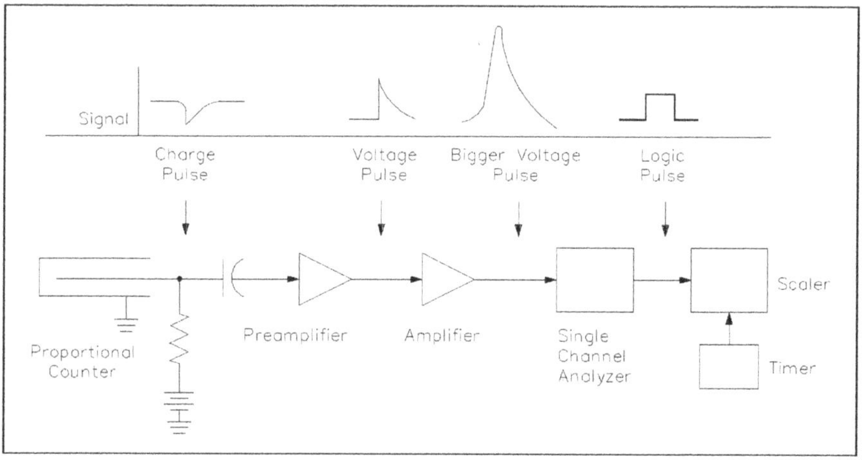

Figure 9 Proportional Counter Circuit

The capacitor converts the charge pulse to a voltage pulse. The voltage is equal to the amount of charge divided by the capacitance of the capacitor, as given in Equation 6-8.

$$V = \frac{Q}{C} \tag{6-8}$$

where

V = voltage pulse (volts)
Q = charge (coulombs)
C = capacitance (farads)

The preamplifier amplifies the voltage pulse. Further amplification is obtained by sending the signal through an amplifier circuit (typically about 10 volts maximum). The pulse size is then determined by a single channel analyzer. Figure 10 shows the operation of a single channel analyzer.

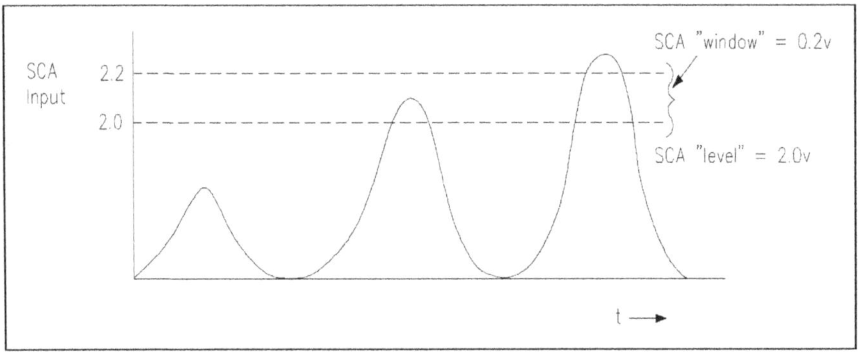

Figure 10 Single Channel Analyzer Operation

The single channel analyzer has two dial settings: a LEVEL dial and a WINDOW dial. For example, when the level is set at 2 volts, and the window at 0.2 volts, the analyzer will give an output pulse only when the input pulse is between 2 and 2.2 volts. The output pulse is usually a standardized height and width logic pulse, as shown in Figure 11.

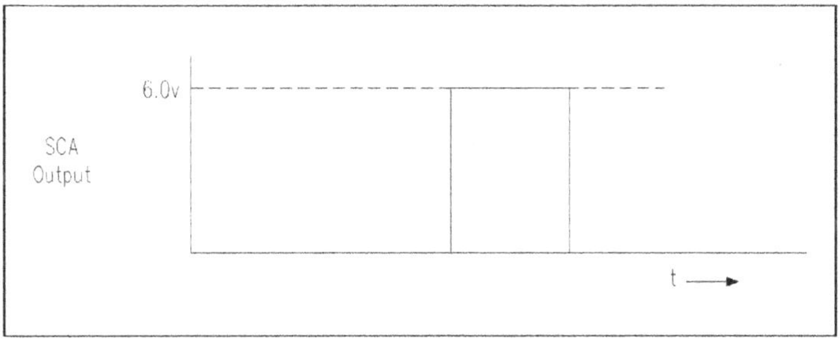

Figure 11 Single Channel Analyzer Output

Since the single channel analyzer can be set so that an output is only produced by a certain pulse size, it provides for the counting of one specific radiation in a mixed radiation field.

This output is fed to a scaler which counts the number of pulses it receives. A timer gates the scaler so that the scaler counts the pulses for a predetermined length of time. Knowing the number of counts per a given time interval allows calculation of the count rate (number of counts per unit time).

Proportional counters can also count neutrons by introducing boron into the chamber. The most common means of introducing boron is by combining it with tri-fluoride gas to form Boron Tri-Fluoride (BF_3). When a neutron interacts with a boron atom, an alpha particle is emitted. The BF_3 counter can be made sensitive to neutrons and not to gamma rays.

Gamma rays can be eliminated because the neutron-induced alpha particles produce more ionizations than gamma rays produce. This is due mainly to the fact that gamma ray-induced electrons have a much longer range than the dimensions of the chamber; the alpha particle energy is, in most cases, greater than gamma rays produced in a reactor. Therefore, neutron pulses are much larger than gamma ray-produced pulses.

By using a discriminator,the scaler can be set to read only the larger pulses produced by the neutron. A discriminator is basically a single channel analyzer with only one setting. Figure 12 illustrates the operation of a discriminator.

If the discriminator is set at 2 volts, then any input pulse $\geq$ 2 volts causes an output pulse.

Figure 13 shows a typical circuit used to measure neutrons with a BF_3 proportional counter.

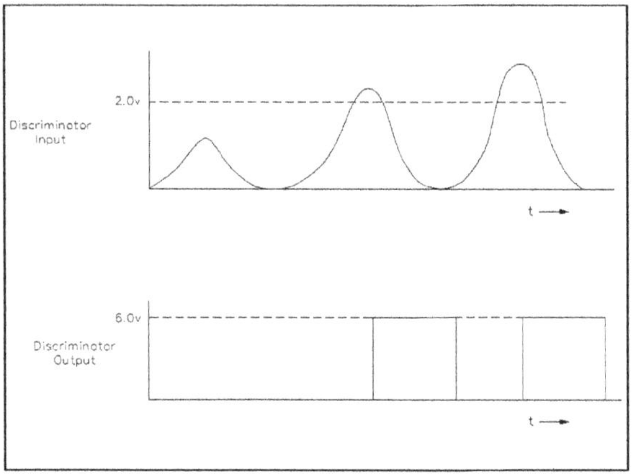

Figure 12 Discriminator

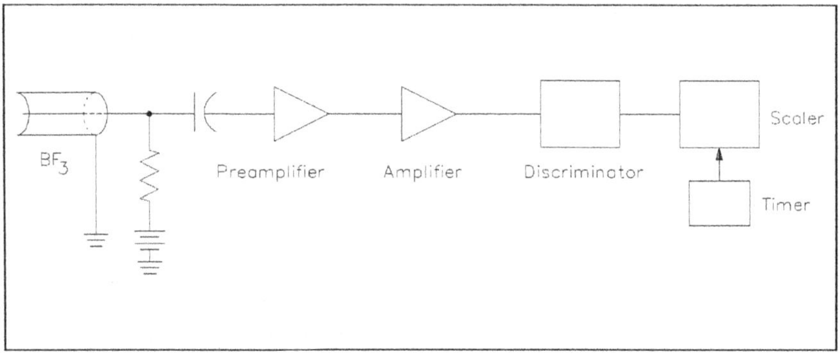

Figure 13 BF_3 Proportional Counter Circuit

The BF_3 proportional counter is used to monitor low power levels in a nuclear reactor. It is used in the "startup" or "source range" channels. Proportional counters cannot be used at high power levels because they are pulse-type detectors. Typically, it takes 10 to 20 microseconds for each pulse to go from 10% of its peak, to its peak, and back to 10%. If another neutron interacts in the chamber during this time, the two pulses are superimposed. The voltage output would never drop to zero between the two pulses, and the chamber would draw a steady current as electrons are being produced.

Summary

Proportional counter circuitry is summarized below.

Proportional Counter Circuitry Summary

- The proportional counter measures the charge produced by each particle of radiation.
- The preamplifier/amplifier amplifies the voltage pulse to a usable size.
- The single channel analyzer/discriminator produces an output only when the input is a certain pulse size.
- The scaler counts the number of pulses received during a predetermined length of time.
- The timer provides the gating signal to the scaler.

IONIZATION CHAMBER

The ionization chamber is a detector that operates in the ionization region.

EO 2.3 DESCRIBE the operation of an ionization chamber to include:

a. Radiation detection

b. Voltage variations

c. Gamma sensitivity reduction

Ionization chambers are electrical devices that detect radiation when the voltage is adjusted so that the conditions correspond to the ionization region (refer to Region II of Figure 6). The charge obtained is the result of collecting the ions produced by radiation. This charge will depend on the type of radiation being detected. Ionization chambers have two distinct disadvantages when compared to proportional counters: they are less sensitive, and they have a slower response time.

There are two types of ionization chambers to be discussed: the pulse counting ionization chamber and the integrating ionization chamber. In the pulse counting ionization chamber, the pulses are detected due to particles traversing the chamber. In the integrating chamber, the pulses add, and the integrated total of the ionizations produced in a predetermined period of time is measured. The same type of ionization chamber may be used for either function. However, as a general rule, the integrating type ionization chamber is used.

Flat plates or concentric cylinders may be utilized in the construction of an ionization chamber. The flat plate design is preferred because it has a well-defined active volume and ensures that ions will not collect on the insulators and cause a distortion of the electric field. The concentric cylinder design does not have a well-defined active volume because of the variation in the electric field as the insulator is approached. Ionization chamber construction differs from the proportional counter (flat plates or concentric cylinders vice a cylinder and central electrode) to allow for the integration of pulses produced by the incident radiation. The proportional counter would require such exact control of the electric field between the electrodes that it would not be practical.

Figure 14 illustrates a simple ionization circuit consisting of two parallel plates of metal with an air space between them. The plates are connected to a battery which is connected in series with a highly sensitive ammeter.

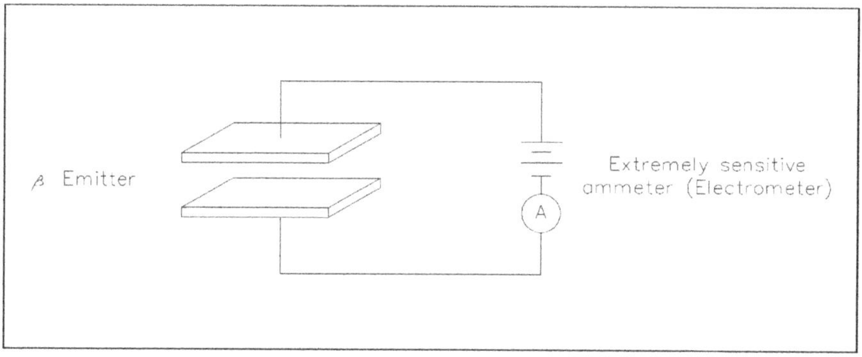

Figure 14 Simple Ionization Circuit

If a radioactive source that is an emitter of beta particles is placed near the detector, the beta particles will pass between the plates and strike atoms in the air. With sufficient energy, the beta particle causes an electron to be ejected from an atom in air. A single beta particle may eject 40 to 50 electrons for each centimeter of path length traveled. The electrons ejected by the beta particle often have enough energy to eject more electrons from other atoms in air. The total number of electrons produced is dependent on the energy of the beta particle and the gas between the plates of the ionization chamber.

In general, a 1 MeV beta particle will eject approximately 50 electrons per centimeter of travel, while a 0.05 MeV beta particle will eject approximately 300 electrons. The lower energy beta ejects more electrons because it has more collisions. Each electron produced by the beta particle, while traveling through air, will produce thousands of electrons. A current of 1 micro-ampere consists of about 10^{12} electrons per second.

If 1 volt is applied to the plates of the ionization chamber shown in Figure 14, some of the free electrons will be attracted to the positive plate of the detector. This attraction is not strong because 1 volt does not create a strong electric field between the two plates. The free electrons will tend to drift toward the positive plate, causing a current to flow, which is indicated on the ammeter. Not all of the free electrons will make it to the positive plate because the positively charged atoms that resulted when an electron was ejected may recapture other free electrons. Therefore, the ammeter will register only a fraction of the number of free electrons between the plates.

When the voltage is increased, the free electrons are more strongly attracted to the positive plate. They will move toward the positive plate more quickly and will have less opportunity to recombine with the positive ions. Figure 15 shows a plot of the number of electrons measured by the ammeter as a function of applied voltage.

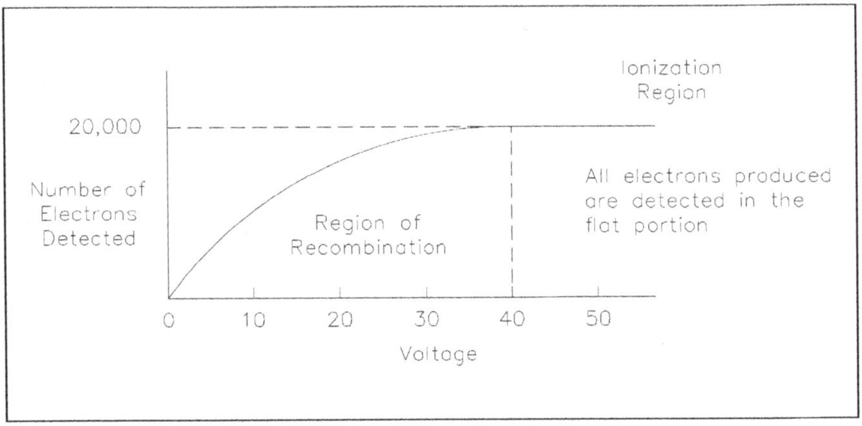

Figure 15 Recombination and Ionization Regions

At zero voltage, no attraction of electrons between the plates occurs. The electrons will eventually recombine, so there is no current flow. As the applied voltage is increased, the positive plate will begin to attract free electrons more strongly, and a higher percentage will reach the positive plate. As the voltage is increased further, a point will be reached in which all of the electrons produced in the chamber will reach the positive plate. Any further increase in voltage has no effect on the number of electrons collected.

The simple ionization chamber shown in Figure 14 can also be utilized for the detection of gamma rays. Since the ammeter is sensitive only to electrons, gamma rays must interact with the atoms in air between the plates to release electrons. The gamma rays interact by compton scattering, photoelectric effect, or pair production. Each of these interactions causes some, or all, of the energy of the incident gamma rays to be converted into the kinetic energy of the ejected electrons. The ejected electrons move at very high speeds and cause other electrons to be ejected from their atoms. All of these electrons can be collected by the positively charged plate and measured by the ammeter.

The plates in an ionization chamber are normally enclosed in metal, as shown by Figure 16.

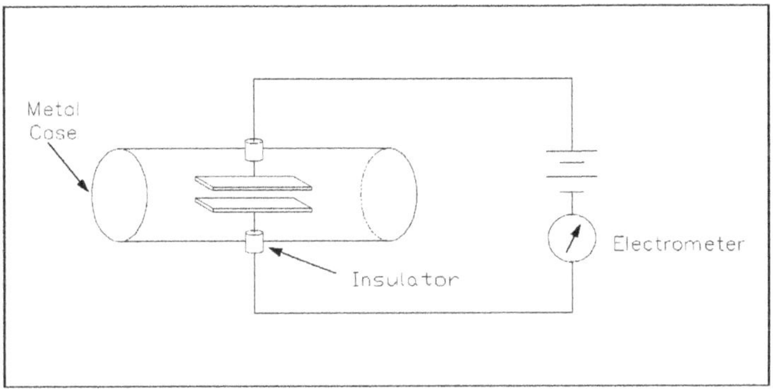

Figure 16 Ionization Chamber

This metal chamber serves to shield the plates from outside electric fields and to contain the air or other gas. Gamma rays have very little trouble in penetrating the metal walls of the chamber. Beta particles and alpha particles, however, are stopped by the metal wall. For alpha and beta particles to be detected, some means must be provided for a thin wall or "window." This window must be thin enough for the alpha and beta particles to penetrate. However, a window of almost any thickness will prevent an alpha particle from entering the chamber.

Neutrons can also be detected by an ionization chamber. As we already know, neutrons are uncharged; therefore, they cause no ionizations themselves. If the inner surface of the ionization chamber is coated with a thin coat of boron, the following reaction can take place.

$$^{10}_{5}B + ^{1}_{0}n \rightarrow ^{7}_{3}Li^{+++} + ^{4}_{2}He^{++} + 5e$$

A neutron is captured by a boron atom, and an energetic alpha particle is emitted. The alpha particle causes ionization within the chamber, and ejected electrons cause further secondary ionizations.

Another method for detecting neutrons using an ionization chamber is to use the gas boron trifluoride (BF_3) instead of air in the chamber. The incoming neutrons produce alpha particles when they react with the boron atoms in the detector gas. Either method may be used to detect neutrons in nuclear reactor neutron detectors.

When using an ionization chamber for detecting neutrons, beta particles can be prevented from entering the chamber by walls thick enough to shield out all of the beta particles. Gamma rays cannot be shielded from the detector; therefore, they always contribute to the total current read by the ammeter. This effect is not desired because the detector responds not only to neutrons, but also to gamma rays. Several ways are available to minimize this problem.

Discrimination is possible because the ionizations produced by the alpha particles differ in energy levels from those produced by gamma rays. A 1 MeV alpha particle moving through the gas loses all of its energy in a few centimeters. Therefore, all of the secondary electrons are produced along a path of only a few centimeters. A 1 MeV gamma ray produces a 1 MeV electron, and this electron has a long range and loses its energy over the entire length of its range. If we make the sensitive volume of the chamber smaller without reducing the area of the coated boron, the sensitivity to gamma rays is reduced.

Figure 17 illustrates how the chamber may be modified to accomplish this reduction.

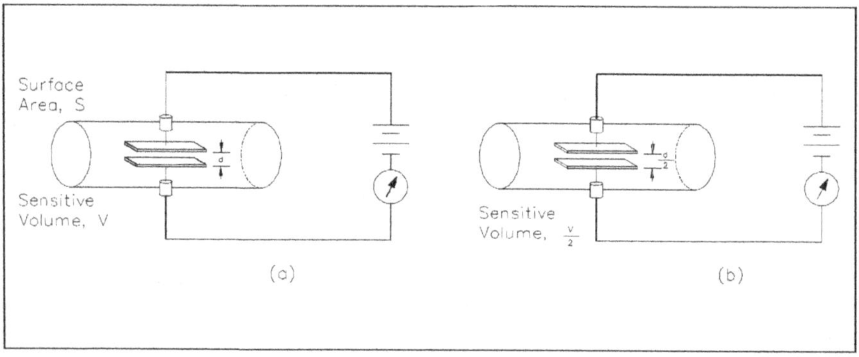

Figure 17 Minimizing Gamma Influence by Size and Volume

In Figure 17(b) there is half as much gas in the sensitive volume as in the chamber in Figure 17(a). As a result, gamma rays have only half as much gas to interact with; therefore, half the number of electrons are produced. The area which is boron-coated has not changed, and both chambers produce the same number of neutron-induced alpha particles. Also, the gamma ray-induced electrons produce fewer ionizations because the range of these electrons is longer than the dimensions of the sensitive volume. The range of neutron-induced alpha particles is short, and all of the energy will be dissipated within the sensitive volume, even when the volume is smaller.

Gamma interference can also be minimized by reducing the pressure of the gas inside the chamber. The reduction in pressure reduces the number of atoms within the sensitive volume and has the same effect as reducing the volume.

Ionization chamber sensitivity to gamma rays can also be reduced by increasing chamber sensitivity to neutrons. This is accomplished by increasing the boron-coated area, as shown in Figure 18. Both ionization chambers shown in Figure 18 have the same sensitive volume.

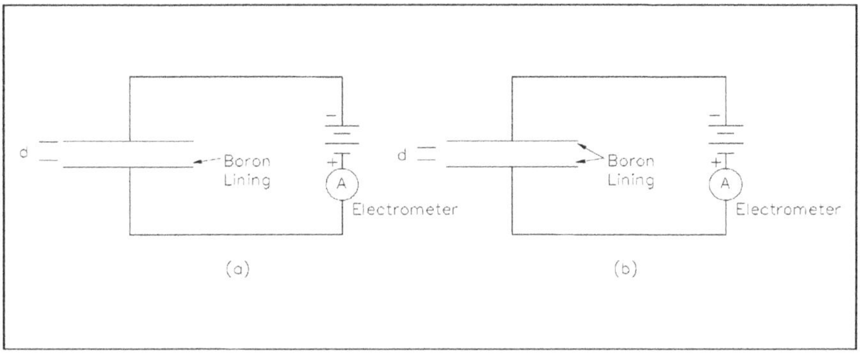

Figure 18 Minimizing Gamma Influence with Boron Coating Area

The ionization chamber in Figure 18(b) has twice the boron area as the ionization chamber in Figure 18(a). The result is that more neutron-induced alpha particles are produced, and neutron sensitivity is increased. Ionization chambers supplied commercially are designed to minimize gamma sensitivity by both of the techniques described previously. Gamma sensitivity can be minimized but not eliminated. For reactors operating near peak power, neutrons are the dominant radiation, and almost all of the current is due to neutrons. These chambers are used at high reactor powers and are referred to as uncompensated ion chambers. The uncompensated ion chamber is not suitable for use at intermediate or low power levels because the gamma response at these power levels can be significant compared to the neutron response.

Summary

Ionization chambers are summarized below.

Ionization Chamber Summary

- When radiation enters an ionization chamber, the detector gas at the point of incident radiation becomes ionized.
- Some of the electrons have sufficient energy to cause additional ionizations.
- The electrons are attracted to the electrode by the voltage potential set up on the detector.
- If the voltage is set high enough, all of the electrons will reach the electrode before recombination takes place.
- Gamma sensitivity reduction is accomplished by either reducing the amount of chamber gas or increasing the boron coated surface area.

COMPENSATED ION CHAMBER

Gamma compensation is required at intermediate reactor power levels to ensure accurate power reading.

EO 2.4 DESCRIBE how a compensated ion chamber compensates for gamma radiation.

Compensating for the response to gamma rays extends the useful range of the ionization chamber. Compensated ionization chambers consist of two separate chambers; one chamber is coated with boron, and one chamber is not. The coated chamber is sensitive to both gamma rays and neutrons, while the uncoated chamber is sensitive only to gamma rays. Instead of having two separate ammeters and subtracting the currents, the subtraction of these currents is done electrically, and the net output of both detectors is read on a single ammeter. If the polarities are arranged so that the two chambers' currents oppose one another, the reading obtained from the ammeter indicates the difference between the two currents. One plate of the compensated ion chamber is common to both chambers; one side is coated with boron, while the other side is not.

Figure 19 shows the basic circuitry for a compensated ion chamber.

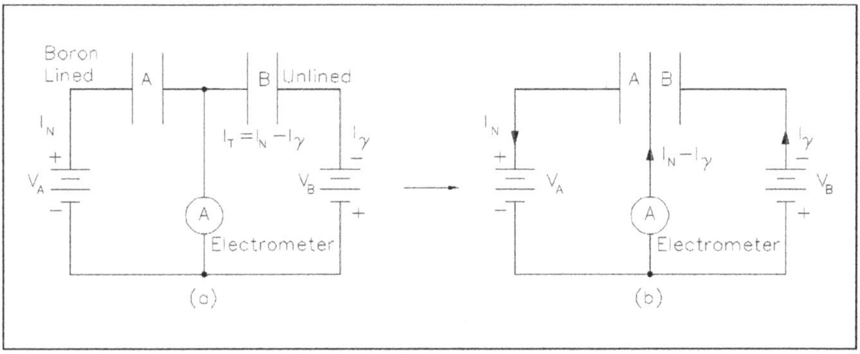

Figure 19 Compensated Ion Chamber

The boron coated chamber is referred to as the working chamber; the uncoated chamber is called the compensating chamber. When exposed to a gamma source, the battery for the working chamber will set up a current flow that deflects the meter in one direction. The compensating chamber battery will set up a current flow that deflects the meter in the opposite direction. If both chambers are identical, and both batteries are of the same voltage, the net current flow is exactly zero. Therefore, the compensating chamber cancels the current due to gamma rays.

The two chambers of a compensated ion chamber are never truly identical; in fact, they are often purposely constructed in different shapes. The chambers are normally constructed as concentric cylinders, as illustrated in Figure 20.

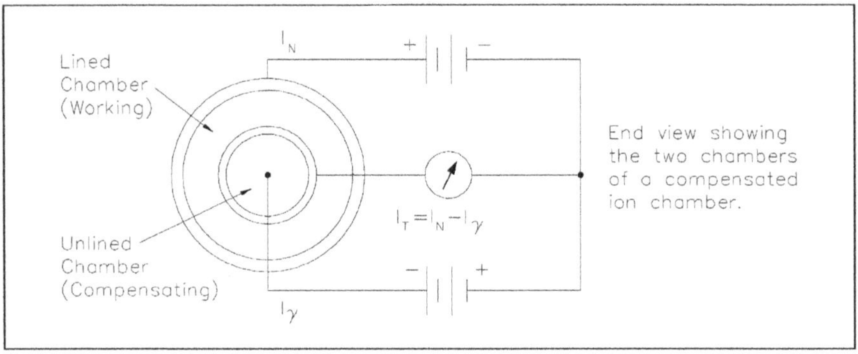

Figure 20 Compensated Ion Chamber with Concentric Cylinders

The use of concentric cylinders has an advantage because both chambers are exposed to nearly the same radiation field. Even though the chambers are not identical, proper selection of the operating voltage eliminates the gamma current. Working chamber operating voltage is given by the manufacturer and is selected to cause operation on the flat portion of the response curve, where very little recombination occurs. If working chamber voltage is increased to operating voltage, and compensating voltage is left at zero, the measured current will be due to gammas only in the working chamber. For this reason, compensating voltage is set while the reactor is shutdown (a minimum number of neutrons are present).

As the compensating chamber voltage is raised, the measured current will decrease as more of the current from the working chamber is canceled by the current from the compensating chamber. Eventually, the voltage becomes large enough so that the two currents cancel. When the currents cancel, the chamber is said to be 100% compensated, and the measured current is zero. At 100% compensation, the detector will respond to neutrons alone.

The compensating chamber usually has a slightly larger sensitive volume than the working chamber. Increasing the compensating current to a value greater than the working chamber current results in a net negative current. In this condition, the chamber is said to be overcompensated. The compensating chamber cancels too much current from the working chamber, and the meter reads low. In this case, the compensating chamber cancels out all of the gamma current and some of the neutron current.

Percent compensation of a compensated ion chamber gives the percentage of the gamma rays which are canceled out. Percent compensation may be calculated based on measured current, when the detector is exposed to gamma rays only as given in Equation 6-9.

$$\text{Percent Compensation} = 1 - \frac{I_{measured}}{I_{operating}} \times 100\% \qquad (6\text{-}9)$$

where

$I_{measured}$ = measured current (milliamps)
$I_{operating}$ = measured current with compensating voltage OFF (milliamps)

If measured current is zero, then percent compensation is 100%. If measured current is positive, the percent compensation is less than 100%, and the chamber is undercompensated. If the measured current is negative, the percent compensation is greater than 100%, and the chamber is overcompensated.

The ionization chamber compensation curve, Figure 21, is a plot of the percent compensation versus compensating voltage. This compensation curve must be plotted prior to using a compensated ion chamber.

In ideal situations, compensated ion chambers operate at 100% compensation, and indicated current is due to neutrons. Small changes in compensating voltage change the percent compensation.

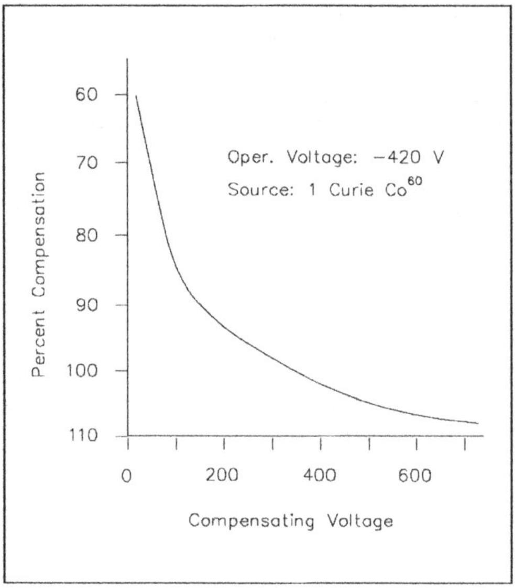

Figure 21 Typical Compensation Curve

The consequences of operating with an overcompensated or undercompensated chamber are important. The purpose of nuclear instrumentation is to detect and measure neutron level, which is the direct measure of core power. If the compensating voltage is set too high, or overcompensated, some neutron current, as well as all of the gamma current, is blocked, and indicated power is lower than actual core power. If compensating voltage is set too low, or undercompensated, not all of the gamma current is blocked, and indicated power is higher than actual core power. At high power, gamma flux is relatively small compared to neutron flux, and the effects of improper compensation may not be noticed. It is extremely important, however, that the chamber be properly compensated during reactor startup and shutdown.

Summary

Compensated ion chambers are summarized below.

Compensated Ion Chamber Summary

- A compensated ion chamber has two concentric cylinders: a boron-coated chamber and an uncoated chamber.
- Both gammas and neutrons interact in the boron-coated chamber.
- Only gammas interact in the uncoated chamber.
- The voltages to each chamber are set so that the current from the gammas in the boron-coated chamber cancels the current from the gammas in the uncoated chamber.

ELECTROSCOPE IONIZATION CHAMBER

The gold-leaf electroscope has been widely used in the past to study ionizing radiation.

EO 2.5 DESCRIBE the operation of an electroscope ionization chamber.

The gold-leaf electroscope has been widely used in the past to study ionizing radiation. The first measurement of the properties of ionizing radiation was accomplished with this instrument. A microscope containing a graduated scale in the eyepiece is used to observe the gold leaf.

The newest electroscope utilizes a quartz fiber and has many advantages over the gold-leaf type. It is portable, less dependent on position, much smaller in size, and more sensitive. The capacity of the quartz fiber electroscope is about 0.2 pico-farads, and its voltage sensitivity is about one volt per division on the scale. The sensitive element is a fine gold plated quartz fiber mounted on a parallel metal support. Figure 22 illustrates a quartz fiber electroscope.

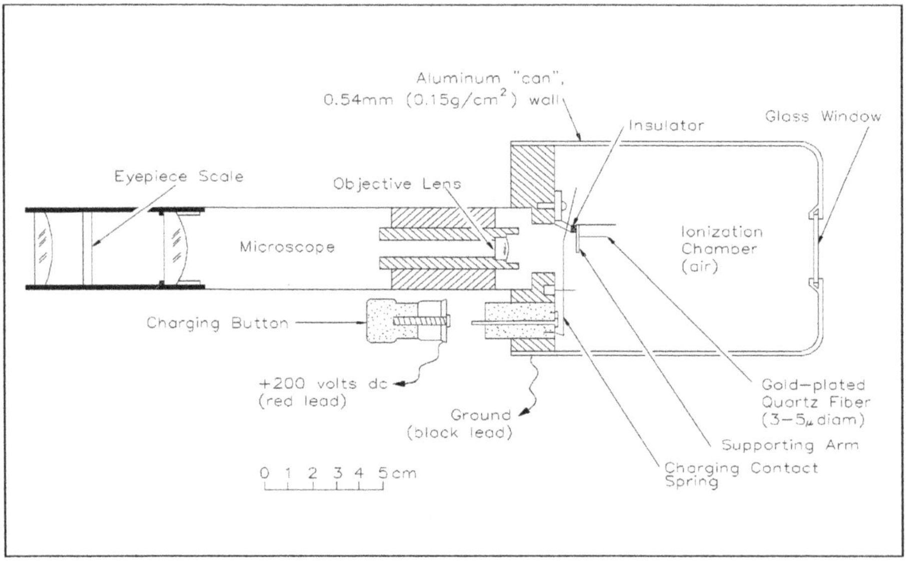

Figure 22 Quartz Fiber Electroscope

A small piece of quartz fiber is mounted across the end of the gold-plated quartz fiber and serves as an index that is viewed through a microscope equipped with an eyepiece scale. The quartz fiber is charged by a battery pressing the charging key. As the quartz fiber is being charged, it is deflected from the support. It takes approximately 200 volts to produce full-scale deflection of the fiber. A glass window at the end of the ionization chamber allows for exposure of the fiber. As the gas (air) is ionized by the incident radiation, the fiber moves toward the position of zero charge. Due to the electroscope's dependability, simplicity, accuracy, and sensitivity, it is widely used in gamma radiation measurement.

A self-reading pocket dosimeter is an example of an electroscope ionization chamber. Pocket dosimeters provide personnel with a means of monitoring their radiation exposure. The dosimeters are available in many ranges of gamma exposures from 0 through 200 milliroentgens to 0 through 1000 roentgens. The sensitivity of the instrument is determined at the time of manufacture. Appropriate scale markings are provided with each dose range.

Summary

The operation of an electroscope ionization chamber is summarized below.

Electroscope Ionization Chamber Summary

- The electroscope ionization chamber is charged using a battery.
- Charging causes the quartz fiber to be deflected from the support.
- When radiation ionizes the gas (air) in the chamber, the charge is reduced, and the fiber moves towards the zero charge position.

GEIGER-M LLER DETECTOR

The Geiger-M ller detector is a radiation detector which operates in the G-M region.

EO 2.6 DESCRIBE the operation of a Geiger-M ller (G-M) detector to include:

a. Radiation detection

b. Quenching

c. Positive ion sheath

The Geiger-M ller or G-M detector is a radiation detector that operates in Region V, or G-M region, as shown on Figure 23. G-M detectors produce larger pulses than other types of detectors. However, discrimination is not possible, since the pulse height is independent of the type of radiation. Counting systems that use G-M detectors are not as complex as those using ion chambers or proportional counters.

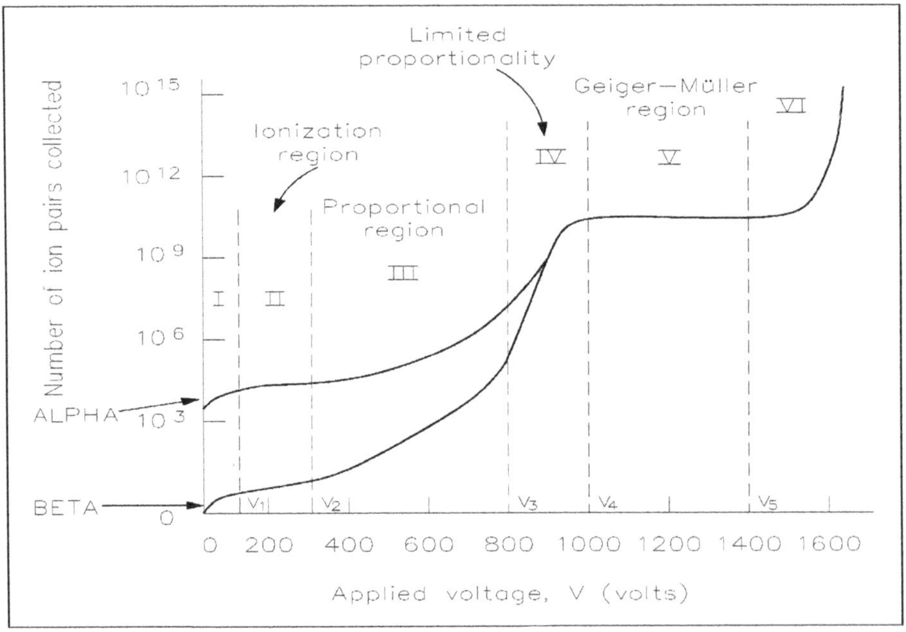

Figure 23 Gas Ionization Curve

The number of electrons collected by a gas-filled detector varies as applied voltage is increased. Once the voltage is increased beyond the proportional region, another flat portion of the curve is reached; this is known as the Geiger-M ller region. The Geiger-M ller region has two important characteristics:

- The number of electrons produced is independent of applied voltage.
- The number of electrons produced is independent of the number of electrons produced by the initial radiation.

This means that the radiation producing one electron will have the same size pulse as radiation producing hundreds or thousands of electrons. The reason for this characteristic is related to the way in which electrons are collected.

When a gamma produces an electron, the electron moves rapidly toward the positively charged central wire. As the electron nears the wire, its velocity increases. At some point its velocity is great enough to cause additional ionizations. As the electrons approach the central wire, the additional ionizations produce a larger number of electrons in the vicinity of the central wire.

As discussed before, for each electron produced there is a positive ion produced. As the applied voltage is increased, the number of positive ions near the central wire increases, and a positively charged cloud (called a positive ion sheath) forms around the central wire. The positive ion sheath reduces the field strength of the central wire and prevents further electrons from reaching the wire. It might appear that a positive ion sheath would increase the effect of the positive central wire, but this is not true; the positive potential is applied to the very thin central wire that makes the strength of the electric field very high. The positive ion sheath makes the central wire appear much thicker and reduces the field strength. This phenomenon is called the detector's space charge. The positive ions will migrate toward the negative chamber picking up electrons. As in a proportional counter, this transfer of electrons can release energy, causing ionization and the liberation of an electron. In order to prevent this secondary pulse, a quenching gas is used, usually an organic compound.

The G-M counter produces many more electrons than does a proportional counter; therefore, it is a much more sensitive device. It is often used in the detection of low-level gamma rays and beta particles for this reason. Electrons produced in a G-M tube are collected very rapidly, usually within a fraction of a microsecond. The output of the G-M detector is a pulse charge and is often large enough to drive a meter without additional amplification. Because the same size pulse is produced regardless of the amount of initial ionization, the G-M counter cannot distinguish radiation of different energies or types. This is the reason G-M counters are not adaptable for use as neutron detectors. The G-M detector is mainly used for portable instrumentation due to its sensitivity, simple counting circuit, and ability to detect low-level radiation.

Summary

The operation of Geiger-M ller detectors are summarized below.

G-M Detector Summary

- The voltage of a Geiger-M ller (G-M) detector is set so that any incident radiation produces the same number of electrons.
- As long as voltage remains in the G-M region, electron production is independent of operating voltage and the initial number of electrons produced by the incident radiation.
- The operation voltage causes a large number of ionizations to occur near the central electrode as the electrons approach.
- The large number of positive ions form a positive ion sheath which prevents additional electrons from reaching the electrode.
- A quenching gas is used in order to prevent a secondary pulse due to ionization by the positive ions.

SCINTILLATION COUNTER

The scintillation counter is a solid state radiation detector.

EO 2.7 DESCRIBE the operation of a scintillation counter to include:
- **a. Radiation detection**
- **b. Three classes of phosphors**
- **c. Photomultiplier tube operation**

The scintillation counter is a solid state radiation detector which uses a scintillation crystal (phosphor) to detect radiation and produce light pulses. Figure 24 is important in the explanation of scintillation counter operation.

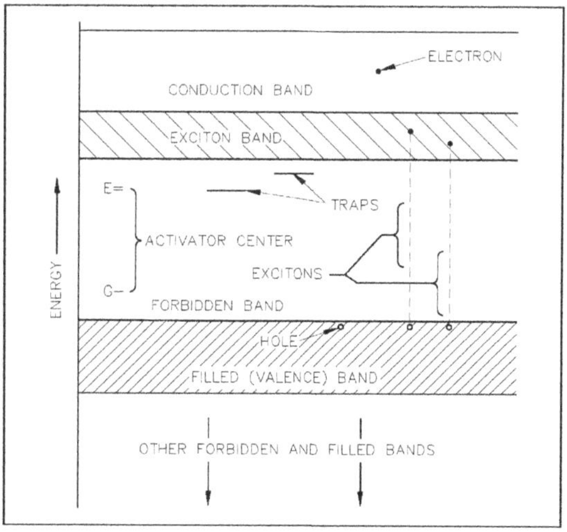

Figure 24 Electronic Energy Band of an Ionic Crystal

As radiation interacts in the scintillation crystal, energy is transferred to bound electrons of the crystal's atoms. If the energy that is transferred is greater than the ionization energy, the electron enters the conduction band and is free from the binding forces of the parent atom. This leaves a vacancy in the valence band and is termed a hole. If the energy transferred is less than the binding energy, the electron remains attached, but exists in an excited energy state. Once again, a hole is created in the valence band. By adding impurities during the growth of the scintillation crystal, the manufacturer is able to produce activator centers with energy levels located within the forbidden energy gap. The activator center can trap a mobile electron, which raises the activator center from its ground state, G, to an excited state, E. When the center de-excites, a photon is emitted. The activator centers in a scintillation crystal are referred to as luminescence centers. The emitted photons are in the visible region of the electromagnetic spectrum.

Scintillation counters are constructed by coupling a suitable scintillation phosphor to a light-sensitive photomultiplier tube. Figure 25 illustrates an example of a scintillation counter using a thallium-activated sodium iodide crystal.

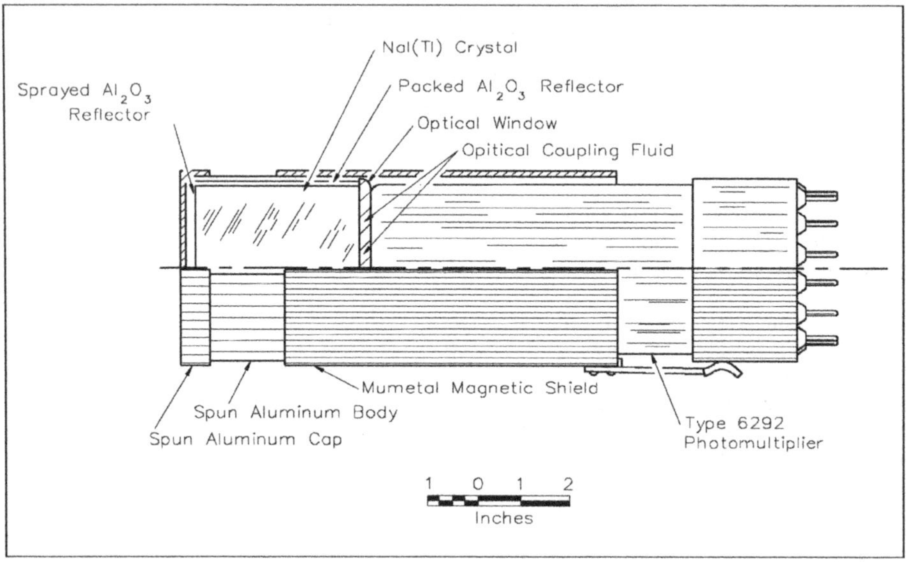

Figure 25 Scintillation Counter

There are three classes of solid state scintillation phosphors: organic crystals, inorganic crystals, and plastic phosphors.

Inorganic crystals include lithium iodide (LiI), sodium iodide (NaI), cesium iodide (CsI), and zinc sulfide (ZnS). Inorganic crystals are characterized by high density, high atomic number, and pulse decay times of approximately 1 microsecond. Thus, they exhibit high efficiency for detection of gamma rays and are capable of handling high count rates.

Organic scintillation phosphors include naphthalene, stilbene, and anthracene. The decay time of this type of phosphor is approximately 10 nanoseconds. This type of crystal is frequently used in the detection of beta particles.

Plastic phosphors are made by adding scintillation chemicals to a plastic matrix. The decay constant is the shortest of the three phosphor types, approaching 1 or 2 nanoseconds. The plastic has a high hydrogen content; therefore, it is useful for fast neutron detectors.

A schematic cross-section of one type of photomultiplier tube is shown in Figure 26. The photomultiplier is a vacuum tube with a glass envelope containing a photocathode and a series of electrodes called dynodes. Light from a scintillation phosphor liberates electrons from the photocathode by the photoelectric effect. These electrons are not of sufficient number or energy to be detected reliably by conventional electronics. However, in the photomultiplier tube, they are attracted by a voltage drop of about 50 volts to the nearest dynode.

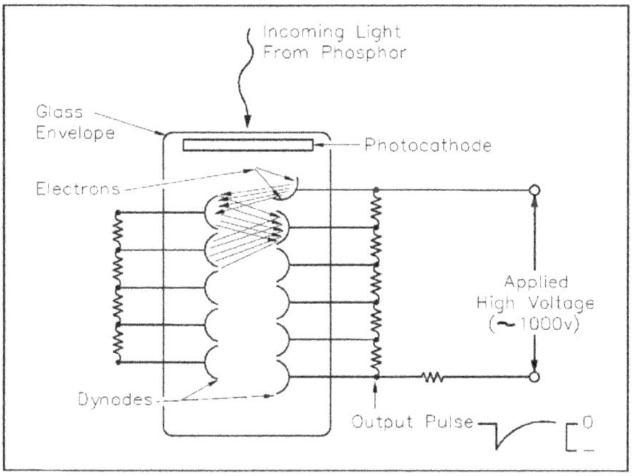

Figure 26 Photomultiplier Tube Schematic Diagram

The photoelectrons strike the first dynode with sufficient energy to liberate several new electrons for each photoelectron. The second-generation electrons are, in turn, attracted to the second dynode where a larger third-generation group of electrons is emitted. This amplification continues through 10 to 12 stages. At the last dynode, sufficient electrons are available to form a current pulse suitable for further amplification by transistor circuits. The voltage drops between dynodes are established by a single external bias, approximately 1000 volts dc, and a network of external resistors to equalize the voltage drops.

The advantages of a scintillation counter are its efficiency and the high precision and counting rates that are possible. These latter attributes are a consequence of the extremely short duration of the light flashes, from about 10^{-9} to 10^{-6} seconds. The intensity of the light flash and the amplitude of the output voltage pulse are proportional to the energy of the particle responsible for the flash. Consequently, scintillation counters can be used to determine the energy, as well as the number, of the exciting particles (or gamma photons). The photomultiplier tube output is very useful in radiation spectrometry (determination of incident radiation energy levels).

Summary

The operation of scintillation counters is summarized below.

Scintillation Counter Summary

- Radiation interactions with a crystal center cause electrons to be raised to an excited state.
- When the center de-excites, the crystal emits a photon in the visible light range.
- Three classes of phosphors are used: inorganic crystals, organic crystals, and plastic phosphors.
- The photon, emitted from the phosphor, interacts with the photocathode of a photomultiplier tube, releasing electrons.
- Using a voltage potential, the electrons are attracted and strike the nearest dynode with enough energy to release additional electrons.
- The second-generation electrons are attracted and strike a second dynode, releasing more electrons.
- This amplification continues through 10 to 12 stages.
- At the final dynode, sufficient electrons are available to produce a pulse of sufficient magnitude for further amplification.

GAMMA SPECTROSCOPY

Gamma spectroscopy is a radiochemistry measurement method which determines the energy and count rate of gamma rays emitted by radioactive substances.

EO 2.8 DESCRIBE the operation of a gamma spectrometer to include:
a. Type of detector used
b. Multichannel analyzer operation

Gamma spectroscopy is a radiochemistry measurement method that determines the energy and count rate of gamma rays emitted by radioactive substances. Gamma spectroscopy is an extremely important measurement. A detailed analysis of the gamma ray energy spectrum is used to determine the identity and quantity of gamma emitters present in a material.

The equipment used in gamma spectroscopy includes a detector, a pulse sorter (multichannel analyzer), and associated amplifiers and data readout devices. The detector is normally a sodium iodide (NaI) scintillation counter. Figure 27 shows a block diagram of a gamma spectrometer.

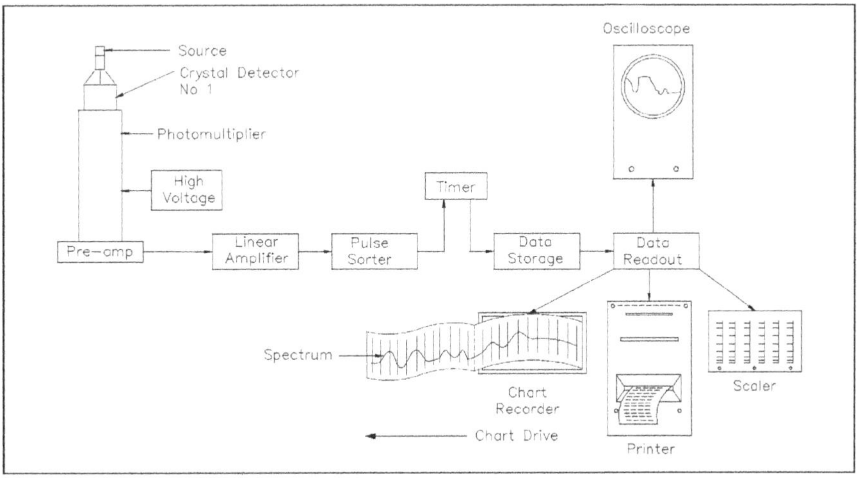

Figure 27 Gamma Spectrometer Block Diagram

The multichannel pulse height analyzer is a device that will separate pulses based on pulse height. Each energy range of pulse height is referred to as a channel. The pulse height is proportional to the energy lost by a gamma ray. Separation of the pulses, based on pulse height, shows the energy spectrum of the gamma rays that are emitted. Multichannel analyzers typically have 100 or 200 channels over an energy range of 0 to 2 MeV. The output is a plot of pulse height and gamma activity, as shown in Figure 28. By analyzing the spectrum of gamma rays emitted, the user can determine the elements which caused the gamma pulses.

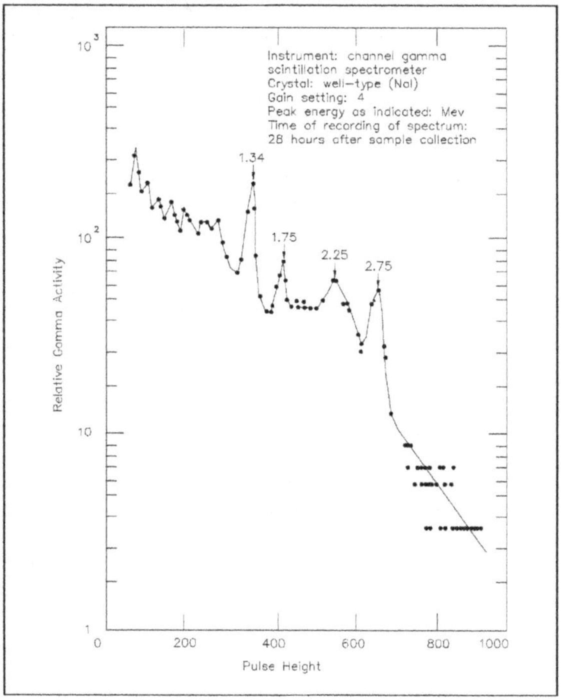

Figure 28 Multichannel Analyzer Output

Summary

The operation of a gamma spectrometer is summarized below.

Gamma Spectrometer Summary

- A gamma spectrometer uses a scintillation counter, normally NaI.
- A multichannel analyzer separates the pulses based on pulse height.
- Since each radioactive material emits gammas of certain energy levels, each pulse height corresponds to a different type of atom.

MISCELLANEOUS DETECTORS

Four other types of radiation detectors are the self-powered neutron detector, wide range fission chamber, flux wire, and photographic film.

EO 2.9 DESCRIBE how the following detect neutrons:
- **a. Self-powered neutron detector**
- **b. Wide range fission chamber**
- **c. Flux wire**

EO 2.10 DESCRIBE how a photographic film is used to measure the following:
- **a. Total radiation dose**
- **b. Neutron dose**

Self-Powered Neutron Detector

In very large reactor plants, the need exists to monitor neutron flux in various portions of the core on a continuous basis. This allows for quick detection of instability in any section of the core. This need brought about the development of the self-powered neutron detector that is small, inexpensive, and rugged enough to withstand the in-core environment. The self-powered neutron detector requires no voltage supply for operation. Figure 29 illustrates a simplified drawing of a self-powered neutron detector.

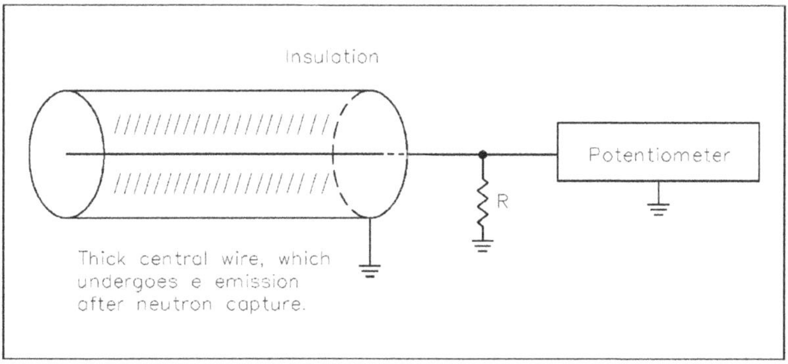

Figure 29 Self-Powered Neutron Detector

The central wire of a self-powered neutron detector is made from a material that absorbs a neutron and undergoes radioactive decay by emitting an electron (beta decay). Typical materials used for the central wire are cobalt, cadmium, rhodium, and vanadium. A good insulating material is placed between the central wire and the detector casing. Each time a neutron interacts with the central wire it transforms one of the wire's atoms into a radioactive nucleus. The nucleus eventually decays by the emission of an electron. Because of the emission of these electrons, the wire becomes more and more positively charged. The positive potential of the wire causes a current to flow in resistor, R. A millivoltmeter measures the voltage drop across the resistor. The electron current from beta decay can also be measured directly with an electrometer.

There are two distinct advantages of the self-powered neutron detector: (a) very little instrumentation is required--only a millivoltmeter or an electrometer, and (b) the emitter material has a much greater lifetime than boron or U^{235} lining (used in wide range fission chambers).

One disadvantage of the self-powered neutron detector is that the emitter material decays with a characteristic half-life. In the case of rhodium and vanadium, which are two of the most useful materials, the half-lives are 1 minute and 3.8 minutes, respectively. This means that the detector cannot respond immediately to a change in neutron flux, but takes as long as 3.8 minutes to reach 63% of steady-state value. This disadvantage is overcome by using cobalt or cadmium emitters which emit their electrons within 10^{-14} seconds after neutron capture. Self-powered neutron detectors which use cobalt or cadmium are called prompt self-powered neutron detectors.

Wide Range Fission Chamber

Fission chambers use neutron-induced fission to detect neutrons. The chamber is usually similar in construction to that of an ionization chamber, except that the coating material is highly enriched U^{235}. The neutrons interact with the U^{235}, causing fission. One of the two fission fragments enters the chamber, while the other fission fragment embeds itself in the chamber wall.

One advantage of using U^{235} coating rather than boron is that the fission fragment has a much higher energy level than the alpha particle from a boron reaction. Neutron-induced fission fragments produce many more ionizations in the chamber per interaction than do the neutron-induced alpha particles. This allows the fission chambers to operate in higher gamma fields than an uncompensated ion chamber with boron lining. Fission chambers are often used as current indicating devices and pulse devices simultaneously. They are especially useful as pulse chambers, due to the very large pulse size difference between neutrons and gamma rays. Because of the fission chamber's dual use, it is often used in "wide range" channels in nuclear instrumentation systems. Fission chambers are also capable of operating over the source and intermediate ranges of neutron levels.

Activation Foils and Flux Wires

Whenever it is necessary to measure reactor neutron flux profiles, a section of wire or foil is inserted directly into the reactor core. The wire or foil remains in the core for the length of time required for activation to the desired level. The cross-section of the flux wire or foil must be known to obtain an accurate flux profile. After activation, the flux wire or foil is rapidly removed from the reactor core and the activity counted.

Activated foils can also discriminate energy levels by placing a cover over the foil to filter out (absorb) certain energy level neutrons. Cadmium covers are typically used for this purpose. The cadmium cover effectively filters out all of the thermal neutrons.

Photographic Film

Photographic film may be utilized in x-ray work and dosimetry. The film tends to darken when exposed to radiation. This general darkening of the film is used to determine overall radiation exposure. Neutron scattering produces individual proton recoil tracks. Counting the tracks yields the film's exposure to fast neutrons. Filters are used to determine the energy and type of radiation. Some typical filters used are aluminum, copper, cadmium, or lead. These filters provide varying amounts of shielding for the attenuation of different energies. By comparing the exposure under the different filters, an approximate spectrum is determined.

Summary

A description of how self-powered neutron detectors, wide range fission chambers, flux wires, and photographic film detect radiation is summarized below.

Miscellaneous Detector Summary

Self-powered neutron detector

- The central wire, made of a neutron-absorbing material, absorbs a neutron and undergoes beta decay.
- As more beta decays occur, the remaining atoms cause the wire to become more positively charged.
- The voltage potential set up causes a current flow in a resistor, which is measured by either a millivoltmeter or electrometer.

Wide range fission chamber

- Neutrons interact with the U^{235} coated chamber causing fission of the U^{235}.
- A highly positive charged fission fragment interacts with the detector gas and causes ionizations.
- The electrons produced are collected as pulses on the electrode.

Flux wire

- The wire is inserted directly into the core and becomes activated by the neutron flux.
- When the desired activation time is reached, the wire is removed from the core and counted.

Photographic film

- Detects total radiation dose by darkening; film darkness determines overall exposure.
- Fast neutron exposure determined by counting individual proton recoil tracks.

CIRCUITRY AND CIRCUIT ELEMENTS

Understanding how the reactor power monitoring detection equipment works requires a working knowledge of basic terminology.

EO 3.1 DEFINE the following terms:

a. Signal-to-noise ratio
b. Discriminator
c. Analog
d. Logarithm
e. Period
f. Decades per minute (DPM)
g. Scalar

EO 3.2 LIST the type of detector used in each of the following nuclear instruments:

a. Source range
b. Intermediate range
c. Power range

Terminology

Understanding how the reactor power monitoring detection equipment works requires a working knowledge of basic terminology.

Signal-to-Noise Ratio

Signal-to-noise ratio is the ratio of the electrical output signal to the electrical noise generated in the cable run or in the instrumentation.

Discriminator

Discrimination in radiation detection circuits refers to the process of distinguishing between different types of radiation on the basis of pulse height. A discriminator circuit selects the minimum or maximum pulse height that is to be counted.

Analog

Analog is defined as a mechanism in which data is represented by continuously variable physical quantities. As it applies to the intermediate range, the output of the intermediate range is an analog current. Due to the wide range of the flux measured, use of logarithmic circuitry is required for indication on a single scale instrument. Analog is used in contrast to digital to refer to circuits in which the magnitude of the signal carries the information. Figure 30(A) illustrates an example of an analog display, and 30(B) illustrates a digital display.

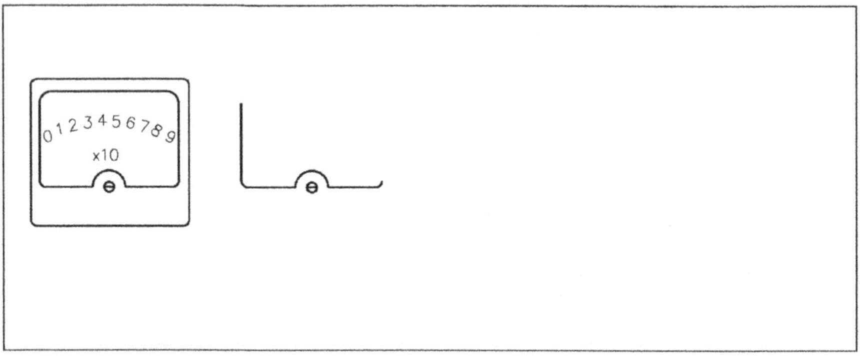

Decades Per Minute (DPM)

Rate circuits are important in the source and intermediate ranges. Rate information is displayed on a meter in decades per minute. These meters indicate how fast reactor power is changing in decades (power of 10) in each minute.

Scalar

This term refers to a measurement or quantity that is capable of being represented on a scale (i.e., neutron flux on source range, intermediate range, and power range meters).

Components

Three ranges are used to monitor the power level of a reactor throughout the full range of reactor operation: source range, intermediate range, and power range. The source range normally uses a proportional counter, while the intermediate and power ranges use ionization chambers. A compensated ion chamber is used for the intermediate range. The power range uses an uncompensated ion chamber. Each of the three different ranges makes use of some or all of the following types of components.

Preamplifiers and Amplifiers

Radiation detector output signals are usually weak and require amplification before they can be used. In radiation detection circuits, the nature of the input pulse and discriminator determines the characteristics that the preamplifier and amplifier must have. Two stages of amplification are used in most detection circuits to increase the signal-to-noise ratio.

Figure 31 shows how a two-stage amplifier increases the signal-to-noise ratio.

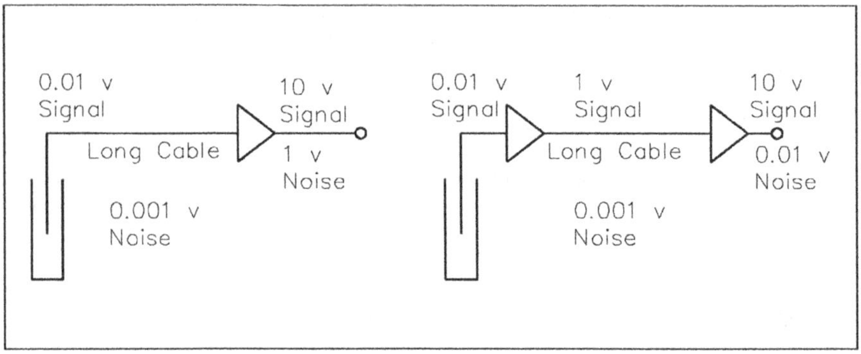

Figure 31 Single and Two-Stage Amplifier Circuits

The radiation detector is located some distance from the readout. A shielded coaxial cable transmits the detector output to the amplifier. The output signal of the detector may be as low as 0.01 volts. A total gain of 1000 is needed to increase this signal to 10 volts, which is a usable output pulse voltage. There is always a pickup of noise in the long cable run; this noise can amount to 0.001 volts.

If all amplification were done at the remote amplifier, the 0.01-volt pulse signal would be 10 volts, and the 0.001 noise signal would be 1 volt. This is a signal-to-noise ratio of 10 and could be significantly reduced by dividing the total gain between two stages of amplification. A preamplifier located near the detector and a remote amplifier could be used. The preamplifier virtually eliminates cable noise because of the short cable length. If, for a total gain of 1000, the preamplifier has a gain of 100 and the amplifier has a gain of 10, the output signal from the preamplifier is 1 volt. The signal transmitted via the long cable run still picks up the 0.001-volt noise. The amplifier amplifies the 1.0-volt pulse signal and the 0.001-volt noise signal by a factor of 10. The result is a 10-volt pulse signal and a 0.01-volt noise signal. This gives a signal-to-noise ratio of 1000.

Discriminator Circuit

A discriminator circuit selects the minimum pulse height. When the input pulse exceeds the discriminator preset level, the discriminator generates an output pulse. The discriminator input is normally an amplified and shaped detector signal. This signal is an analog signal because the amplitude is proportional to the energy of the incident particle.

The biased diode circuit is the simplest form of discriminator. Figure 32 shows a biased diode discriminator circuit with its associated input and output signals.

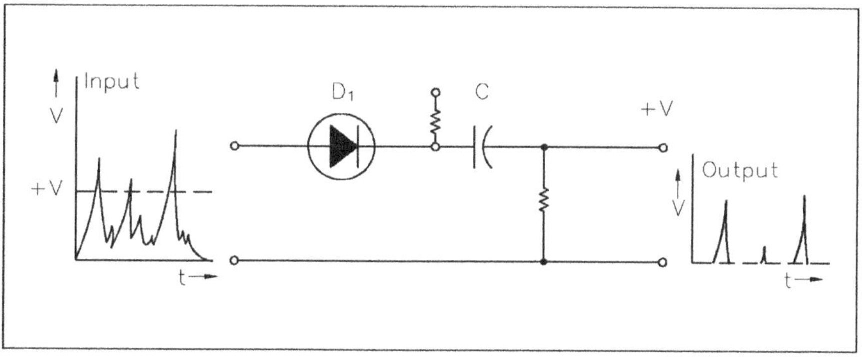

Figure 32 Biased Diode Discriminator

Diode D_1 is shown with its cathode connected to a positive voltage source +V. A diode cannot conduct unless the voltage across the anode is positive with respect to the cathode. As long as the voltage at the anode is less than that of the cathode, diode D_1 does not conduct, and there is no output. At some point, anode voltage exceeds the bias value +V, and the diode conducts. The input signal is allowed to pass to the output.

Figure 32 illustrates input and output signals and how the discriminator acts to eliminate all pulses that are below the preset level. The output pulses of this circuit have the same relative amplitudes as the input pulses.

Logarithmic Meters

Radiation detection circuit currents or pulse rates vary over a wide range of values. The current output of an ionization chamber may vary by 8 orders of magnitude. For example, the range may be from 10^{-13} amps to 10^{-5} amps. The most accurate method to display this range would be to utilize a linear current meter with several scales, and the capability to switch those scales. This is not practical. A single scale which covers the entire range of values is used. This scale is referred to as logarithmic.

The logarithmic output meter must be provided with a signal which is proportional to the logarithm of the input signal. This is easily done by using a diode when the input signal is from an ionization chamber. The voltage across the diode equals the logarithm of the current through the diode. Using this principle, the simplified circuit, shown in Figure 33, is used to convert ionization chamber current to a voltage proportional to the logarithm of this current.

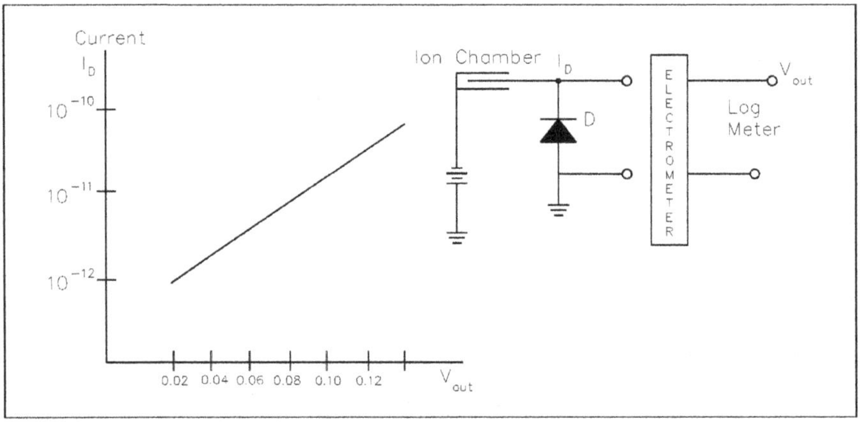

Figure 33 Log Count Rate Meter

Period Meters and Startup Rate

In many applications it is essential to know the rate of change of power. This rate normally increases or decreases exponentially with time. The time constant for this change is referred to as the period. A period of five seconds means that the value changes by a factor of e (2.718) in five seconds. Figure 34 shows a basic period meter circuit.

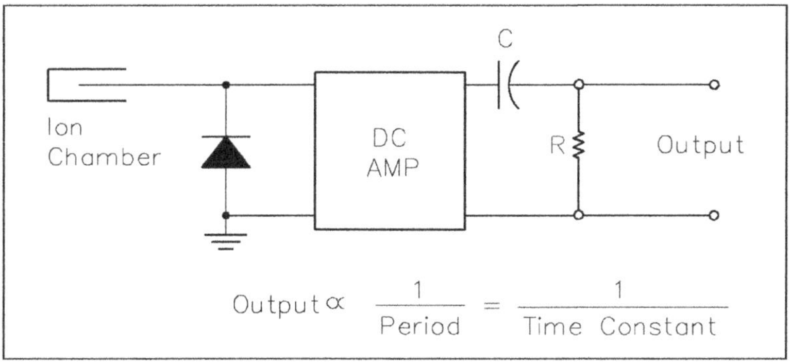

Figure 34 Period Meter Circuit

Placing the signal through an RC circuit causes a voltage that is proportional to the reciprocal of the period. If the current output from the ionization chamber is constant, no current flows through resistor R, and the output voltage is zero. This corresponds to an infinite period. As the ion chamber output current changes, there is a voltage transient across capacitor C, and current flows through resistor R. The more rapid the transient, the greater the voltage drop across resistor R, and the shorter the period.

Rate information is displayed on a meter in decades per minute, and since it is used by the operator to monitor the rate of change of power during startup, it is termed startup rate. Startup rate (SUR) equates to reactor period using Equation 6-10.

$$SUR = \frac{26.06}{\tau} \qquad (6\text{-}10)$$

where

SUR = startup rate in decades per minute
26.06 = constant
τ = reactor period in seconds

The reactor operator adjusts control rods so that an upper limit, such as 1 DPM, is not exceeded. This allows an orderly increase in reactor power.

Summary

The source range uses a proportional counter. The intermediate range uses a compensated ion chamber. The power range uses an uncompensated ion chamber. Terms used to describe the electrical circuits are summarized below.

Circuit Terminology Summary

- Signal-to-noise ratio is the ratio of the electrical output signal to the electrical noise generated.
- A discriminator selects the minimum pulse height to be counted.
- Analog is a mechanism in which data is represented by continuously variable physical quantities.
- Logarithm is the exponent that indicates the power to which a number is raised to produce a given number.
- Reactor period is that amount of time required for neutron flux to change by a factor of e.
- Decades per minute is the rate at which neutron flux is changing by a power of 10 in each minute.
- Scalar is a measurement or quantity which is capable of being represented on a scale.
- Startup rate is the rate at which neutron flux is changing measured in decades per minute.

SOURCE RANGE NUCLEAR INSTRUMENTATION

Three ranges are used to monitor the power level of a reactor throughout the full range of reactor operation. The source range makes use of a proportional counter.

EO 3.3 **Given a block diagram of a typical source range instrument, STATE the purpose of major components.**

a. Linear amplifier
b. Discriminator
c. Pulse integrator
d. Log count rate amplifier
e. Differentiator

Source range instrumentation normally consists of two redundant count rate channels, each composed of a high-sensitivity proportional counter and associated signal measuring equipment. These channels are typically used over a counting range of 0.1 to 10^6 counts per second, but vary based on reactor design. Their outputs are displayed on meters in terms of the logarithm of the count rate.

Source range instrumentation also measures the rate of change of the count rate. The rate of change is displayed on meters in terms of the startup rate from -1 to +10 decades per minute. Protective functions are not normally associated with source range instrumentation because of inherent limitations in this range. However, interlocks may be incorporated.

Many reactor plants have found it necessary to place source range proportional counters in lead shielding to reduce gamma flux at the detectors. This serves two functions: (a) it increases the low end sensitivity of the detector, and (b) it adds to detector life. Another means by which detector life is extended is to disable the high voltage power supply to the detector and short the signal lead when neutron flux has passed into the intermediate range. There are some reactor plants that have made provisions for moving the source range detectors from their operating positions to a position of reduced neutron flux level, once the flux level increases above the source range.

Figure 35 shows a typical source range channel in functional form.

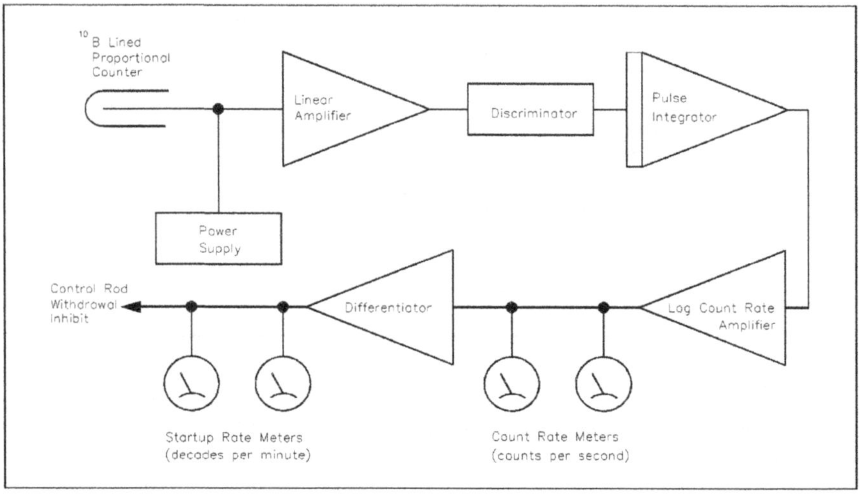

Figure 35 Source Range Channel

B^{10} lined or BF_3 gas-filled proportional counters are normally used as source range detectors. Proportional counter output is in the form of one pulse for every ionizing event; therefore, there is a series of random pulses varying in magnitude representing neutron and gamma ionizing events.

The pulse height may only be a few millivolts, which is too low to be directly used without amplification. The linear amplifier amplifies the input signal by a factor of several thousand to raise the pulse height to several volts.

The discriminator excludes passage of pulses that are less than a predetermined level. The function of the discriminator is to exclude noise and gamma pulses that are lower in magnitude than neutron pulses.

The pulses are then sent to the pulse integrator where they are integrated to give a signal that is proportional to the logarithm of the count rate.

The log count rate amplifier then amplifies the signal, which varies directly as the logarithm of the pulse rate, in the detector. The logarithmic count rate is then displayed on a meter with a logarithmic scale in counts per second.

The logarithmic count rate signal is differentiated to measure the rate of change in neutron flux. The differentiator output is proportional to reactor period. The value of reactor period is inversely proportional to the actual rate of change of reactor power and relates to power changes by factors of e (2.718). The power rate change based on factors of 10, in decades per minute, is more meaningful to the reactor operator. Therefore, the output of the differentiator is converted from reactor period to decades per minute through the meter scale used.

Summary

The purposes of source range components are summarized below.

Source Range Instrumentation Summary

- The **linear amplifier** amplifies the input signal by a factor of several thousand to raise the pulse height to several volts.
- The **discriminator** excludes passage of pulses that are less than a predetermined level.
- The **pulse integrator** provides an output signal proportional to the logarithm of the count rate.
- The **log count rate amplifier** amplifies the signal for display on a meter.
- The **differentiator** provides an output signal proportional to the rate of power change.

INTERMEDIATE RANGE NUCLEAR INSTRUMENTATION

Three ranges are used to monitor the power level of a reactor throughout the full range of reactor operation. The intermediate range makes use of a compensated ion chamber.

EO 3.4 Given a block diagram of a typical intermediate range instrument, STATE the purpose of major components.

a. Log n amplifier
b. Differentiator
c. Reactor protection interface

Intermediate-range nuclear instrumentation consists of a minimum of two redundant channels. Each of these channels is made up of a boron-lined or boron gas-filled compensated ion chamber and associated signal measuring equipment of which the output is a steady current produced by the neutron flux.

The compensated ion chamber is utilized in the intermediate range because the current output is proportional to the relatively stable neutron flux, and it compensates for signals from gamma flux. This range of indication also provides a measure of the rate of change of neutron level. This rate of change is displayed on meters in terms of startup rate in decades per minute (-1 to +10 decades per minute). High startup rate on either channel may initiate a protective action. This protective action may be in the form of a control rod withdrawal inhibit and alarm, or a high startup rate reactor trip.

Figure 36 shows a typical intermediate-range channel.

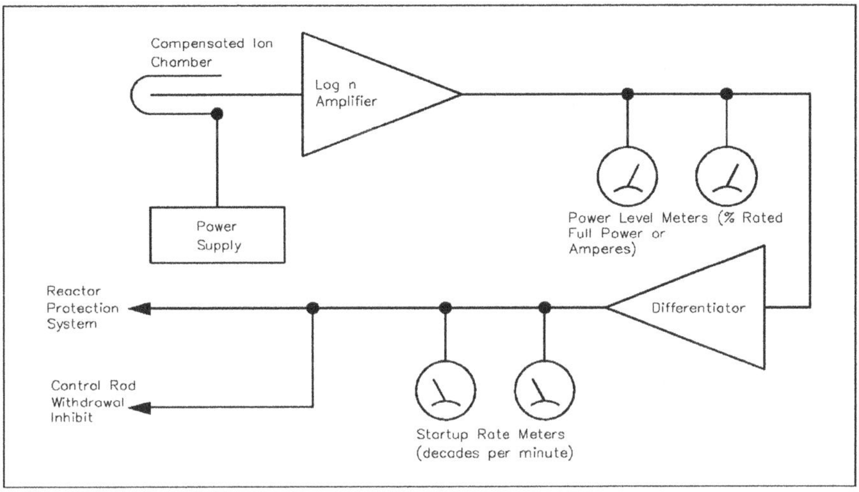

Figure 36 Intermediate Range Channel

Typically, the compensated ion chamber output is an analog current ranging from 10^{-11} to 10^{-3} amperes, but varies with reactor design. The log n amplifier is a logarithmic current amplifier that converts the detector output to a signal proportional to the logarithm of the detector current. This logarithmic output is proportional to the logarithm of the neutron level.

The determination of rate change of the logarithm of the neutron level, as in the source range, is accomplished by the differentiator. The differentiator measures reactor period or startup rate. Startup rate in the intermediate range is more stable because the neutron level signal is subject to less sudden large variations. For this reason, intermediate-range startup rate is often used as an input to the reactor protection system.

The reactor protective interface provides signals for protective actions. Examples of protective actions include control rod withdrawal interlocks and startup rate reactor trips.

Summary

The purposes of intermediate range components are summarized below.

Intermediate Range Instrumentation Summary

- The log n amplifier converts the detector output signal to a signal proportional to the logarithm of the detector current.
- The differentiator provides an output proportional to the rate of change of power.
- The reactor protection interface provides signals for protective actions.

POWER RANGE NUCLEAR INSTRUMENTATION

Three ranges are used to monitor the power level of a reactor throughout the full range of reactor operation. The power range makes use of an uncompensated ion chamber.

EO 3.5 **STATE the reason gamma compensation is NOT required in the power range.**

EO 3.6 **Given a block diagram of a typical power range instrument, STATE the purpose of major components.**
- **a. Linear amplifier**
- **b. Reactor protection interface**

Power range nuclear instrumentation normally consists of four identical linear power level channels which originate in eight uncompensated ion chambers. The output is a steady current produced by the neutron flux. Uncompensated ion chambers are utilized in the power range because gamma compensation is unnecessary; the neutron-to-gamma flux ratio is high. Having a high neutron-to-gamma flux ratio means that the number of gammas is insignificant compared to the number of neutrons.

The output of each power range channel is directly proportional to reactor power and typically covers a range from 0% to 125% of full power, but varies with each reactor. The output of each channel is displayed on a meter in terms of power level in percent of full rated power. The gain of each instrument is adjustable which provides a means for calibrating the output. This adjustment is normally determined by using a plant heat balance. Protective actions may be initiated by high power level on any two channels; this is termed coincidence operation.

Figure 37 shows a typical power range channel.

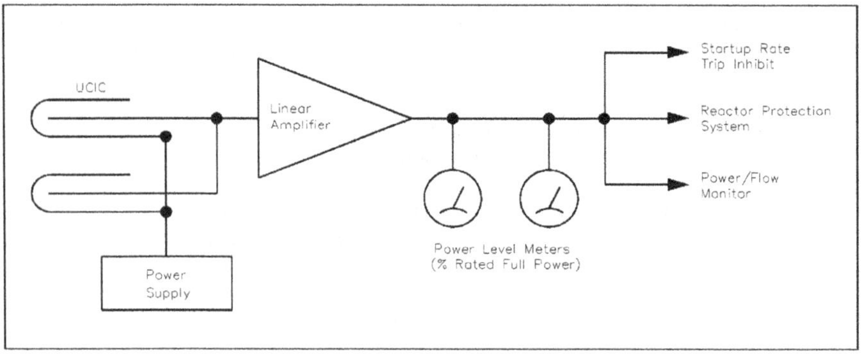

Figure 37 Power Range Channel

Two detectors in each channel are functionally connected in parallel so that the measured signal is the sum of the two detectors. This output drives a linear amplifier which amplifies the signal to a useful level.

The reactor protective interface provides signals for protective actions. Examples of protective action signals provided by the power range include:

- A signal to the reactor protection system at a selected value (normally 10% reactor power) to disable the high startup rate reactor trip
- A signal to protective systems when reactor power level exceeds predetermined values
- A signal for use in the reactor control system
- A signal to the power-to-flow circuit

Summary

Gamma compensation is NOT required in the power range since neutrons outnumber gammas by such a large number that gammas are insignificant. The purposes of power range components are summarized below.

Power Range Instrumentation Summary

- The **linear amplifier** amplifies the signal to a useful level.
- The **reactor protective** interface provides signals for protective actions.

Intentionally Left Blank

Department of Energy
Fundamentals Handbook

INSTRUMENTATION AND CONTROL
Module 7
Process Controls

TABLE OF CONTENTS

LIST OF FIGURES iv

LIST OF TABLES vi

REFERENCES vii

OBJECTIVES viii

PRINCIPLES OF CONTROL SYSTEMS 1

Introduction 1
Terminology 2
Automatic Control System 4
Functions of Automatic Control 4
Elements of Automatic Control 4
Feedback Control 5
Summary 6

CONTROL LOOP DIAGRAMS 7

Terminology 7
Feedback Control System Block Diagram 9
Process Time Lags 13
Stability of Automatic Control Systems 13
Summary 16

TWO POSITION CONTROL SYSTEMS 17

Controllers 17
Two Position Controller 18
Example of Two Position Control 19
Modes of Automatic Control 19
Summary 21

PROPORTIONAL CONTROL SYSTEMS 22

Control Mode 22
Proportional Band 22
Example of a Proportional Process Control System 23
Summary 27

TABLE OF CONTENTS (Cont.)

RESET (INTEGRAL) CONTROL SYSTEMS 28

Reset Control (Integral) 28
Definition of Integral Control 28
Example of an Integral Flow Control System 29
Properties of Integral Control 32
Summary 32

PROPORTIONAL PLUS RESET CONTROL SYSTEMS 33

Proportional Plus Reset 33
Example of Proportional Plus Reset Control 34
Reset Windup 35
Summary 36

PROPORTIONAL PLUS RATE CONTROL SYSTEMS 37

Proportional-Derivative 37
Definition of Derivative Control 37
Example of Proportional Plus Rate Control 40
Applications 41
Summary 42

PROPORTIONAL-INTEGRAL-DERIVATIVE CONTROL SYSTEMS 43

Proportional-Integral-Derivative 43
Proportional Plus Reset Plus Rate Controller Actions 43
Summary 46

CONTROLLERS 47

Controllers 47
Control Stations 47
Self-Balancing Control Stations 50
Summary 53

TABLE OF CONTENTS (Cont.)

VALVE ACTUATORS 54

Actuators 54
Pneumatic Actuators 54
Hydraulic Actuators 57
Electric Solenoid Actuators 58
Electric Motor Actuators 59
Summary 60

LIST OF FIGURES

Figure 1 Open-Loop Control System 2

Figure 2 Closed-Loop Control System 3

Figure 3 Feedback in a Closed-Loop Control System 3

Figure 4 Relationships of Functions and Elements in an Automatic Control System 5

Figure 5 Block and Arrows 8

Figure 6 Summing Points 8

Figure 7 Takeoff Point 9

Figure 8 Feedback Control System Block Diagram 9

Figure 9 Lube Oil Cooler Temperature Control System and Equivalent Block Diagram 11

Figure 10 Types of Oscillations 14

Figure 11 Process Control System Operation 17

Figure 12 Two Position Controller Input/Output Relationship 18

Figure 13 Two Position Control System 19

Figure 14 Relation Between Valve Position and Controlled Variable Under Proportional Mode 20

Figure 15 Proportional System Controller 22

Figure 16 Proportional Temperature Control System 24

Figure 17 Combined Controller and Final Control Element Action 25

Figure 18 Controller Characteristic Curve 26

Figure 19 Integral Output for a Fixed Input 29

LIST OF FIGURES (Cont.)

Figure 20 Integral Flow Rate Controller 30

Figure 21 Reset Controller Response 31

Figure 22 Response of Proportional Plus Reset Control 33

Figure 23 Heat Exchanger Process System 34

Figure 24 Effects of Disturbance on Reverse Acting Controller 35

Figure 25 Derivative Output for a Constant Rate of Change Input 38

Figure 26 Rate Control Output 38

Figure 27 Response of Proportional Plus Rate Control 39

Figure 28 Heat Exchanger Process 40

Figure 29 Effect of Disturbance on Proportional Plus Rate Reverse Acting Controller 41

Figure 30 PID Control Action Responses 44

Figure 31 PID Controller Response Curves 45

Figure 32 Typical Control Station 48

Figure 33 Deviation Indicator 49

Figure 34 Self-Balancing Control Station 51

Figure 35 Pneumatic Actuator: Air-to-Close/Spring-to-Open 54

Figure 36 Pneumatic Actuator with Controller and Positioner 56

Figure 37 Hydraulic Actuator 57

Figure 38 Electric Solenoid Actuator 58

Figure 39 Electric Motor Actuator 59

LIST OF TABLES

NONE

REFERENCES

- Anderson, N.A., Instrumentation for Process Measurement and Control, Second Edition, Chilton Company, Philadelphia, PA, 1972.
- Considine, D.M., Process Instruments and Controls Handbook, Second Edition, McGraw-Hill Book Company, Inc., New York, NY, 1974.
- Distefano, J.J. III, Feedback and Control Systems, Schaum's Outline Series, 1967.
- Kirk, Franklin W. and Rimboi, Nicholas R., Instrumentation, Third Edition, American Technical Publishers, ISBN 0-8269-3422-6.
- Academic Program for Nuclear Power Plant Personnel, Volume IV, General Physics Corporation, Library of Congress Card #A 397747, April 1982.
- Fozard, B., Instrumentation and Control of Nuclear Reactors, ILIFFE Books Ltd., London.
- Wightman, E.J., Instrumentation in Process Control, CRC Press, Cleveland, Ohio.
- Rhodes, T.J. and Carroll, G.C., Industrial Instruments for Measurement and Control, Second Edition, McGraw-Hill Book Company.
- Process Measurement Fundamentals, Volume I, General Physics Corporation, ISBN 0-87683-001-7, 1981.

TERMINAL OBJECTIVE

1.0 Given a process control system, **SUMMARIZE** the operation of the system based on changing system inputs.

ENABLING OBJECTIVES

1.1 **DEFINE** the following process control terms:
- a. Control system
- b. Control system input
- c. Control system output
- d. Open-loop system
- e. Closed-loop system
- f. Feedback
- g. Controlled variable
- h. Manipulated variable

1.2 **DESCRIBE** the operation of a control loop diagram including the following components:
- a. Controlled system
- b. Controlled elements
- c. Feedback elements
- d. Reference point
- e. Controlled output
- f. Feedback signal
- g. Actuating signal
- h. Manipulated variable
- i. Disturbance

1.3 **EXPLAIN** how capacitance, resistance, and transportation time affect a control system's lag time.

1.4 **DESCRIBE** the characteristics of the following types of automatic control systems:
- a. Two position control system
- b. Proportional control system
- c. Integral control
- d. Proportional plus reset control system
- e. Proportional plus rate control
- f. Proportional plus reset plus rate control

ENABLING OBJECTIVES (Cont.)

1.5 **STATE** the purpose of the following components of a typical control station:
   a. Setpoint indicator
   b. Setpoint adjustment
   c. Deviation indicator
   d. Output meter
   e. Manual-automatic transfer switch
   f. Manual output adjust knob

1.6 **DESCRIBE** the operation of a self-balancing control station.

1.7 **DESCRIBE** the operation of the following types of actuators:
   a. Pneumatic
   b. Hydraulic
   c. Solenoid
   d. Electric motor

Intentionally Left Blank

PRINCIPLES OF CONTROL SYSTEMS

Control systems integrate elements whose function is to maintain a process variable at a desired value or within a desired range of values.

EO 1.1 DEFINE the following process control terms:

a. Control system
b. Control system input
c. Control system output
d. Open-loop system
e. Closed-loop system
f. Feedback
g. Controlled variable
h. Manipulated variable

Introduction

Instrumentation provides the various indications used to operate a nuclear facility. In some cases, operators record these indications for use in day-to-day operation of the facility. The information recorded helps the operator evaluate the current condition of the system and take actions if the conditions are not as expected.

Requiring the operator to take all of the required corrective actions is impractical, or sometimes impossible, especially if a large number of indications must be monitored. For this reason, most systems are controlled automatically once they are operating under normal conditions. Automatic controls greatly reduce the burden on the operator and make his or her job manageable.

Process variables requiring control in a system include, but are not limited to, flow, level, temperature, and pressure. Some systems do not require all of their process variables to be controlled. Think of a central heating system. A basic heating system operates on temperature and disregards the other atmospheric parameters of the house. The thermostat monitors the temperature of the house. When the temperature drops to the value selected by the occupants of the house, the system activates to raise the temperature of the house. When the temperature reaches the desired value, the system turns off.

Automatic control systems neither replace nor relieve the operator of the responsibility for maintaining the facility. The operation of the control systems is periodically checked to verify proper operation. If a control system fails, the operator must be able to take over and control the process manually. In most cases, understanding how the control system works aids the operator in determining if the system is operating properly and which actions are required to maintain the system in a safe condition.

Terminology

A ***control system*** is a system of integrated elements whose function is to maintain a process variable at a desired value or within a desired range of values. The control system monitors a process variable or variables, then causes some action to occur to maintain the desired system parameter. In the example of the central heating unit, the system monitors the temperature of the house using a thermostat. When the temperature of the house drops to a preset value, the furnace turns on, providing a heat source. The temperature of the house increases until a switch in the thermostat causes the furnace to turn off.

Two terms which help define a control system are input and output. ***Control system input*** is the stimulus applied to a control system from an external source to produce a specified response from the control system. In the case of the central heating unit, the control system input is the temperature of the house as monitored by the thermostat.

Control system output is the actual response obtained from a control system. In the example above, the temperature dropping to a preset value on the thermostat causes the furnace to turn on, providing heat to raise the temperature of the house.

In the case of nuclear facilities, the input and output are defined by the purpose of the control system. A knowledge of the input and output of the control system enables the components of the system to be identified. A control system may have more than one input or output.

Control systems are classified by the control action, which is the quantity responsible for activating the control system to produce the output. The two general classifications are open-loop and closed-loop control systems.

An ***open-loop control system*** is one in which the control action is independent of the output. An example of an open-loop control system is a chemical addition pump with a variable speed control (Figure 1). The feed rate of chemicals that maintain proper chemistry of a system is determined by an operator, who is not part of the control system. If the chemistry of the system changes, the pump cannot respond by adjusting its feed rate (speed) without operator action.

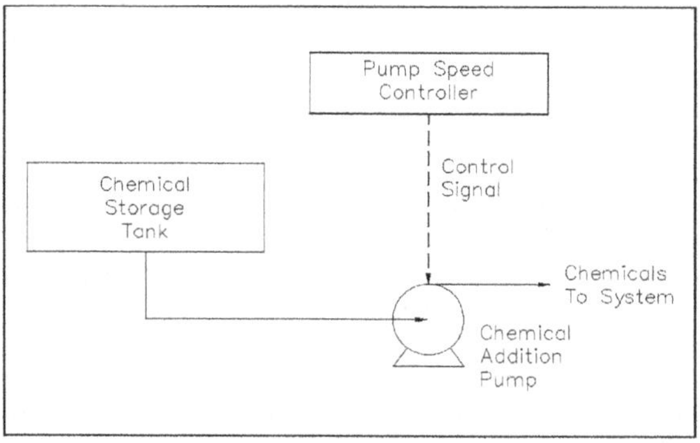

Figure 1 Open-Loop Control System

A ***closed-loop control system*** is one in which control action is dependent on the output. Figure 2 shows an example of a closed-loop control system. The control system maintains water level in a storage tank. The system performs this task by continuously sensing the level in the tank and adjusting a supply valve to add more or less water to the tank. The desired level is preset by an operator, who is not part of the system.

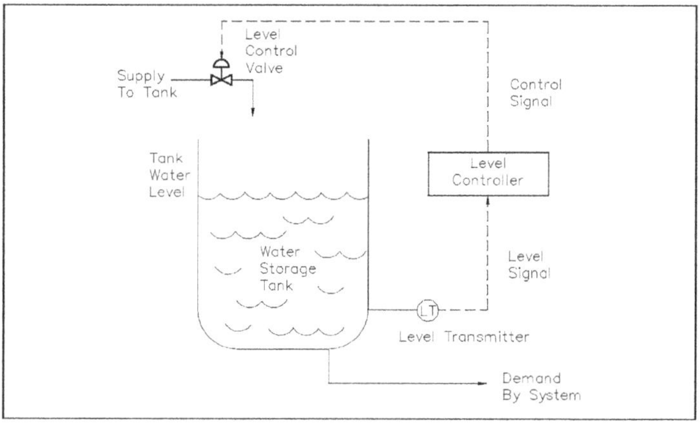

Figure 2 Closed-Loop Control System

Feedback is information in a closed-loop control system about the condition of a process variable. This variable is compared with a desired condition to produce the proper control action on the process. Information is continually "fed back" to the control circuit in response to control action. In the previous example, the actual storage tank water level, sensed by the level transmitter, is feedback to the level controller. This feedback is compared with a desired level to produce the required control action that will position the level control as needed to maintain the desired level. Figure 3 shows this relationship.

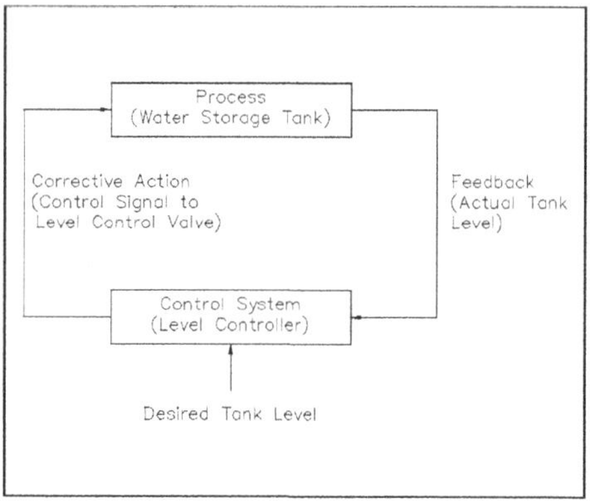

Figure 3 Feedback in a Closed-Loop Control System

Automatic Control System

An automatic control system is a preset closed-loop control system that requires no operator action. This assumes the process remains in the normal range for the control system. An automatic control system has two process variables associated with it: a controlled variable and a manipulated variable.

A ***controlled variable*** is the process variable that is maintained at a specified value or within a specified range. In the previous example, the storage tank level is the controlled variable.

A ***manipulated variable*** is the process variable that is acted on by the control system to maintain the controlled variable at the specified value or within the specified range. In the previous example, the flow rate of the water supplied to the tank is the manipulated variable.

Functions of Automatic Control

In any automatic control system, the four basic functions that occur are:

- Measurement
- Comparison
- Computation
- Correction

In the water tank level control system in the example above, the level transmitter measures the level within the tank. The level transmitter sends a signal representing the tank level to the level control device, where it is compared to a desired tank level. The level control device then computes how far to open the supply valve to correct any difference between actual and desired tank levels.

Elements of Automatic Control

The three functional elements needed to perform the functions of an automatic control system are:

- A measurement element
- An error detection element
- A final control element

Relationships between these elements and the functions they perform in an automatic control system are shown in Figure 4. The measuring element performs the measuring function by sensing and evaluating the controlled variable. The error detection element first compares the value of the controlled variable to the desired value, and then signals an error if a deviation exists between the actual and desired values. The final control element responds to the error signal by correcting the manipulated variable of the process.

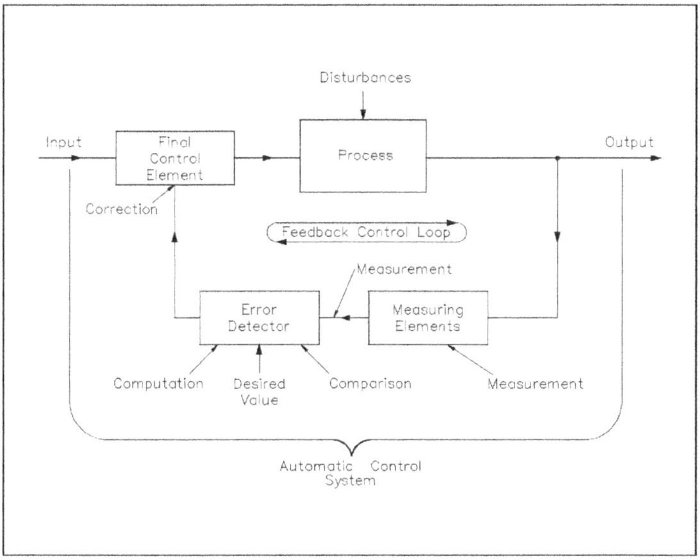

Figure 4 Relationships of Functions and Elements in an Automatic Control System

Feedback Control

An automatic controller is an error-sensitive, self-correcting device. It takes a signal from the process and feeds it back into the process. Therefore, closed-loop control is referred to as feedback control.

Summary

Basic process control terms are summarized below.

Process Control Term Definitions Summary

- A *control system* is a system of integrated elements whose function is to maintain a process variable at a desired value or within a desired range of values.
- *Control system input* is the stimulus applied to a control system from an external source to produce a specified response from the control system.
- *Control system output* is the actual response obtained from a control system.
- An *open-loop control system* is one in which the control action is independent of the output.
- A *closed-loop control system* is one in which control action is dependent on the output.
- *Feedback* is information in a closed-loop control system about the condition of a process variable.
- A *controlled variable* is the process variable that is maintained at a specified value or within a specified range.
- A *manipulated variable* is the process variable that is acted on by the control system to maintain the controlled variable at the specified value or within the specified range.

CONTROL LOOP DIAGRAMS

A loop diagram is a "roadmap" that traces process fluids through the system and designates variables that can disrupt the balance of the system.

EO 1.2 DESCRIBE the operation of a control loop diagram including the following components:
- **a. Controlled system**
- **b. Controlled elements**
- **c. Feedback elements**
- **d. Reference point**
- **e. Controlled output**
- **f. Feedback signal**
- **g. Actuating signal**
- **h. Manipulated variable**
- **i. Disturbance**

EO 1.3 EXPLAIN how capacitance, resistance, and transportation time affect a control system's lag time.

Terminology

A *block diagram* is a pictorial representation of the cause and effect relationship between the input and output of a physical system. A block diagram provides a means to easily identify the functional relationships among the various components of a control system.

The simplest form of a block diagram is the *block and arrows diagram.* It consists of a single block with one input and one output (Figure 5A). The block normally contains the name of the element (Figure 5B) or the symbol of a mathematical operation (Figure 5C) to be performed on the input to obtain the desired output. Arrows identify the direction of information or signal flow.

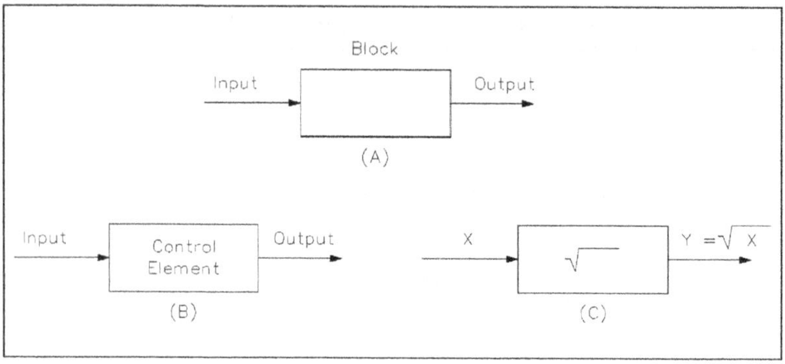

Figure 5 Block and Arrows

Although blocks are used to identify many types of mathematical operations, operations of addition and subtraction are represented by a circle, called a *summing point*. As shown in Figure 6, a summing point may have one or several inputs. Each input has its own appropriate plus or minus sign. A summing point has only one output and is equal to the algebraic sum of the inputs.

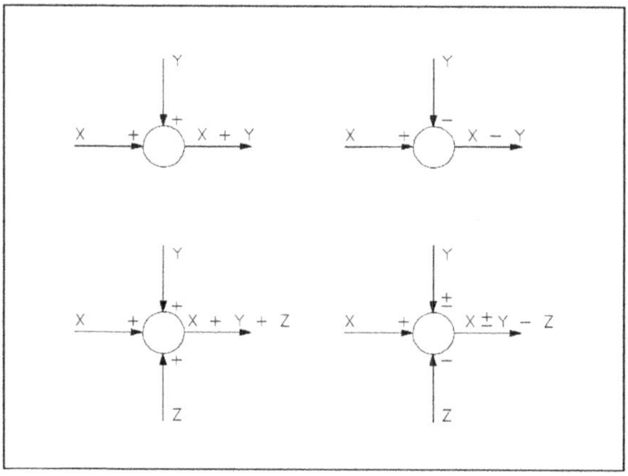

Figure 6 Summing Points

A *takeoff point* is used to allow a signal to be used by more than one block or summing point (Figure 7).

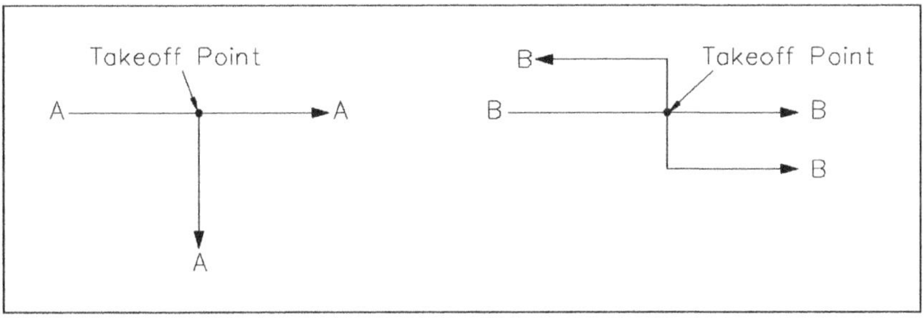

Figure 7 Takeoff Point

Feedback Control System Block Diagram

Figure 8 shows basic elements of a feedback control system as represented by a block diagram. The functional relationships between these elements are easily seen. An important factor to remember is that the block diagram represents flowpaths of control signals, but does not represent flow of energy through the system or process.

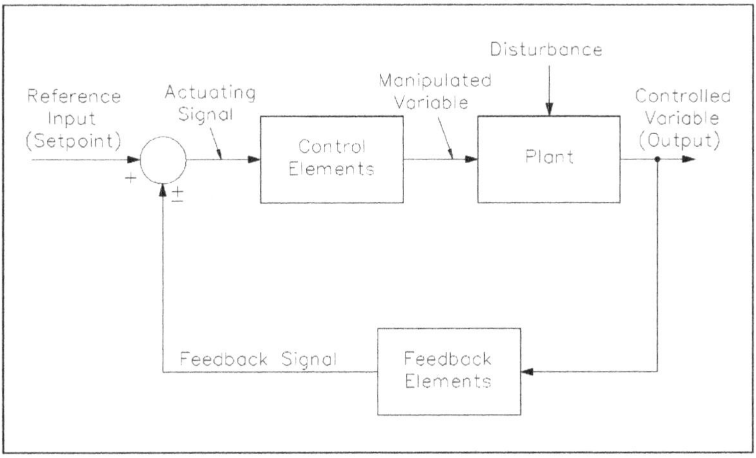

Figure 8 Feedback Control System Block Diagram

Below are several terms associated with the closed-loop block diagram.

The plant is the system or process through which a particular quantity or condition is controlled. This is also called the *controlled system*.

The *control elements* are components needed to generate the appropriate control signal applied to the plant. These elements are also called the "controller."

The *feedback elements* are components needed to identify the functional relationship between the feedback signal and the controlled output.

The *reference point* is an external signal applied to the summing point of the control system to cause the plant to produce a specified action. This signal represents the desired value of a controlled variable and is also called the "setpoint."

The *controlled output* is the quantity or condition of the plant which is controlled. This signal represents the controlled variable.

The *feedback signal* is a function of the output signal. It is sent to the summing point and algebraically added to the reference input signal to obtain the actuating signal.

The *actuating signal* represents the control action of the control loop and is equal to the algebraic sum of the reference input signal and feedback signal. This is also called the "error signal."

The *manipulated variable* is the variable of the process acted upon to maintain the plant output (controlled variable) at the desired value.

The *disturbance* is an undesirable input signal that upsets the value of the controlled output of the plant.

Figure 9 shows a typical application of a block diagram to identify the operation of a temperature control system for lubricating oil. (A) in Figure 9 shows a schematic diagram of the lube oil cooler and its associated temperature control system.

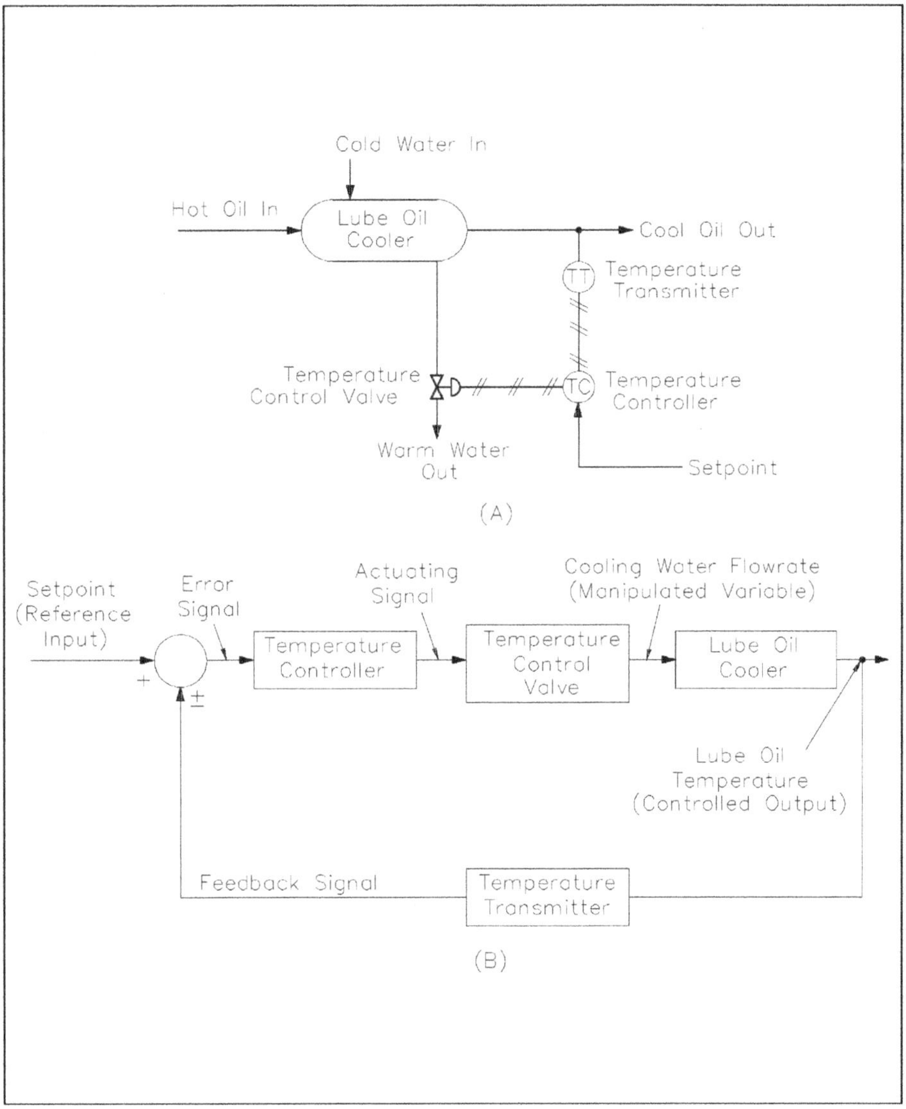

Figure 9 Lube Oil Cooler Temperature Control System and Equivalent Block Diagram

Lubricating oil reduces friction between moving mechanical parts and also removes heat from the components. As a result, the oil becomes hot. This heat is removed from the lube oil by a cooler to prevent both breakdown of the oil and damage to the mechanical components it serves.

The lube oil cooler consists of a hollow shell with several tubes running through it. Cooling water flows inside the shell of the cooler and around the outside of the tubes. Lube oil flows inside the tubes. The water and lube oil never make physical contact.

As the water flows through the shell side of the cooler, it picks up heat from the lube oil through the tubes. This cools the lube oil and warms the cooling water as it leaves the cooler.

The lube oil must be maintained within a specific operating band to ensure optimum equipment performance. This is accomplished by controlling the flow rate of the cooling water with a *temperature control loop.*

The temperature control loop consists of a temperature transmitter, a temperature controller, and a temperature control valve. The diagonally crossed lines indicate that the control signals are air (pneumatic).

The lube oil temperature is the controlled variable because it is maintained at a desired value (the setpoint). Cooling water flow rate is the manipulated variable because it is adjusted by the temperature control valve to maintain the lube oil temperature. The temperature transmitter senses the temperature of the lube oil as it leaves the cooler and sends an air signal that is proportional to the temperature controller. Next, the temperature controller compares the actual temperature of the lube oil to the setpoint (the desired value). If a difference exists between the actual and desired temperatures, the controller will vary the control air signal to the temperature control valve. This causes it to move in the direction and by the amount needed to correct the difference. For example, if the actual temperature is greater than the setpoint value, the controller will vary the control air signal and cause the valve to move in the open direction.

This results in more cooling water flowing through the cooler and lowers the temperature of the lube oil leaving the cooler.

(B) in Figure 9 represents the lube oil temperature control loop in block diagram form. The lube oil cooler is the plant in this example, and its controlled output is the lube oil temperature. The temperature transmitter is the feedback element. It senses the controlled output and lube oil temperature and produces the feedback signal.

The feedback signal is sent to the summing point to be algebraically added to the reference input (the setpoint). Notice the setpoint signal is positive, and the feedback signal is negative. This means the resulting actuating signal is the difference between the setpoint and feedback signals.

The actuating signal passes through the two control elements: the temperature controller and the temperature control valve. The temperature control valve responds by adjusting the manipulated variable (the cooling water flow rate). The lube oil temperature changes in response to the different water flow rate, and the control loop is complete.

Process Time Lags

In the last example, the control of the lube oil temperature may initially seem easy. Apparently, the operator need only measure the lube oil temperature, compare the actual temperature to the desired (setpoint), compute the amount of error (if any), and adjust the temperature control valve to correct the error accordingly. However, processes have the characteristic of delaying and retarding changes in the values of the process variables. This characteristic greatly increases the difficulty of control.

Process time lags is the general term that describes these process delays and retardations.

Process time lags are caused by three properties of the process. They are: *capacitance, resistance*, and *transportation time.*

Capacitance is the ability of a process to store energy. In Figure 9, for example, the walls of the tubes in the lube oil cooler, the cooling water, and the lube oil can store heat energy. This energy-storing property gives the ability to retard change. If the cooling water flow rate is increased, it will take a period of time for more energy to be removed from the lube oil to reduce its temperature.

Resistance is that part of the process that opposes the transfer of energy between capacities. In Figure 9, the walls of the lube oil cooler oppose the transfer of heat from the lube oil inside the tubes to the cooling water outside the tubes.

Transportation time is time required to carry a change in a process variable from one point to another in the process. If the temperature of the lube oil (Figure 9) is lowered by increasing the cooling water flow rate, some time will elapse before the lube oil travels from the lube oil cooler to the temperature transmitter. If the transmitter is moved farther from the lube oil cooler, the transportation time will increase. This time lag is not just a slowing down or retardation of a change; it is an actual time delay during which no change occurs.

Stability of Automatic Control Systems

All control modes previously described can return a process variable to a steady value following a disturbance. This characteristic is called "stability."

Stability is the ability of a control loop to return a controlled variable to a steady, non-cyclic value, following a disturbance.

Control loops can be either stable or unstable. Instability is caused by a combination of process time lags discussed earlier (i.e., capacitance, resistance, and transport time) and inherent time lags within a control system. This results in slow response to changes in the controlled variable. Consequently, the controlled variable will continuously cycle around the setpoint value.

Oscillations describes this cyclic characteristic. There are three types of oscillations that can occur in a control loop. They are *decreasing amplitude, constant amplitude,* and *increasing amplitude*. Each is shown in Figure 10.

Decreasing amplitude (Figure 10A). These oscillations decrease in amplitude and eventually stop with a control system that opposes the change in the controlled variable. This is the condition desired in an automatic control system.

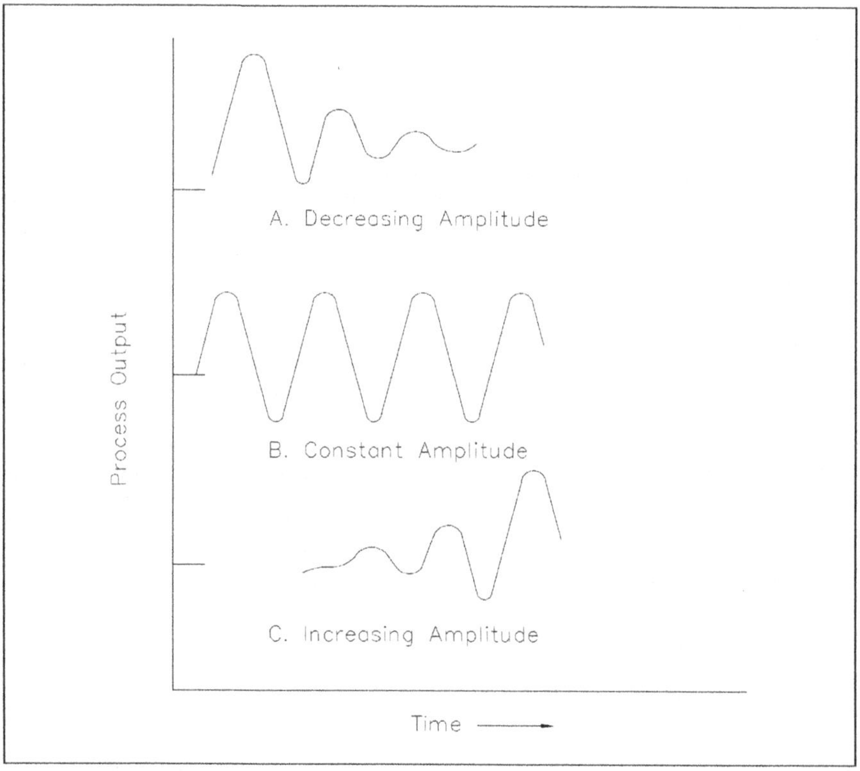

Figure 10 Types of Oscillations

Constant amplitude (Figure 10B). Action of the controller sustains oscillations of the controlled variable. The controlled variable will never reach a stable condition; therefore, this condition is not desired.

Increasing amplitude (Figure 10C). The control system not only sustains oscillations but also increases them. The control element has reached its full travel limits and causes the process to go out of control.

Summary

The important information in this chapter is summarized below.

Control Loop Diagrams Summary

- A controlled system is the system or process through which a particular quantity or condition is controlled.
- Control elements are components needed to generate the appropriate control signal applied to the plant. These elements are also called the "controller."
- Feedback elements are components needed to identify the functional relationship between the feedback signal and the controlled output.
- Reference point is an external signal applied to the summing point of the control system to cause the plant to produce a specified action.
- Controlled output is the quantity or condition of the plant which is controlled. This signal represents the controlled variable.
- Feedback signal is a function of the output signal. It is sent to the summing point and algebraically added to the reference input signal to obtain the actuating signal.
- The actuating signal represents the control action of the control loop and is equal to the algebraic sum of the reference input signal and feedback signal. This is also called the "error signal."
- The manipulated variable is the variable of the process acted upon to maintain the plant output (controlled variable) at the desired value.
- A disturbance is an undesirable input signal that upsets the value of the controlled output of the plant.
- Process time lags are affected by capacitance, which is the ability of a process to store energy; resistance, the part of the process that opposes the transfer of energy between capacities; and transportation time, the time required to carry a change in a process variable from one point to another in the process. This time lag is not just a slowing down of a change, but rather the actual time delay during which no change occurs.

TWO POSITION CONTROL SYSTEMS

A two position controller is the simplest type of controller.

EO 1.4 DESCRIBE the characteristics of the following types of automatic control systems:
a. Two position control system

Controllers

A controller is a device that generates an output signal based on the input signal it receives. The input signal is actually an error signal, which is the difference between the measured variable and the desired value, or setpoint.

This input error signal represents the amount of deviation between where the process system is actually operating and where the process system is desired to be operating. The controller provides an output signal to the final control element, which adjusts the process system to reduce this deviation. The characteristic of this output signal is dependent on the type, or mode, of the controller. This chapter describes the simplest type of controller, which is the two position, or ON-OFF, mode controller.

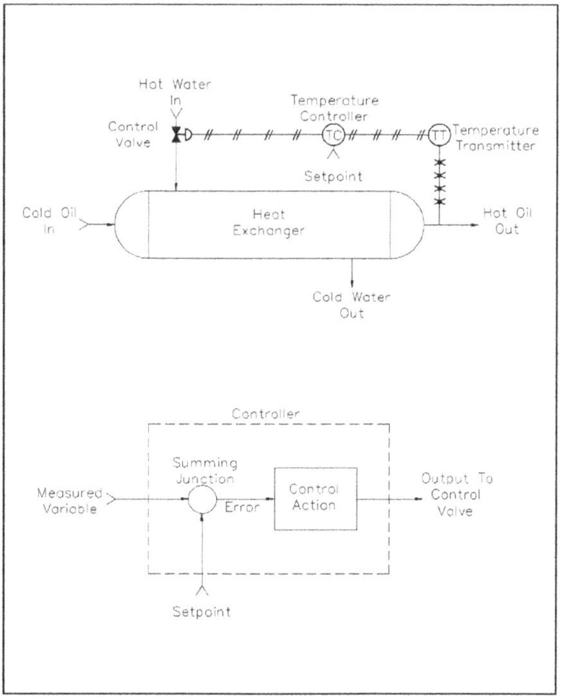

Figure 11 Process Control System Operation

Two Position Controller

A two position controller is a device that has two operating conditions: completely on or completely off.

Figure 12 shows the input to output, characteristic waveform for a two position controller that switches from its "OFF" state to its "ON" state when the measured variable increases above the setpoint. Conversely, it switches from its "ON" state to its "OFF" state when the measured variable decreases below the setpoint. This device provides an output determined by whether the error signal is above or below the setpoint. The magnitude of the error signal is above or below the setpoint. The magnitude of the error signal past that point is of no concern to the controller.

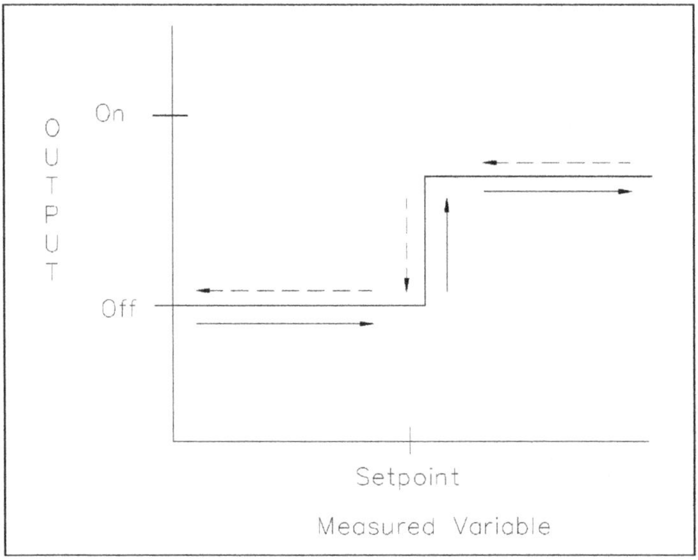

Figure 12 Two Position Controller Input/Output Relationship

Example of Two Position Control

A system using a two position controller is shown in Figure 13.

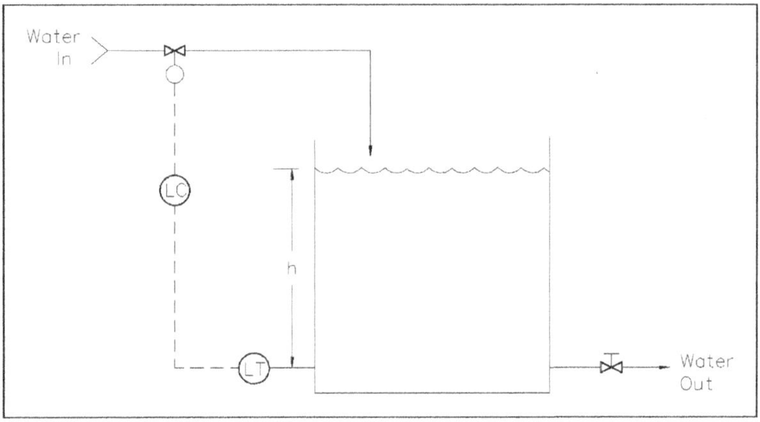

Figure 13 Two Position Control System

The controlled process is the volume of water in the tank. The controlled variable is the level in the tank. It is measured by a level detector that sends information to the controller. The output of the controller is sent to the final control element, which is a solenoid valve, that controls the flow of water into the tank.

As the water level decreases initially, a point is reached where the measured variable drops below the setpoint. This creates a positive error signal. The controller opens the final control element fully. Water is subsequently injected into the tank, and the water level rises. As soon as the water level rises above the setpoint, a negative error signal is developed. The negative error signal causes the controller to shut the final control element. This opening and closing of the final control element results in a cycling characteristic of the measured variable.

Modes of Automatic Control

The mode of control is the manner in which a control system makes corrections relative to an error that exists between the desired value (setpoint) of a controlled variable and its actual value. The mode of control used for a specific application depends on the characteristics of the process being controlled. For example, some processes can be operated over a wide band, while others must be maintained very close to the setpoint. Also, some processes change relatively slowly, while others change almost immediately.

Deviation is the difference between the setpoint of a process variable and its actual value. This is a key term used when discussing various modes of control.

Four modes of control commonly used for most applications are:

proportional
proportional plus reset (PI)
proportional plus rate (PD)
proportional plus reset plus rate (PID)

Each mode of control has characteristic advantages and limitations. The modes of control are discussed in this and the next several sections of this module.

In the *proportional (throttling) mode*, there is a continuous linear relation between value of the controlled variable and position of the final control element. In other words, amount of valve movement is proportional to amount of deviation.

Figure 14 shows the relationship between valve position and controlled variable (temperature) characteristics of proportional mode. Notice that valve position changes in exact proportion to deviation. Also, the proportional mode responds only to amount of deviation and is insensitive to rate or duration of deviation. At the 2 minute and 4 minute marks, when the temperature returns to its setpoint value, the valve returns to its initial position. There is no valve correction without deviation.

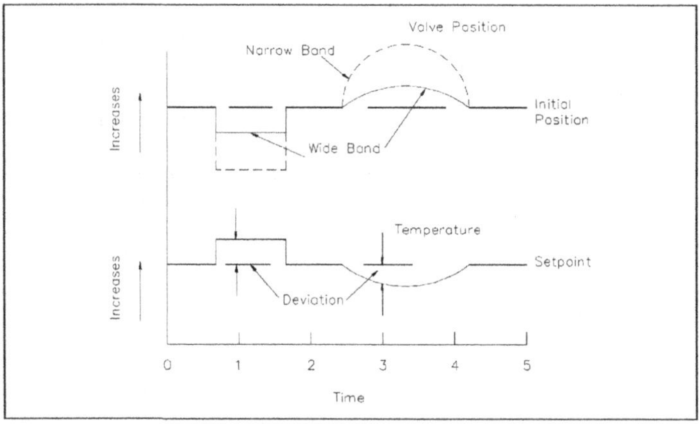

Figure 14 Relation Between Valve Position and Controlled Variable Under Proportional Mode

Three terms commonly used to describe the proportional mode of control are *proportional band*, *gain*, and *offset*.

Proportional band, (also called *throttling range*), is the change in value of the controlled variable that causes full travel of the final control element. Figure 14 shows the relationship between valve position and temperature band for two different proportional bands.

The proportional band of a particular instrument is expressed as a percent of full range. For example, if full range of an instrument is 200°F and it takes a 50°F change in temperature to cause full valve travel, the percent proportional band is 50°F in 200°F, or 25%. Proportional bands may range from less than 1% to well over 200%. However, proportional bands over 100% cannot cause full valve travel even for full range change of the controlled variable.

Gain, also called *sensitivity*, compares the ratio of amount of change in the final control element to amount of change in the controlled variable. Mathematically, gain and sensitivity are reciprocal to proportional band.

Offset, also called *droop*, is deviation that remains after a process has stabilized. Offset is an inherent characteristic of the proportional mode of control. In other words, the proportional mode of control will not necessarily return a controlled variable to its setpoint.

Summary

The important information in this chapter is summarized below:

Two Position Controller Summary

- It is a device that has two operating conditions: completely on or completely off.
- This device provides an output determined by whether the error signal is above or below the setpoint.
- *Deviation* is the difference between the setpoint of a process variable and its actual value.
- In the proportional (throttling) mode, the amount of valve movement is proportional to the amount of deviation. *Gain* compares the ratio of amount of change in the final control element to change in the controlled variable, and *offset* is the deviation that remains after a process has been stabilized.

PROPORTIONAL CONTROL SYSTEMS

Proportional control is also referred to as throttling control.

EO 1.4 DESCRIBE the characteristics of the following types of automatic control systems:
b. Proportional control system

Control Mode

In the proportional control mode, the final control element is throttled to various positions that are dependent on the process system conditions. For example, a proportional controller provides a linear stepless output that can position a valve at intermediate positions, as well as "full open" or "full shut." The controller operates within a band that is between the 0% output point and the 100% output point and where the output of the controller is proportional to the input signal.

Proportional Band

With proportional control, the final control element has a definite position for each value of the measured variable. In other words, the output has a linear relationship with the input. Proportional band is the change in input required to produce a full range of change in the output due to the proportional control action. Or simply, it is the percent change of the input signal required to change the output signal from 0% to 100%.

The proportional band determines the range of output values from the controller that operate the final control element. The final control element acts on the manipulated variable to determine the value of the controlled variable. The controlled variable is maintained within a specified band of control points around a setpoint.

To demonstrate, let's look at Figure 15.

In this example of a proportional level control system, the flow of supply water into the tank is controlled to maintain the tank water level within prescribed limits. The demand that disturbances placed on the process system are such

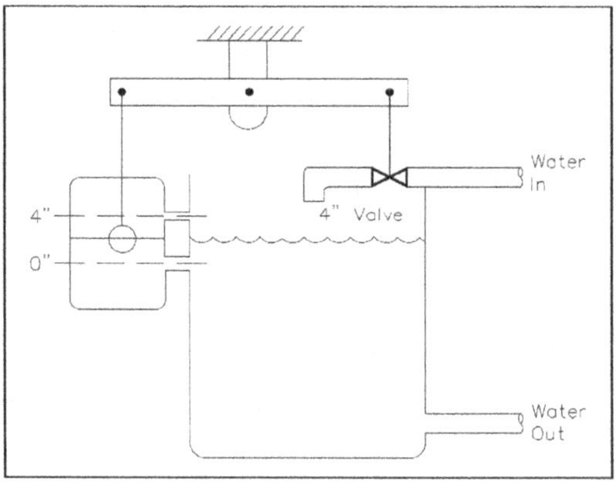

Figure 15 Proportional System Controller

that the actual flow rates cannot be predicted. Therefore, the system is designed to control tank level within a narrow band in order to minimize the chance of a large demand disturbance causing overflow or runout. A fulcrum and lever assembly is used as the proportional controller. A float chamber is the level measuring element, and a 4-in stroke valve is the final control element. The fulcrum point is set such that a level change of 4-in causes a full 4-in stroke of the valve. Therefore, a 100% change in the controller output equals 4-in.

The proportional band is the input band over which the controller provides a proportional output and is defined as follows:

$$\text{Proportional band} = \frac{\text{\% change in input}}{\text{\% change in output}} \times 100\%$$

For this example, the fulcrum point is such that a full 4-in change in float height causes a full 4-in stroke of the valve.

$$\text{P.B.} = \frac{\text{100\% change in input}}{\text{100\% change in output}} \times 100\%$$

Therefore:

$$\text{P.B.} = 100\%$$

The controller has a proportional band of 100%, which means the input must change 100% to cause a 100% change in the output of the controller.

If the fulcrum setting was changed so that a level change of 2 in, or 50% of the input, causes the full 3-in stroke, or 100% of the output, the proportional band would become 50%. The proportional band of a proportional controller is important because it determines the range of outputs for given inputs.

Example of a Proportional Process Control System

Figure 16 illustrates a process system using a proportional temperature controller for providing hot water.

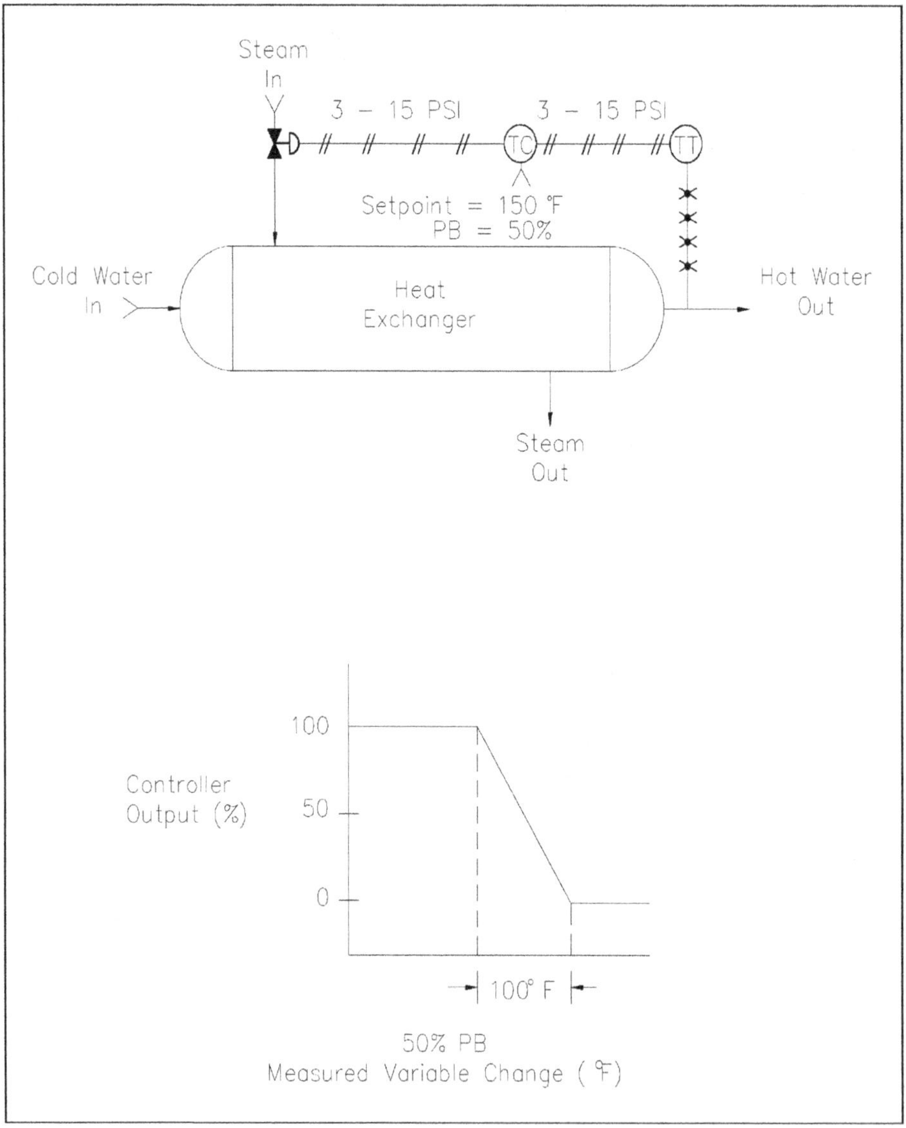

Figure 16 Proportional Temperature Control System

Steam is admitted to the heat exchanger to raise the temperature of the cold water supply. The temperature detector monitors the hot water outlet and produces a 3 to 15 psi output signal that represents a controlled variable range of 100° to 300°F. The controller compares the measured variable signal with the setpoint and sends a 3 to 15 psi output to the final control element, which is a 3-in control valve.

The controller has been set for a proportional band of 50%. Therefore, a 50% change in the 200°F span, or a change of 100°F, causes a 100% controller output change.

The proportional controller is reverse-acting so that the control valve throttles down to reduce steam flow as the hot water outlet temperature increases; the control valve will open further to increase steam flow as the water temperature decreases.

The combined action of the controller and control valve for different changes in the measured variable is shown in Figure 17.

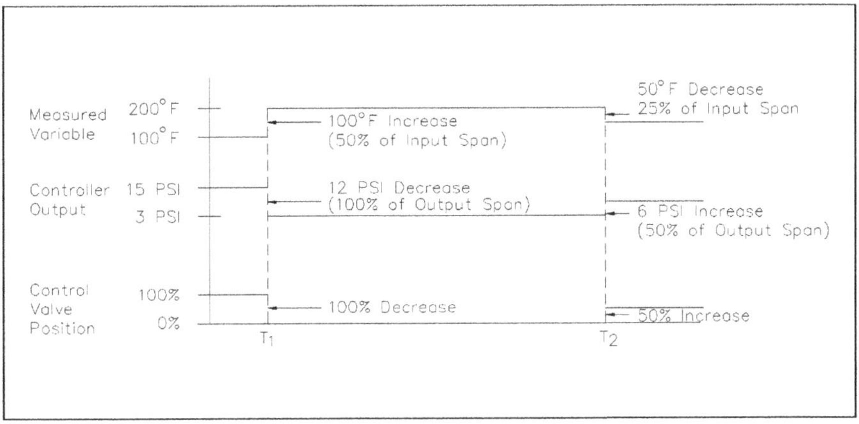

Figure 17 Combined Controller and Final Control Element Action

Initially, the measured variable value is equal to 100°F. The controller has been set so that this value of measured variable corresponds to a 100% output, or 15 psi, which in turn, corresponds to a "full open" control valve position.

At time t_1, the measured variable increases by 100°F, or 50%, of the measured variable span. This 50% controller input change causes a 100% controller output change due to the controller's proportional band of 50%. The direction of the controller output change is decreasing because the controller is reverse-acting. The 100% decrease corresponds to a decrease in output for 15 psi to 3 psi, which causes the control valve to go from fully open to fully shut.

At time t_2, the measured variable decreases by 50°F, or 25%, of the measured variable span. The 25% controller input decrease causes a 50% controller output increase. This results in a controller output increase from 3 psi to 9 psi, and the control valve goes from fully shut to 50% open.

The purpose of this system is to provide hot water at a setpoint of 150°F. The system must be capable of handling demand disturbances that can result in the outlet temperature increasing or decreasing from the setpoint. For that reason, the controller is set up such that the system functions as shown in Figure 18.

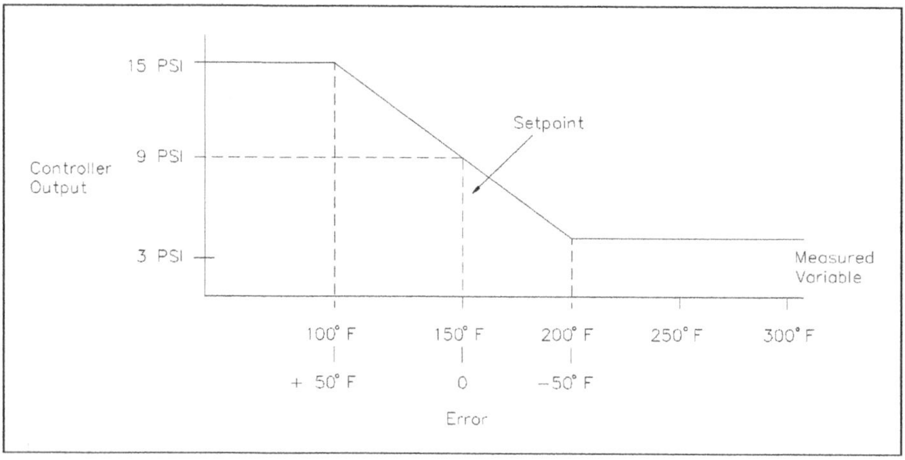

Figure 18 Controller Characteristic Curve

If the measured variable drops below the setpoint, a positive error is developed, and the control valve opens further. If the measured variable goes above the setpoint, a negative error is developed, and the control valve throttles down (opening is reduced). The 50% proportional band causes full stroke of the valve between a +50°F error and a -50°F error.

When the error equals zero, the controller provides a 50%, or 9 psi, signal to the control valve. As the error goes above and below this point, the controller produces an output that is proportional to the magnitude of the error, determined by the value of the proportional band. The control valve is then capable of being positioned to compensate for the demand disturbances that can cause the process to deviate from the setpoint in either direction.

Summary

The important information in this chapter is summarized below.

Proportional Control Summary

- In the proportional control mode, the final control element is throttled to various positions that are dependent on the process system conditions.
- With proportional control, the output has a linear relationship with the input.
- The proportional band is the change in input required to produce a full range of change in the output due to the proportional control action.
- The controlled variable is maintained within a specified band of control points around a setpoint.

RESET (INTEGRAL) CONTROL SYSTEMS

The output rate of change of an integral controller is dependent on the magnitude of the input.

EO 1.4 DESCRIBE the characteristics of the following types of automatic control systems:
c. Integral control

Reset Control (Integral)

Integral control describes a controller in which the output rate of change is dependent on the magnitude of the input. Specifically, a smaller amplitude input causes a slower rate of change of the output. This controller is called an integral controller because it approximates the mathematical function of integration. The integral control method is also known as reset control.

Definition of Integral Control

A device that performs the mathematical function of integration is called an integrator. The mathematical result of integration is called the integral. The integrator provides a linear output with a rate of change that is directly related to the amplitude of the step change input and a constant that specifies the function of integration.

For the example shown in Figure 19, the step change has an amplitude of 10%, and the constant of the integrator causes the output to change 0.2% per second for each 1% of the input.

The integrator acts to transform the step change into a gradually changing signal. As you can see, the input amplitude is repeated in the output every 5 seconds. As long as the input remains constant at 10%, the output will continue to ramp up every 5 seconds until the integrator saturates.

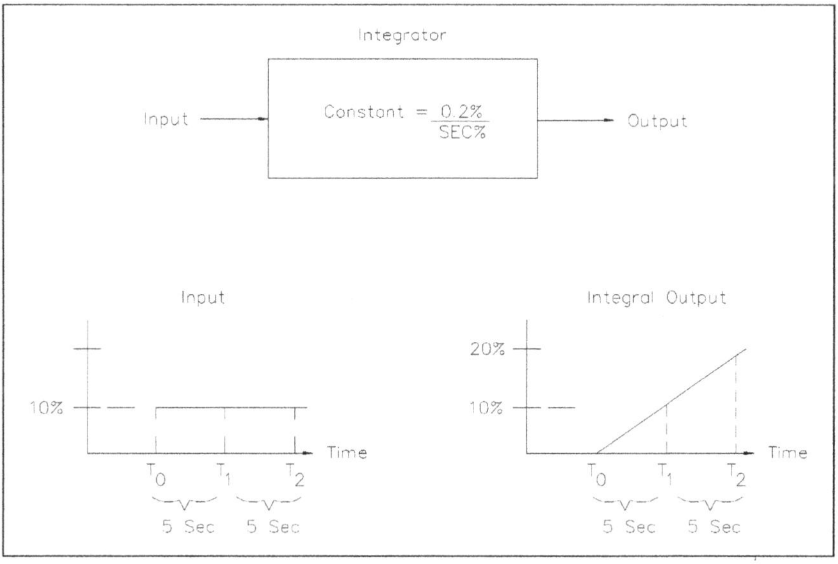

Figure 19 Integral Output for a Fixed Input

Example of an Integral Flow Control System

With integral control, the final control element's position changes at a rate determined by the amplitude of the input error signal. Recall that:

Error = Setpoint - Measured Variable

If a large difference exists between the setpoint and the measured variable, a large error results. This causes the final control element to change position rapidly. If, however, only a small difference exists, the small error signal causes the final control element to change position slowly.

Figure 20 illustrates a process using an integral controller to maintain a constant flow rate. Also included is the equivalent block diagram of the controller.

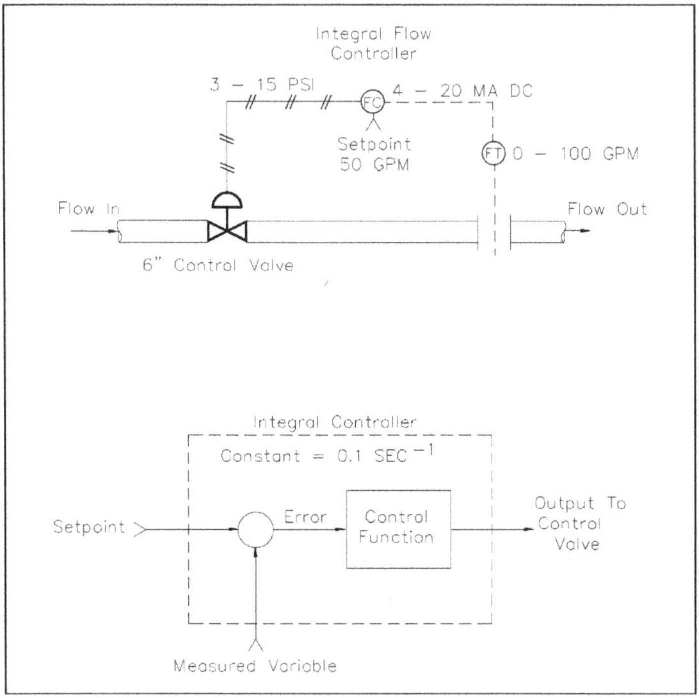

Figure 20 Integral Flow Rate Controller

Initially, the system is set up on an anticipated flow demand of 50 gpm, which corresponds to a control valve opening of 50%. With the setpoint equal to 50 gpm and the actual flow measured at 50 gpm, a zero error signal is sent to the input of the integral controller. The controller output is initially set for a 50%, or 9 psi, output to position the 6-in control valve to a position of 3 in open. The output rate of change of this integral controller is given by:

Output rate of change = Integral constant x % Error

If the measured variable decreases from its initial value of 50 gpm to a new value of 45 gpm, as seen in Figure 21, a positive error of 5% is produced and applied to the input of the integral controller. The controller has a constant of 0.1 seconds^{-1}, so the controller output rate of change is 0.5% per second.

The positive 0.5% per second indicates that the controller output increases from its initial point of 50% at 0.5% per second. This causes the control valve to open further at a rate of 0.5% per second, increasing flow.

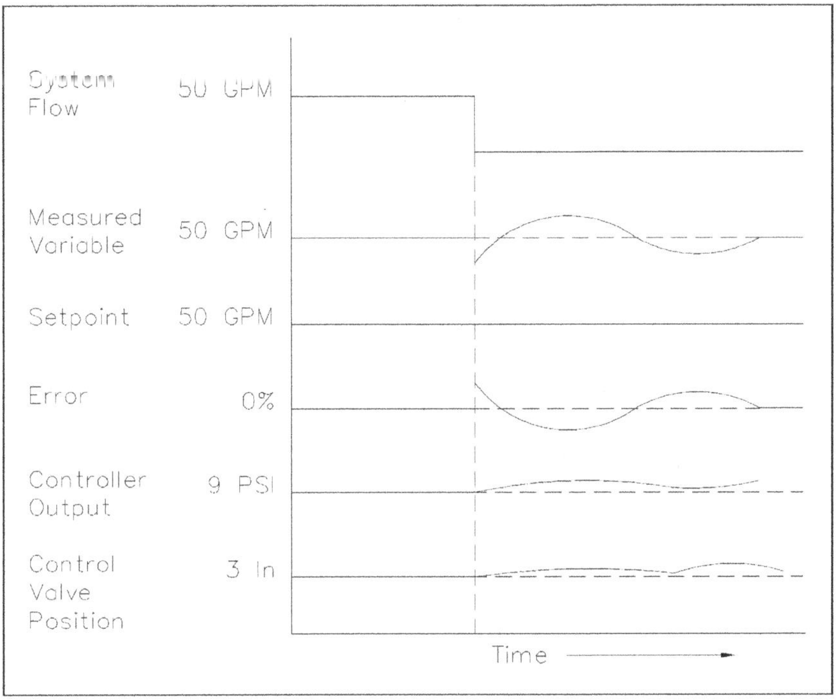

Figure 21 Reset Controller Response

The controller acts to return the process to the setpoints. This is accomplished by the repositioning of the control valve. As the controller causes the control valve to reposition, the measured variable moves closer to the setpoint, and a new error signal is produced. The cycle repeats itself until no error exists.

The integral controller responds to both the amplitude and the time duration of the error signal. Some error signals that are large or exist for a long period of time can cause the final control element to reach its "fully open" or "fully shut" position before the error is reduced to zero. If this occurs, the final control element remains at the extreme position, and the error must be reduced by other means in the actual operation of the process system.

Properties of Integral Control

The major advantage of integral controllers is that they have the unique ability to return the controlled variable back to the exact setpoint following a disturbance.

Disadvantages of the integral control mode are that it responds relatively slowly to an error signal and that it can initially allow a large deviation at the instant the error is produced. This can lead to system instability and cyclic operation. For this reason, the integral control mode is not normally used alone, but is combined with another control mode.

Summary

Integral controllers are summarized below.

Integral Control Summary

- An integral controller provides an output rate of change that is determined by the magnitude of the error and the integral constant.
- The controller has the unique ability to return the process back to the exact setpoint.
- The integral control mode is not normally used by itself because of its slow response to an error signal.

PROPORTIONAL PLUS RESET CONTROL SYSTEMS

Proportional plus reset control is a combination of the proportional and integral control modes.

EO 1.4 DESCRIBE the characteristics of the following types of automatic control systems:

d. Proportional plus reset control system

Proportional Plus Reset

This type control is actually a combination of two previously discussed control modes, proportional and integral. Combining the two modes results in gaining the advantages and compensating for the disadvantages of the two individual modes.

The main advantage of the proportional control mode is that an immediate proportional output is produced as soon as an error signal exists at the controller as shown in Figure 22. The proportional controller is considered a fast-acting device. This immediate output change enables the proportional controller to reposition the final control element within a relatively short period of time in response to the error.

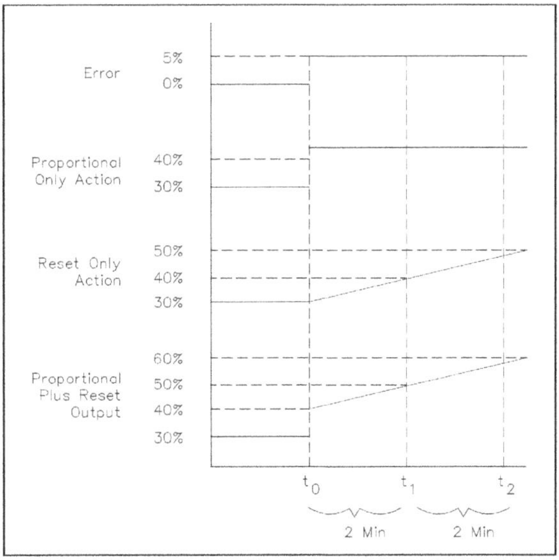

Figure 22 Response of Proportional Plus Reset Control

The main disadvantage of the proportional control mode is that a residual offset error exists between the measured variable and the setpoint for all but one set of system conditions.

The main advantage of the integral control mode is that the controller output continues to reposition the final control element until the error is reduced to zero. This results in the elimination of the residual offset error allowed by the proportional mode.

The main disadvantage of the integral mode is that the controller output does not immediately direct the final control element to a new position in response to an error signal. The controller output changes at a defined rate of change, and time is needed for the final control element to be repositioned.

The combination of the two control modes is called the proportional plus reset (PI) control mode. It combines the immediate output characteristics of a proportional control mode with the zero residual offset characteristics of the integral mode.

Example of Proportional Plus Reset Control

Let's once more refer to our heat exchanger example (see Figure 23). This time we will apply a proportional plus reset controller to the process system.

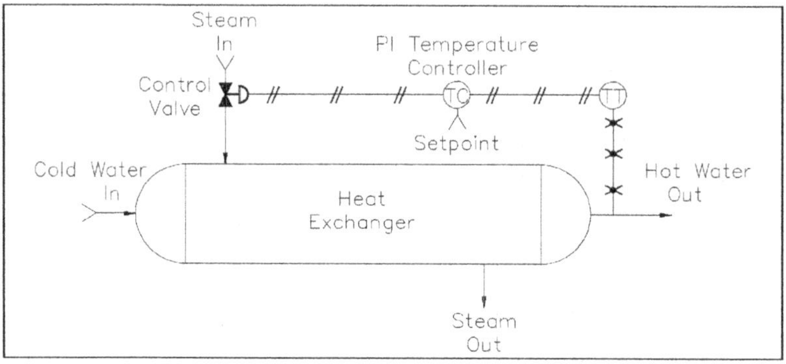

Figure 23 Heat Exchanger Process System

The response curves shown in Figure 24 illustrate only the demand and the measured variable which represents the hot water outlet temperature.

Assume the process undergoes a demand disturbance which reduces the flow of the hot water out of the heat exchanger. The temperature and flow rate of the steam into the heat exchanger remain the same. As a result, the temperature of the hot water out will begin to rise.

The proportional action of the proportional plus reset controller, if acting alone, would respond to the disturbance and reposition the control valve to a position that would return the hot water out to a new control point, as illustrated by the response curves. You'll note that a residual error would still exist.

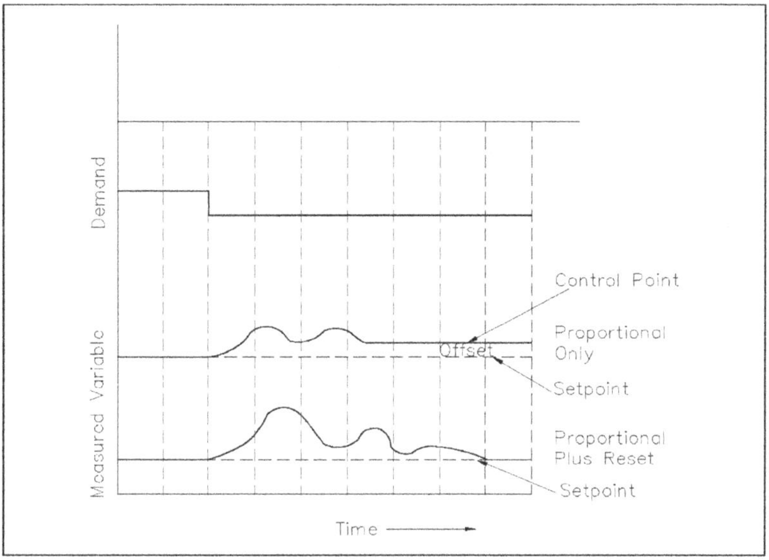

Figure 24 Effects of Disturbance on Reverse Acting Controller

By adding the reset action to the proportional action the controller produces a larger output for the given error signal and causes a greater adjustment of the control valve. This causes the process to come back to the setpoint more quickly. Additionally, the reset action acts to eliminate the offset error after a period of time.

Reset Windup

Proportional plus reset controllers act to eliminate the offset error found in proportional control by continuing to change the output after the proportional action is completed and by returning the controlled variable to the setpoint.

An inherent disadvantage to proportional plus reset controllers is the possible adverse effects caused by large error signals. The large error can be caused by a large demand deviation or when initially starting up the system. This is a problem because a large sustained error signal will eventually cause the controller to drive to its limit, and the result is called "reset windup."

Because of reset windup, this control mode is not well-suited for processes that are frequently shut down and started up.

Summary

The proportional plus reset control mode is summarized below.

Proportional Plus Reset Control Summary

- Proportional plus reset control eliminates any offset error that would occur with proportional control only.
- Reset windup is an inherent disadvantage of proportional plus reset controllers that are subject to large error signals.

PROPORTIONAL PLUS RATE CONTROL SYSTEMS

Proportional plus rate control is a control mode in which a derivative section is added to the proportional controller.

EO 1.4 DESCRIBE the characteristics of the following types of automatic control systems:

e. Proportional plus rate control

Proportional-Derivative

Proportional plus rate describes a control mode in which a derivative section is added to a proportional controller. This derivative section responds to the rate of change of the error signal, not the amplitude; this derivative action responds to the rate of change the instant it starts. This causes the controller output to be initially larger in direct relation with the error signal rate of change. The higher the error signal rate of change, the sooner the final control element is positioned to the desired value. The added derivative action reduces initial overshoot of the measured variable, and therefore aids in stabilizing the process sooner.

This control mode is called proportional plus rate (PD) control because the derivative section responds to the rate of change of the error signal.

Definition of Derivative Control

A device that produces a derivative signal is called a differentiator. Figure 25 shows the input versus output relationship of a differentiator.

The differentiator provides an output that is directly related to the rate of change of the input and a constant that specifies the function of differentiation. The derivative constant is expressed in units of seconds and defines the differential controller output.

The differentiator acts to transform a changing signal to a constant magnitude signal as shown in Figure 26. As long as the input rate of change is constant, the magnitude of the output is constant. A new input rate of change would give a new output magnitude.

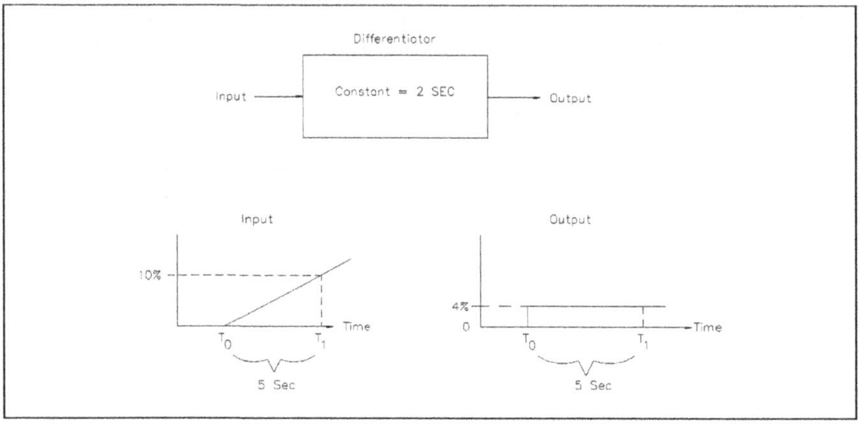

Figure 25 Derivative Output for a Constant Rate of Change Input

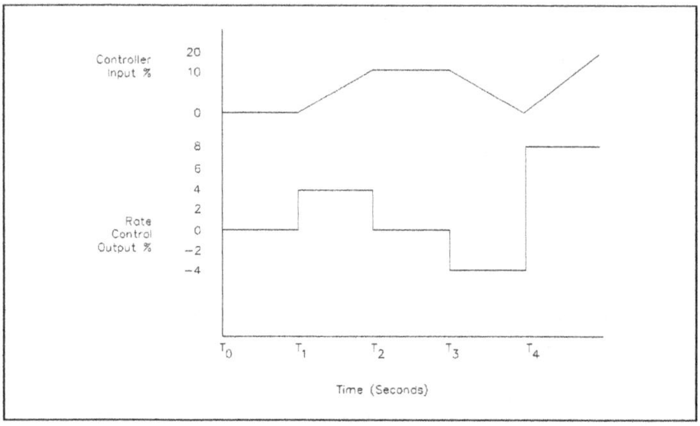

Figure 26 Rate Control Output

Derivative cannot be used alone as a control mode. This is because a steady-state input produces a zero output in a differentiator. If the differentiator were used as a controller, the input signal it would receive is the error signal. As just described, a steady-state error signal corresponds to any number of necessary output signals for the positioning of the final control element. Therefore, derivative action is combined with proportional action in a manner such that the proportional section output serves as the derivative section input.

Proportional plus rate controllers take advantage of both proportional and rate control modes.

As seen in Figure 27, proportional action provides an output proportional to the error. If the error is not a step change, but is slowly changing, the proportional action is slow. Rate action, when added, provides quick response to the error.

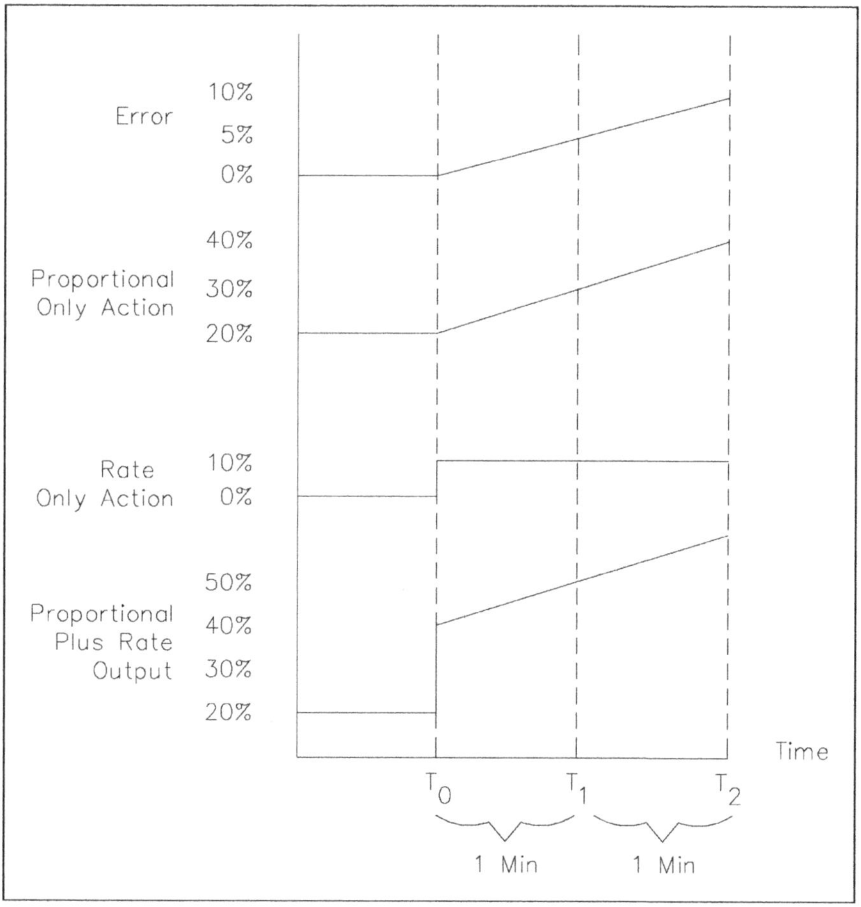

Figure 27 Response of Proportional Plus Rate Control

Example of Proportional Plus Rate Control

To illustrate proportional plus rate control, we will use the same heat exchanger process that has been analyzed in previous chapters (see Figure 28). For this example, however, the temperature controller used is a proportional plus rate controller.

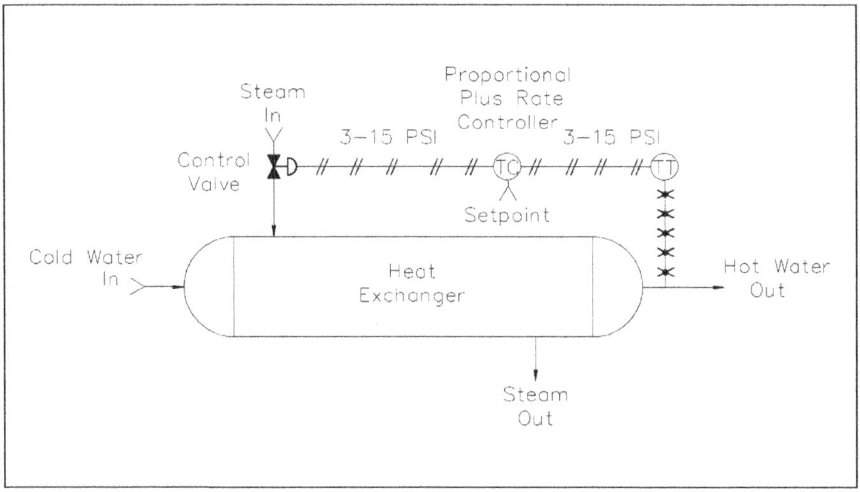

Figure 28 Heat Exchanger Process

As illustrated in Figure 29, the proportional only control mode responds to the decrease in demand, but because of the inherent characteristics of proportional control, a residual offset error remains. Adding the derivative action affects the response by allowing only one small overshoot and a rapid stabilization to the new control point. Thus, derivative action provides increased stability to the system, but does not eliminate offset error.

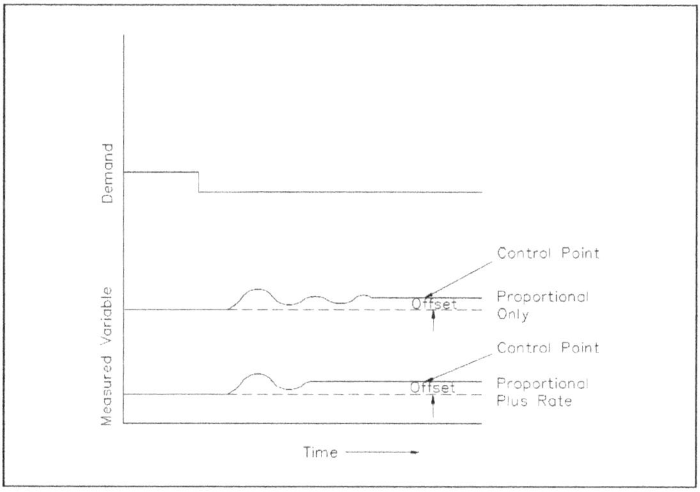

Figure 29 Effect of Disturbance on Proportional Plus Rate Reverse Acting Controller

Applications

Proportional plus rate control is normally used with large capacity or slow-responding processes such as temperature control. The leading action of the controller output compensates for the lagging characteristics of large capacity, slow processes.

Rate action is not usually employed with fast responding processes such as flow control or noisy processes because derivative action responds to any rate of change in the error signal, including the noise.

Proportional plus rate controllers are useful with processes which are frequently started up and shut down because it is not susceptible to reset windup.

Summary

The proportional plus rate control mode is summarized below.

Proportional Plus Rate Control Summary

- Derivative action is added to a controller to make it respond to the rate of change of the error signal.
- Derivative action cannot be used as a control mode alone.
- Proportional plus rate control does not eliminate offset error.
- Proportional plus rate control increases system stability.

PROPORTIONAL-INTEGRAL-DERIVATIVE CONTROL SYSTEMS

Proportional plus reset plus rate controllers combine proportional control actions with integral and derivative actions.

EO 1.4 DESCRIBE the characteristics of the following types of automatic control systems:
f. Proportional plus reset plus rate control

Proportional-Integral-Derivative

For processes that can operate with continuous cycling, the relatively inexpensive two position controller is adequate. For processes that cannot tolerate continuous cycling, a proportional controller is often employed. For processes that can tolerate neither continuous cycling nor offset error, a proportional plus reset controller can be used. For processes that need improved stability and can tolerate an offset error, a proportional plus rate controller is employed.

However, there are some processes that cannot tolerate offset error, yet need good stability. The logical solution is to use a control mode that combines the advantages of proportional, reset, and rate action. This chapter describes the mode identified as proportional plus reset plus rate, commonly called Proportional-Integral-Derivative (PID).

Proportional Plus Reset Plus Rate Controller Actions

When an error is introduced to a PID controller, the controller's response is a combination of the proportional, integral, and derivative actions, as shown in Figure 30.

Assume the error is due to a slowly increasing measured variable. As the error increases, the proportional action of the PID controller produces an output that is proportional to the error signal. The reset action of the controller produces an output whose rate of change is determined by the magnitude of the error. In this case, as the error continues to increase at a steady rate, the reset output continues to increase its rate of change. The rate action of the controller produces an output whose magnitude is determined by the rate of change. When combined, these actions produce an output as shown in Figure 30.

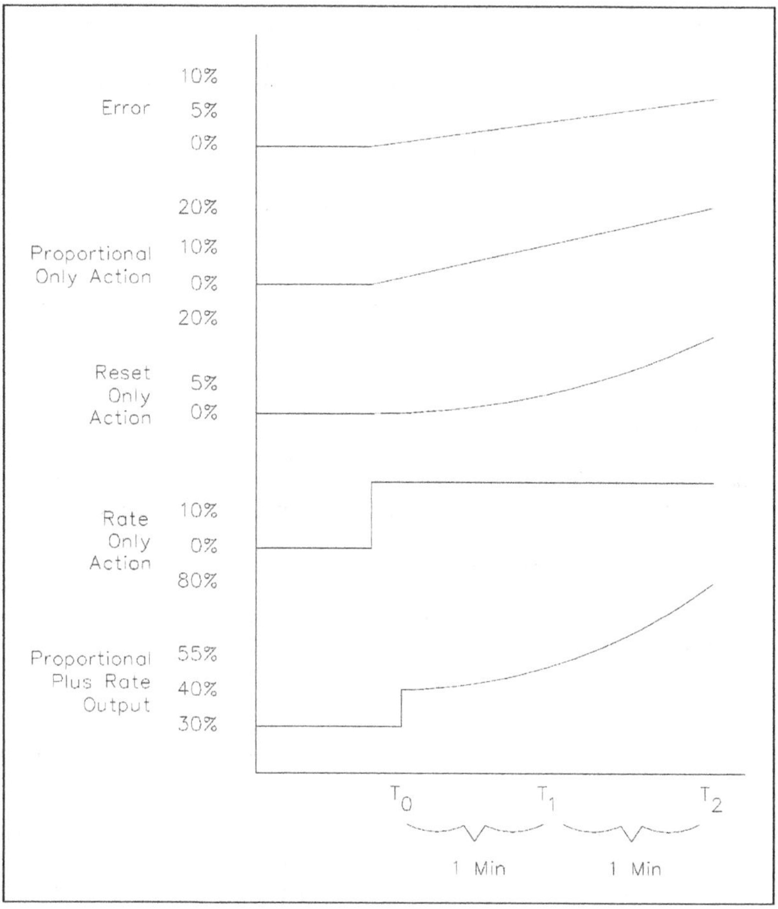

Figure 30 PID Control Action Responses

As you can see from the combined action curve, the output produced responds immediately to the error with a signal that is proportional to the magnitude of the error and that will continue to increase as long as the error remains increasing.

You must remember that these response curves are drawn assuming no corrective action is taken by the control system. In actuality, as soon as the output of the controller begins to reposition the final control element, the magnitude of the error should begin to decrease. Eventually, the controller will bring the error to zero and the controlled variable back to the setpoint.

Figure 31 demonstrates the combined controller response to a demand disturbance. The proportional action of the controller stabilizes the process. The reset action combined with the proportional action causes the measured variable to return to the setpoint. The rate action combined with the proportional action reduces the initial overshoot and cyclic period.

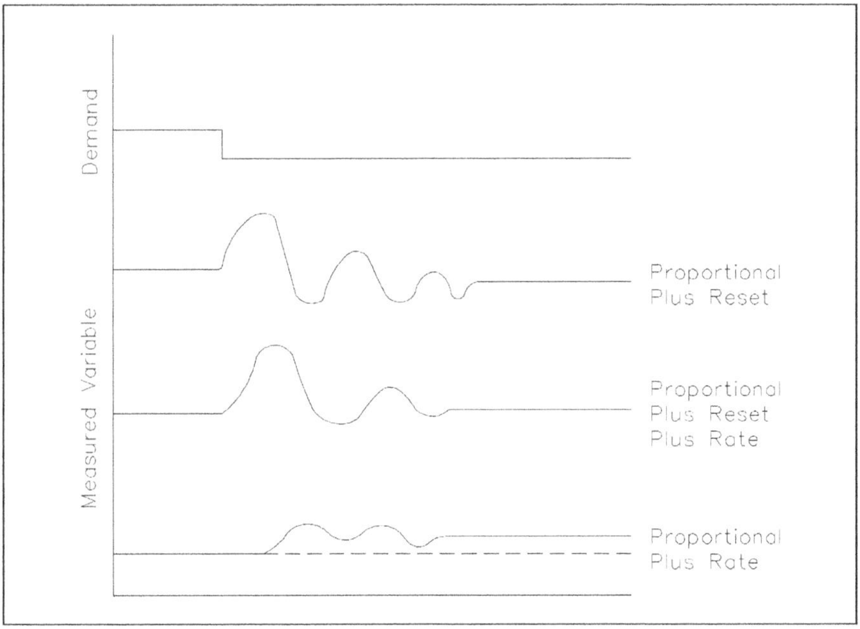

Figure 31 PID Controller Response Curves

Summary

The PID control mode is summarized below.

Proportional Plus Reset Plus Rate Control Summary

- The PID controller combines the three individual modes to achieve the advantages of each.
- The proportional action responds to the error amplitude.
- The integral action eliminates the offset error.
- The derivative action provides additional stability to the process.
- PID controllers can be used to control most processes, even those that are difficult to control.

CONTROLLERS

Mechanical "watchdogs" called controllers are installed in a system to maintain process variables within a given parameter.

EO 1.5 **STATE the purpose of the following components of a typical control station:**
- **a. Setpoint indicator**
- **b. Setpoint adjustment**
- **c. Deviation indicator**
- **d. Output meter**
- **e. Manual-automatic transfer switch**
- **f. Manual output adjust knob**

EO 1.6 **DESCRIBE the operation of a self-balancing control station.**

Controllers

Controllers are the controlling element of a control loop. Their function is to maintain a process variable (pressure, temperature, level, etc.) at some desired value. This value may or may not be constant.

The function is accomplished by comparing a setpoint signal (desired value) with the actual value (controlled variable). If the two values differ, an error signal is produced.

The error signal is amplified (increased in strength) to produce a controller output signal. The output signal is sent to a final control element which alters a manipulated variable and returns the controlled variable to setpoint.

This chapter will describe two controllers commonly found in nuclear facility control rooms. Although plants may have other types of controllers, information presented here will generally apply to those controllers as well.

Control Stations

Control stations perform the function of a controller and provide additional controls and indicators to allow an operator to manually adjust the controller output to the final control element.

Figure 32 shows the front panel of a typical control station. It contains several indicators and controls. Each will be discussed.

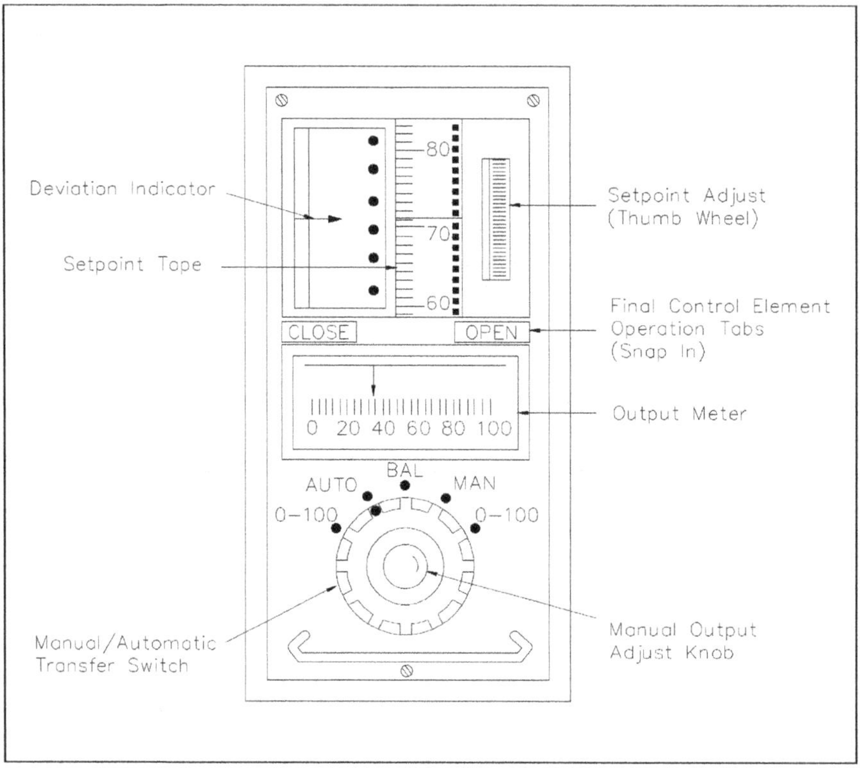

Figure 32 Typical Control Station

The *setpoint indicator*, located in the center of the upper half of the controller, indicates the setpoint (desired value) selected for the controller. The scale may be marked 0% to 100% or correspond directly to the controlled variable (e.g., 0 - 1000 psig or -20°F to +180°F).

The *setpoint adjustment*, located right of the setpoint indicator, is a thumbwheel type adjustment dial that allows the operator to select the setpoint value. By rotating the thumbwheel, the scale moves under the setpoint index line.

The *deviation indicator*, located left of the setpoint indicator, displays any error (+10% to -10%) between setpoint value and actual controlled variable value. With no error, the deviation pointer stays at mid-scale, in line with the setpoint index mark. If the controlled variable is lower than setpoint, the deviation indicator deflects downward. If higher, the indicator deflects upward. An example of this is shown in Figure 33.

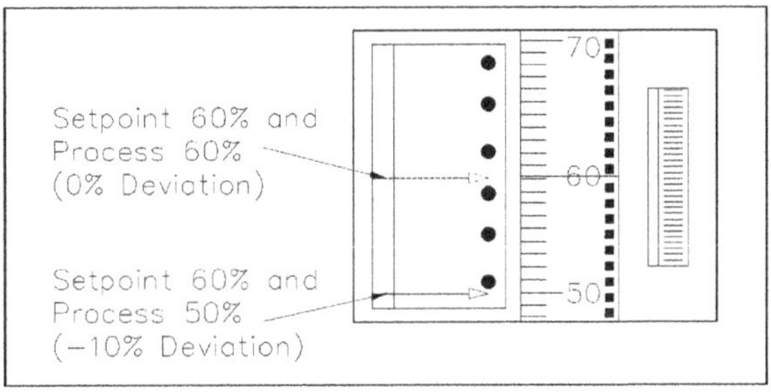

Figure 33 Deviation Indicator

The *output meter* is the horizontally positioned meter below the deviation and setpoint indicators. It indicates controller output signal in percent. This particular controller ranges from zero to 100% current. However, this will correspond to an air signal for pneumatic controllers.

Snap-in tabs, above each end of the output meter, indicate the direction the final control element moves for a change in the output signal. Tabs normally read "open-close" for control valves and "slow-fast" for variable-speed motors, or other appropriate designations.

The *manual-automatic (M-A) transfer switch*, immediately below the output meter, selects operating mode of the controller.

A *manual output adjust knob*, in the center of the M-A transfer switch, varies the controller output signal in manual mode of operation. The knob is rotated clockwise to increase the signal and counterclockwise to decrease the signal.

The M-A transfer switch has five positions that alter the mode of operation. The indication is provided by the deviation meter.

AUTO. This is the normal position of the M-A transfer switch. It places the controller in the automatic mode of operation. Also, the deviation meter indicates any deviation between controlled variable and setpoint.

0 - 100 (AUTO side). In this position, the controller is still in automatic mode. However, the deviation meter now indicates the approximate value of the controlled variable. The deviation meter deflects full down for zero variable value, and full up for 100% variable value.

MAN. This position places the controller in the manual mode of operation. Controller output is now varied by adjusting the manual output adjust knob. This adjustment is indicated on the output meter. The deviation meter indicates any deviation between controlled variable and setpoint.

0 - 100 (MAN side). The controller is still in the manual mode of operation, and the deviation meter indicates controlled variable value (0% to 100%) as it did in the 0-100 (AUTO side) position.

BAL. In many cases, controller output signals of the automatic mode and manual mode may not be the same. If the controller were directly transferred from automatic to manual or manual to automatic, the controller output signal could suddenly change from one value to another. As a result, the final control element would experience a sudden change in position or "bump." This can cause large swings in the value of the process variable and possible damage to the final control element.

Bumpless transfer is the smooth transfer of a controller from one operating mode to another. The balance (BAL) position provides this smooth transfer when transferring the controller from the automatic to manual mode. In the BAL position, the controller is still in the automatic mode of operation, but the deviation meter now indicates the difference between outputs of manual and automatic modes of control. The manual output is adjusted until the deviation meter shows no deflection. Now, the controller can be transferred smoothly from automatic to manual.

To ensure a bumpless transfer from manual to automatic, the manual output signal, indicated by the output meter, is adjusted to match the controlled variable value to setpoint. This will be indicated by no deflection of the deviation meter. Once matched, the M-A transfer switch can be switched from manual (MAN) to automatic (AUTO) control.

Self-Balancing Control Stations

The self-balancing M-A control station shown in Figure 34 has several controls and indicators that are basically the same as those shown on the M-A control station in Figure 32. However, there are some which differ. In addition, the controller does not require a balancing procedure prior to shifting from one mode (manual or automatic) to another.

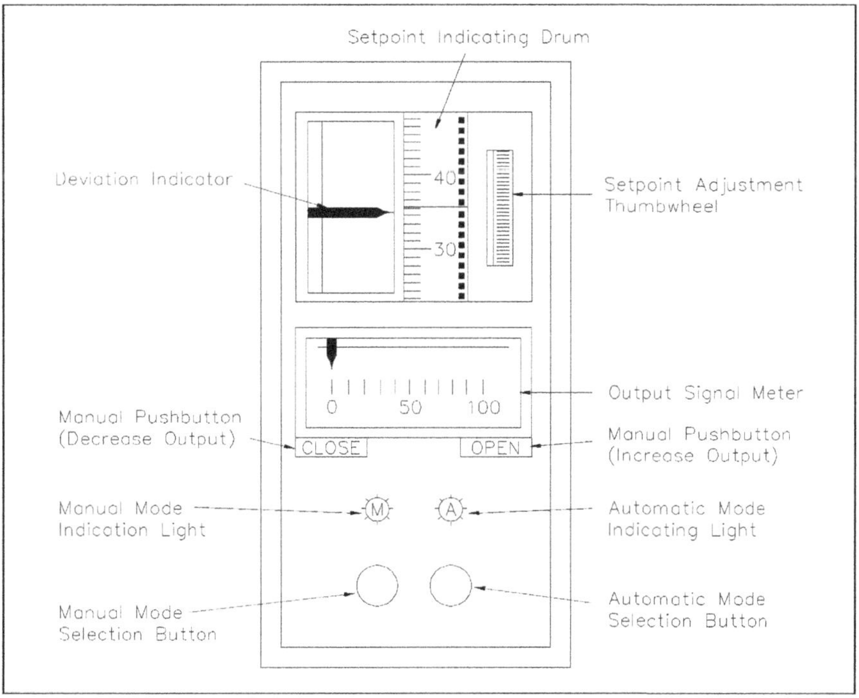

Figure 34 Self-Balancing Control Station

Self-balancing describes a control station in which the non-operating mode output signal follows (tracks) the operating mode output signal. When the control station is in the automatic mode, the manual output signal will follow the automatic output signal. Once the controller is transferred to the manual mode, the output signal will remain at its previous value until one of the manual push buttons (discussed below) is depressed. Then, the output will vary. When the controller is in manual mode, the automatic output signal will track the manual output signal. Once the controller is transferred from the manual to automatic mode, the automatic output signal will initially remain at the manual mode value. If a deviation did exist in the manual mode, the automatic output signal would change slowly and return the controlled variable to setpoint.

The deviation indicator, setpoint indicator, setpoint adjustment thumbwheel, and output meter of the controller in Figure 34 function essentially the same as those in Figure 32. The remaining controls and indicators are quite different. Therefore, each will be discussed.

Manual push buttons. These buttons are located below each end of the output meter and are used in the manual mode of operation. Buttons are labeled to indicate their effect on the final control element. The labels are "open-close" for valves and "slow-fast" for variable speed devices. The left push button decreases the output signal. The right push button increases the output signal. Either button can be depressed at two different positions, half-in and full-in. At the half-in position, the output signal changes slowly. At the full-in position, the output signal changes about ten times faster.

Mode indicating lights. Located directly below the manual push buttons, these lights indicate the operating mode of the controller. When in manual mode, the left light, labeled "M", will be lit; when in the automatic mode, the right light, labeled "A", will be lit.

Mode selection buttons. Located directly under each mode indicating light, each button will select its respective mode of control. If the button below the "M" mode light is depressed, the controller will be in the manual mode of operation; if the button below the "A" mode light is depressed, the controller will be in the automatic mode of operation.

As previously discussed, a particular plant will probably have controllers different from the two described here. Although most information provided can be generally applied, it is extremely important that the operator know the specific plant's controllers and their applications.

Final control elements are devices that complete the control loop. They link the output of the controlling elements with their processes. Some final control elements are designed for specific applications. For example, neutron-absorbing control rods of a reactor are specifically designed to regulate neutron-power level. However, the majority of final control elements are general application devices such as valves, dampers, pumps, and electric heaters. Valves and dampers have similar functions. Valves regulate flow rate of a liquid while dampers regulate flow of air and gases. Pumps, like valves, can be used to control flow of a fluid. Heaters are used to control temperature.

These devices can be arranged to provide a type of "on-off" control to maintain a variable between maximum and minimum values. This is accomplished by opening and shutting valves or dampers or energizing and de-energizing pumps or heaters. On the other hand, these devices can be modulated over a given operating band to provide a proportional control. This is accomplished by positioning valves or dampers, varying the speed of a pump, or regulating the current through electric heater. There are many options to a process control.

Of the final control elements discussed, the most widely used in power plants are valves. Valves can be easily adapted to control liquid level in a tank, temperature of a heat exchanger, or flow rate.

Summary

The important information in this chapter is summarized below.

Controllers Summary

- The *setpoint indicator* displays the desired value for the controller.
- The dial adjustment used to vary the setpoint value is the *setpoint adjustment.*
- The *deviation indicator* displays the difference in percentages between the setpoint value and the actual controlled variable value.
- Percentage display for the output signal is indicated on the *output meter*.
- The *manual-automatic transfer switch* is a five position switch that alters the mode of operation.
- Located in the center of the transfer switch, the *manual output adjustment knob* varies the controller output signal in the manual mode of operation.
- A self-balancing control station's non-operating mode output signal follows the operating mode output signal.

VALVE ACTUATORS

Remote operation of a valve is easily managed by one of the four types of actuators.

EO 1.7 DESCRIBE the operation of the following types of actuators:
a. Pneumatic
b. Hydraulic
c. Solenoid
d. Electric motor

Actuators

By themselves, valves cannot control a process. Manual valves require an operator to position them to control a process variable. Valves that must be operated remotely and automatically require special devices to move them. These devices are called actuators. Actuators may be pneumatic, hydraulic, or electric solenoids or motors.

Pneumatic Actuators

A simplified diagram of a pneumatic actuator is shown in Figure 35. It operates by a combination of force created by air and spring force. The actuator positions a control valve by transmitting its motion through the stem.

A rubber diaphragm separates the actuator housing into two air chambers. The upper chamber receives supply air through an opening in the top of the housing.

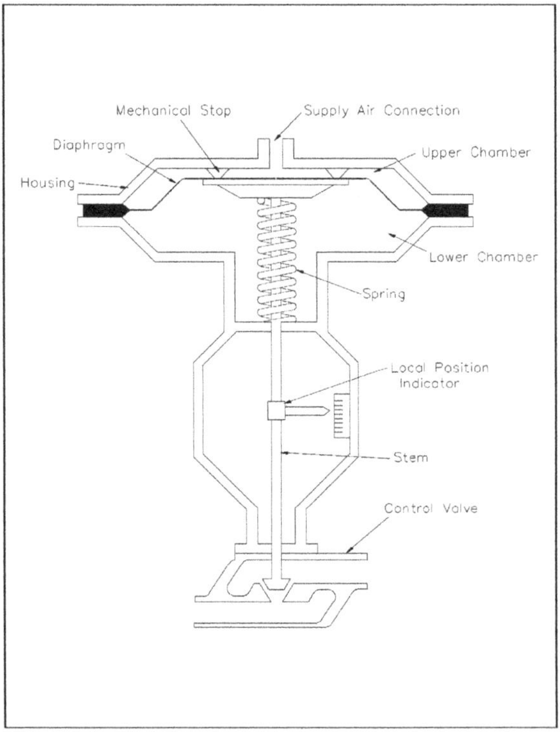

Figure 35 Pneumatic Actuator: Air-to-Close/Spring-to-Open

The bottom chamber contains a spring that forces the diaphragm against mechanical stops in the upper chamber. Finally, a local indicator is connected to the stem to indicate the position of the valve.

The position of the valve is controlled by varying supply air pressure in the upper chamber. This results in a varying force on the top of the diaphragm. Initially, with no supply air, the spring forces the diaphragm upward against the mechanical stops and holds the valve fully open. As supply air pressure is increased from zero, its force on top of the diaphragm begins to overcome the opposing force of the spring. This causes the diaphragm to move downward and the control valve to close. With increasing supply air pressure, the diaphragm will continue to move downward and compress the spring until the control valve is fully closed. Conversely, if supply air pressure is decreased, the spring will begin to force the diaphragm upward and open the control valve. Additionally, if supply pressure is held constant at some value between zero and maximum, the valve will position at an intermediate position. Therefore, the valve can be positioned anywhere between fully open and fully closed in response to changes in supply air pressure.

A positioner is a device that regulates the supply air pressure to a pneumatic actuator. It does this by comparing the actuator's demanded position with the control valve's actual position. The demanded position is transmitted by a pneumatic or electrical control signal from a controller to the positioner. The pneumatic actuator in Figure 35 is shown in Figure 36 with a controller and positioner added.

The controller generates an output signal that represents the demanded position. This signal is sent to the positioner. Externally, the positioner consists of an input connection for the control signal, a supply air input connection, a supply air output connection, a supply air vent connection, and a feedback linkage. Internally, it contains an intricate network of electrical transducers, air lines, valves, linkages, and necessary adjustments. Other positioners may also provide controls for local valve positioning and gauges to indicate supply air pressure and control air pressure (for pneumatic controllers). From an operator's viewpoint, a description of complex internal workings of a positioner is not needed. Therefore, this discussion will be limited to inputs to and outputs from the positioner.

In Figure 36, the controller responds to a deviation of a controlled variable from setpoint and varies the control output signal accordingly to correct the deviation. The control output signal is sent to the positioner, which responds by increasing or decreasing the supply air to the actuator. Positioning of the actuator and control valve is fed back to the positioner through the feedback linkage. When the valve has reached the position demanded by the controller, the positioner stops the change in supply air pressure and holds the valve at the new position. This, in turn, corrects the controlled variable's deviation from setpoint.

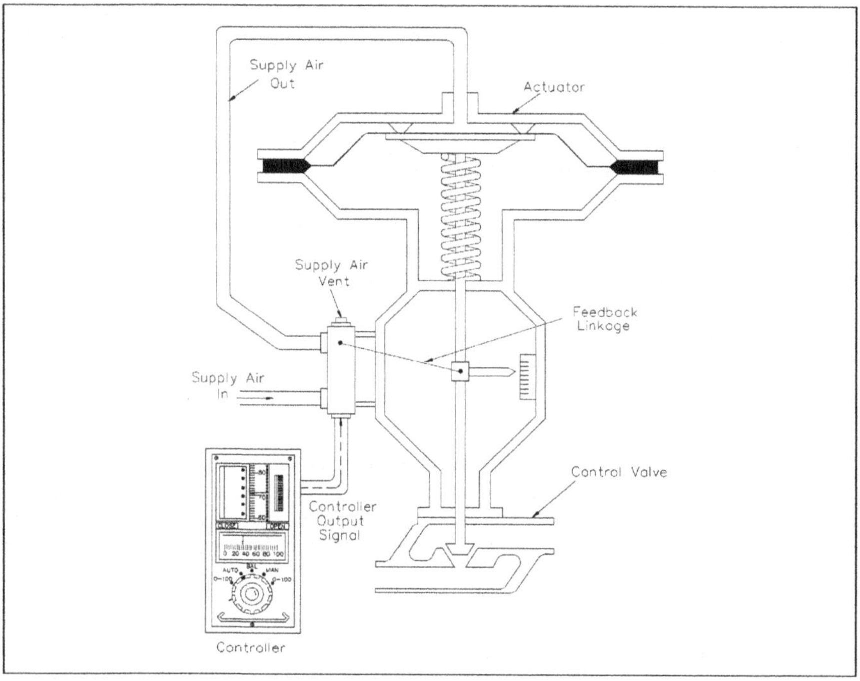

Figure 36 Pneumatic Actuator with Controller and Positioner

For example, as the control signal increases, a valve inside the positioner admits more supply air to the actuator. As a result, the control valve moves downward. The linkage transmits the valve position information back to the positioner. This forms a small internal feedback loop for the actuator. When the valve reaches the position that correlates to the control signal, the linkage stops supply air flow to the actuator. This causes the actuator to stop. On the other hand, if the control signal decreases, another valve inside the positioner opens and allows the supply air pressure to decrease by venting the supply air. This causes the valve to move upward and open. When the valve has opened to the proper position, the positioner stops venting air from the actuator and stops movement of the control valve.

An important safety feature is provided by the spring in an actuator. It can be designed to position a control valve in a safe position if a loss of supply air occurs. On a loss of supply air, the actuator in Figure 36 will fail open. This type of arrangement is referred to as "air-to-close, spring-to-open" or simply "fail-open." Some valves fail in the closed position. This type of actuator is referred to as "air-to-open, spring-to-close" or "fail-closed." This "fail-safe" concept is an important consideration in nuclear facility design.

Hydraulic Actuators

Pneumatic actuators are normally used to control processes requiring quick and accurate response, as they do not require a large amount of motive force. However, when a large amount of force is required to operate a valve (for example, the main steam system valves), hydraulic actuators are normally used. Although hydraulic actuators come in many designs, piston types are most common.

A typical piston-type hydraulic actuator is shown in Figure 37. It consists of a cylinder, piston, spring, hydraulic supply and return line, and stem. The piston slides vertically inside the cylinder and separates the cylinder into two chambers. The upper chamber contains the spring and the lower chamber contains hydraulic oil.

The hydraulic supply and return line is connected to the lower chamber and allows hydraulic fluid to flow to and from the lower chamber of the actuator. The stem transmits the motion of the piston to a valve.

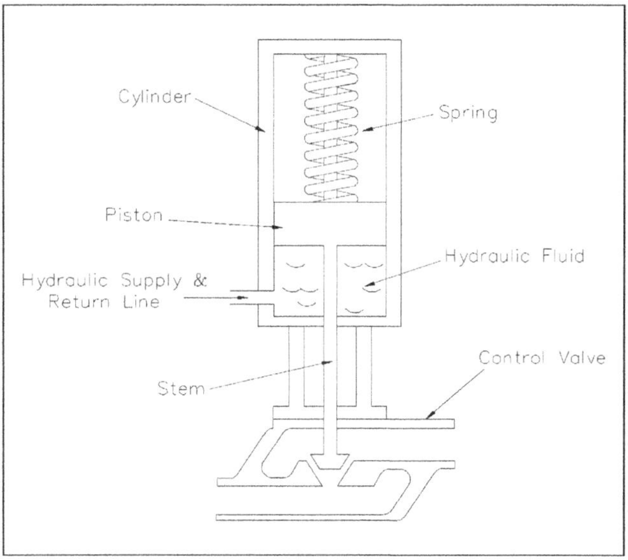

Figure 37 Hydraulic Actuator

Initially, with no hydraulic fluid pressure, the spring force holds the valve in the closed position. As fluid enters the lower chamber, pressure in the chamber increases. This pressure results in a force on the bottom of the piston opposite to the force caused by the spring. When the hydraulic force is greater than the spring force, the piston begins to move upward, the spring compresses, and the valve begins to open. As the hydraulic pressure increases, the valve continues to open. Conversely, as hydraulic oil is drained from the cylinder, the hydraulic force becomes less than the spring force, the piston moves downward, and the valve closes. By regulating amount of oil supplied or drained from the actuator, the valve can be positioned between fully open and fully closed.

The principles of operation of a hydraulic actuator are like those of the pneumatic actuator. Each uses some motive force to overcome spring force to move the valve. Also, hydraulic actuators can be designed to fail-open or fail-closed to provide a fail-safe feature.

Electric Solenoid Actuators

A typical electric solenoid actuator is shown in Figure 38. It consists of a coil, armature, spring, and stem.

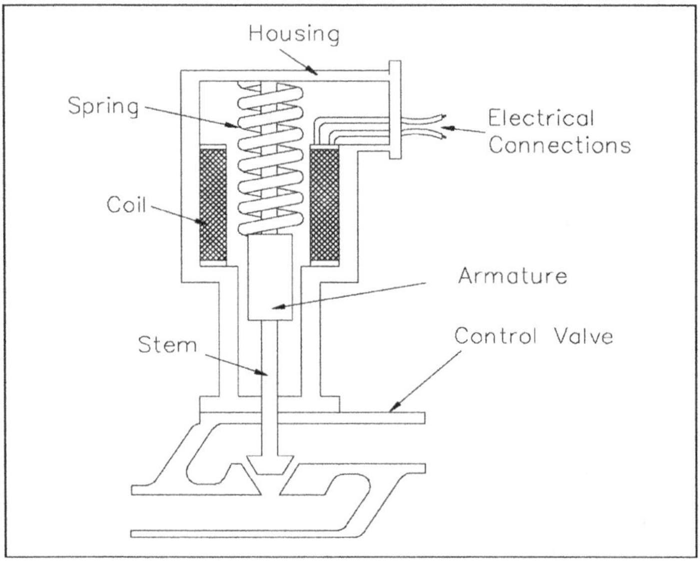

Figure 38 Electric Solenoid Actuator

The coil is connected to an external current supply. The spring rests on the armature to force it downward. The armature moves vertically inside the coil and transmits its motion through the stem to the valve.

When current flows through the coil, a magnetic field forms around the coil. The magnetic field attracts the armature toward the center of the coil. As the armature moves upward, the spring collapses and the valve opens. When the circuit is opened and current stops flowing to the coil, the magnetic field collapses. This allows the spring to expand and shut the valve.

A major advantage of solenoid actuators is their quick operation. Also, they are much easier to install than pneumatic or hydraulic actuators. However, solenoid actuators have two disadvantages. First, they have only two positions: fully open and fully closed. Second, they don't produce much force, so they usually only operate relatively small valves.

Electric Motor Actuators

Electric motor actuators vary widely in their design and applications. Some electric motor actuators are designed to operate in only two positions (fully open or fully closed). Other electric motors can be positioned between the two positions. A typical electric motor actuator is shown in Figure 39. Its major parts include an electric motor, clutch and gear box assembly, manual handwheel, and stem connected to a valve.

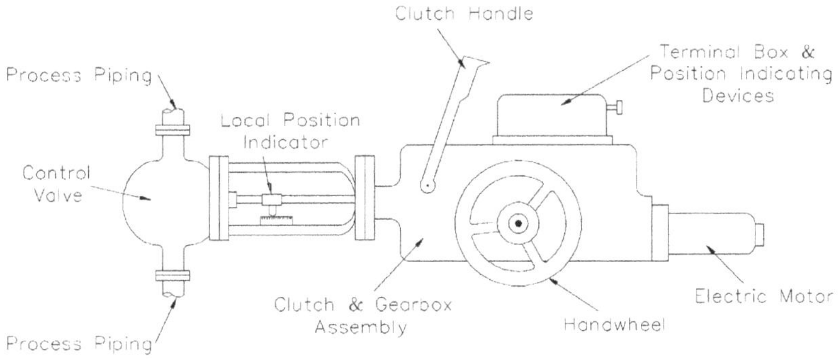

Figure 39 Electric Motor Actuator

The motor moves the stem through the gear assembly. The motor reverses its rotation to either open or close the valve. The clutch and clutch lever disconnects the electric motor from the gear assembly and allows the valve to be operated manually with the handwheel.

Most electric motor actuators are equipped with limit switches, torque limiters, or both. Limit switches de-energize the electric motor when the valve has reached a specific position. Torque limiters de-energize the electric motor when the amount of turning force has reached a specified value. The turning force normally is greatest when the valve reaches the fully open or fully closed position. This feature can also prevent damage to the actuator or valve if the valve binds in an intermediate position.

Summary

The important information in this chapter is summarized below.

Valve Actuator Summary

- Pneumatic actuators utilize combined air and spring forces for quick accurate responses for almost any size valve with valve position ranging from 0-100%.
- Hydraulic actuators use fluid displacement to move a piston in a cylinder positioning the valve as needed for 0-100% fluid flow. This type actuator is incorporated when a large amount of force is necessary to operate the valve.
- Solenoid actuators are used on small valves and employ an electromagnet to move the stem which allows the valve to either be fully open or fully closed.
- Equipped with limit switches and/or torque limiters, the electric motor actuator has the capability of 0-100% control and has not only a motor but also a manual handwheel, and a clutch and gearbox assembly.

end of text.

CONCLUDING MATERIAL

Review activities:

DOE - ANL-W, BNL, EG&G Idaho,
EG&G Mound, EG&G Rocky Flats,
LLNL, LANL, MMES, ORAU, REECo,
WHC, WINCO, WEMCO, and WSRC.

Preparing activity:

DOE - NE-73
Project Number 6910-0019/2